1971

The Tailoring
of Melville's
White-Jacket

The Tailoring

of Melville's

White-Jacket

by Howard P. Vincent

EVANSTON
NORTHWESTERN UNIVERSITY PRESS
1970

Howard P. Vincent, author of *Daumier and His World*
and *The Trying-Out of Moby-Dick,* is University Professor
at Kent State University.

Material from the following books has been quoted with permission of the pub-
lishers: *Selected Poems 1928–1958* by Stanley Kunitz, Little, Brown and Company,
1958. *The Collected Poems of Wallace Stevens* by Wallace Stevens, Alfred A.
Knopf, Inc., copyright 1954. *The Cantos of Ezra Pound,* copyright 1948 by Ezra
Pound, reprinted by permission of New Directions Publishing Corporation and
Faber and Faber Ltd. *Improvisation* from *The Killer and Other Plays* by Eugène
Ionesco, translated by Donald Watson, copyright © by John Calder (Publishers)
Ltd. 1960, published by Grove Press, Inc. and John Calder (Publishers) Ltd.
Collected Poems by Conrad Aiken, copyright 1953 by Conrad Aiken, reprinted
by permission of Oxford University Press. *Collected Poems* by Herbert Read,
copyright 1966, with the permission of the publishers, Horizon Press, New York,
and Faber and Faber Ltd. *Collected Later Poems* by William Carlos Williams,
copyright 1948 by William Carlos Williams, reprinted by permission of New
Directions Publishing Corporation and MacGibbon & Kee Ltd. *A Way of Looking* by Elizabeth Jennings, copyright 1956 by Elizabeth Jennings, reprinted by
permission of Harold Ober Associates Inc. and Macmillan & Co. Ltd. *Complete Poems* by Elizabeth Bishop, copyright 1940, 1946, 1947, 1948, 1949, 1951,
1952, 1955, 1969 by Elizabeth Bishop, reprinted with permission of Farrar, Straus
& Giroux. "For Once, Then, Something" from *The Poetry of Robert Frost,*
edited by Edward Connery Lathem, copyright 1923, © 1969 by Holt, Rinehart
and Winston, Inc., copyright 1951 by Robert Frost, reprinted by permission of
Holt, Rinehart and Winston, Inc.

Contents

CONTENTS

DEDICATED TO

HARRISON HAYFORD

Introduction

His craze was this: he heard a call
Ever from heaven: O scribe, write, write!
Write this—that write—to these indite—
To them! For ever it was—write!
Well, write he did, as here you see.
What is it all?

Clarel, III, xxvii, 118–123

•

THIS is a study of the genesis of Herman Melville's fifth book, *White-Jacket.* Except for *Israel Potter,* it has been less studied and analyzed than any of Melville's works, and yet many critics have placed it high in the canon, after *Moby-Dick* and *Billy Budd.*

It has a staying power and a wide appeal which has kept it alive for more than a century. It has good ingredients—the sea, shiplife, brutality, heroism, foreign sights, national pride—skillfully blended for our pleasure. No man was ever bored by *White-Jacket*—although some women might be.

White-Jacket in its genesis reveals the developing art of Melville far better than *Moby-Dick,* in which that art is fully developed. R. P. Blackmur put it well: ". . . it is often in his relative failures that an artist's drive is most clearly defined; if only because in his purest successes there is the sense of the self-born, self-driven, and self-complete and these qualities escape definition."

White-Jacket immediately preceded *Moby-Dick,* and as we examine it minutely in its genesis we see that Melville is trying out new techniques and new themes which appear, mastered, in the later book; we also watch the same process of creation, of borrowing and altering and adding, which produced the masterpiece, so that the lesser book illuminates the greater.

•

"There is," said Wallace Stevens, "about every poet a vast world of other people from which he derives himself and through himself his poetry." Part of that world, as Emerson told us in *The American Scholar,* is the world of books. Melville was a borrower, an incorrigible appropriator. He took straws to make them into haystacks. Melville took what he wanted wherever he found it; he made it his own and thus he made it ours. By watching this process we may perhaps increase our appreciation of creation itself but, more important, of the thing created; *White-Jacket* (yes, and *Moby-Dick,* too) may be seen in a new and clearer light. That is the hope of this book.

•

The scholar as well as the poet has a "vast world of other people from which he derives himself and through himself" his publications. *The Tailoring of White-Jacket* is itself a piece of patchwork; Melville's metaphor for his own book applies to this book about it. Many of the scholar's patches are cut from the work of previous scholars, a fabric only suggested in the citations here and in footnotes and bibliography.

No one can write about *White-Jacket* without having mastered the basic study of *White-Jacket* included in Charles R. Anderson's *Melville in the South Seas* (New York: Columbia University Press, 1939). Every finding of his has been valuable, and almost every conjecture of his has been verified. In four chapters he searchingly studied the "actual" and the fictional elements in *White-Jacket,* so that although I have since gone over the same ground he covered, especially the Muster Roll and Log Book of the *United States,* I have not needed to use them extensively. On the other hand, Anderson did little to study Melville's literary manipulations—not so much of facts as of books.

It might seem that with Anderson exhaustively studying the personal record (which has also been the subject of articles by Wilson Hefflin and Harrison Hayford), and with Keith Huntress, Thomas Philbrick, Page Proctor, and John Seelye turning up some of Melville's most significant literary sources, that *White-Jacket* has been exposed completely. Such, however, is far from the situation, nor will such complete exposure have been accomplished in this book. Finality in studying Melville's methods must never be assumed—that is scholarly *hubris.* Further sources *have* been found (and further ones will be found tomorrow), interesting in themselves and for filling out the record. Furthermore, the re-examination of the published sources has yielded new information, including details of considerable significance. Even more important, however, is that the study of all the sources together, those previously found and those new-found, gives an entirely different perspective on Melville's writing of *White-Jacket,* of his compositional process. It is another instance of the six blind men and the elephant. The scholarly study of the sources of a long literary work by means of separate, short articles—one source here, one source there—are misleading, much as though art critics were to analyze a painting only in minute and discretely treated sections, in short articles—one to study only the painter's use of blue, the second the red, the third the yellow, and so on—all of which would be interesting but which would leave the total picture undisclosed since it is, creatively, all of the colors at once juxtaposed, interacting. The study of interlacings and interactions, the sources in their totality rather than in isolation, is the purpose of this study of *White-Jacket.*

I wish to thank the librarians and archivists of the Public Records Office, London, the National Archives, Washington, the British Museum, the New York Public Library, the Boston Public Library, and the Kent State University Library, for their special help. The Kent State University Research Committee generously gave me a summer fellowship which enabled me to finish the final draft of my study, and another grant to pay for typing. ·

Two personal debts are extensive. Merton Sealts gave an early draft a close and intelligent reading which noted many errors and helped me in construction. Harrison Hayford has helped at every stage of my work. Indeed, we first began separately to trace the sources of *White-Jacket* early in the 1940's. Later we agreed on a collaborative study, but pressing commitments, especially to the General Editorship of the Northwestern-Newberry Edition of the Writings of Herman Melville, forced him to withdraw. With characteristic generosity he turned over all of his materials for my unrestricted use. He has advised, corrected, criticized, and encouraged every step of my progress. Many of the discoveries—such as, for example, the Schiller passage—which seem to be mine were really his. He may properly claim an active share in any virtues which this book may have, and a total uninvolvement in any of its defects.

The Tailoring
of Melville's
White-Jacket

· I ·

The Publication
of *White-Jacket*

Moreover the very occupation with an author, and the business of
exhibiting him, disposes us to affirm and amplify his importance.
Matthew Arnold, "The Study of Poetry"

•

WHITE-JACKET was composed at great speed during the summer of
1849. During May and June, Melville had been busy writing *Redburn,*
which by 20 July was "now going thro' the press," so that soon after, presumably, he set to work upon *White-Jacket.* He wrote to his
father-in-law:

They are two *jobs*, which I have done for money—being forced to it, as other men are to sawing wood. And while I have felt obliged to refrain from writing the kind of book I would wish to; yet, in writing these two books, I have not repressed myself much—so far as *they* are concerned; but have spoken pretty much as I feel.[1]

By 5 September Evert Duyckinck wrote to his brother, "Melville is hard at work with proof of the new book [*White-Jacket*]. I have the entire sheets of Redburn—Defoe on the ocean." Thus close came the two books, almost twinned.

On October 11, Melville boarded the *Southampton* to take *White-Jacket* to an English publisher. On 9 January 1850 the title-page was deposited for American copyright, and on 26 March the book itself was deposited. Meanwhile it had been published in England.

The reviews were unanimously favorable.[2] Several critics expressed relief at the return of Melville to the fold of prose normalcy, while all were delighted with the strong sense of ship and sea which Melville evoked. They welcomed the genuine, realist Melville thoroughly cured of his late allegorizing disease: "on the right ground at last. When we read his 'Mardi,' or rather *tried* to read it . . . we feared that the author had mistaken his bent." Their praise was virtually unanimous, to be summed up by the *Biblical Repository and Classical Review* as that the book had "wonderful power. The life of a man-of-war is painted with such consummate skill and intense energy of expression, that its horrible features glare upon you like a living being, and can never be effaced from the mind. In this line lies its chief value; and for power in this respect it surpasses any book ever read." The writer for *John Bull* said that "the rattling youngster has grown into a thoughtful man, who, without any abatement of his rich and ever sparkling wit, has obtained the mastery of his own fancy," while the critic for *Bentley's Miscellany* thought *White-Jacket*:

Remarkable for the concentration of rare qualities—brilliance and profundity, shrewdness, vivacity, and energy. The sad and solemn,

1. *The Letters of Herman Melville,* edited by Merrell R. Davis and William H. Gilman (New Haven: Yale University Press, 1960), pp. 91–92.
2. Hugh W. Hetherington, *Melville's Reviewers, British and American, 1846–1891* (Chapel Hill: The University of North Carolina Press, 1961), Chapter 6, "*White Jacket*," pp. 157–188. Jay Leyda, *The Melville Log: A Documentary of Herman Melville, 1819–1891* (New York: Harcourt, Brace, 1951), *passim*. An excellent gathering of Melville criticism can be found in *The Recognition of Herman Melville: Selected Criticism Since 1846,* edited by Hershel Parker (Ann Arbor: The University of Michigan Press, 1967).

the gay and playful, the thoughtful and picturesque, are mixed up fantastically in its pages, wondrous forms and images float before us; the wild waste of waters is stirred with spiritual life; while real men and their actions, on constant movement on ship-board, loom out palpable through the gorgeous mist.

The unanimity of praise for *White-Jacket* must have pleased Melville, especially since he had anticipated trouble from the critics who might have been disturbed by the roughness and forthrightness of much in the book. Before publication Melville wrote to Richard Henry Dana, Jr., mentioning his fears and hoping, possibly, for Dana's defense:

I shall be away, in all probability, for some months after the publication of the book. If it is taken hold of in an unfair or ignorant way; & if you should possibly think, that from your peculiar experiences in sea-life, you would be able to say a word to the purpose—may I hope that you will do so, if you can spare the time, & are generous enough to bestow the trouble?—Your name would do a very great deal.[3]

As we have seen, such expert support was not needed in public press. That Melville's fears were well grounded, however, has been discovered by Anderson[4] in his exposure of several sailor attacks on Melville's book—attacks, however, which remained in manuscript, not to be published until scholarship exposed them. These sailor carpings came from a misreading, or inconsideration, of Melville's purpose as stated in both the English and American prefaces to *White-Jacket*, explanations which tried to suggest, through the personal experiences of the author, veracity and authenticity, but which also denied one-to-one identifications of men and events and insisted that this was a general view of life in the navy, drawn from a variety of materials. It was, however, as we shall see in what follows, the very *variety* of Melville's sources—books and memories in puzzling and concealed juxtaposition—and their complex blending by Melville which misled the literalist sailor minds. Indicative of the sailor objections is a comment scribbled by Harrison Robertson in his copy of *White-Jacket* (now in the Lilly Collection of the University of Indiana):

3. *Letters*, p. 93 (October 6, 1849). The two letters to Dana were discovered by Hayford and opened up significant glimpses of Melville's literary life.

4. See especially the slashing and detailed attack in Charles R. Anderson, "A Reply to Herman Melville's *White-Jacket* by Rear-Admiral Thomas O. Selfridge, Sr.," *American Literature*, VII (May 1935), pp. 123–144.

Some of the incidents & characters described in this book, occurred on board the Frigate "United States"—in which I returned home, via Cape Horn, in 1844. Other incidents described are either purely imaginary, or happened at some other time & place—The author probably has made his book not from personal experience wholly, but has patched together scraps picked up from some other person's journal, or conversation—Most of the characters & incidents described are grossly caricatured, or exaggerated.

Robertson was perceptive of Melville's method, but the pejorative tone of "caricatured, or exaggerated" is one which critics reverse, finding in the caricatures (Cadwallader Cuticle, for example) or in the exaggerations (John J. Chase) admirable instances of Melville's art—an art that, as Robertson dimly sensed but could not define, partook of both journalism and fiction.

White-Jacket sold quickly; according to *The Home Journal*, 6 April 1850, "The first edition of Melville's new work, the 'White-Jacket,' was sold as soon as published."

Meritorious though *White-Jacket* is, such a rapid sellout of the first edition argues that its topical temper was in part responsible for its success. The law banning flogging in the Navy had long been debated in Congress and was shortly coming up for a vote. It has been alleged, without proof, that a copy of *White-Jacket* was placed on each Congressman's desk[5] and that the book was thus the final nudge which produced the votes to pass the law. Whatever the truth of this pretty story may be—and it should be true if it isn't—the reviews made no special point of the book's topicality although they did remark on, and highly praise in a general way, the pages against flogging. Something more than a mere propaganda blast was responsible for its sale then and since.

The reason is plain—*White-Jacket* is an excellent book. It is a document of interesting and authoritative detail, valuable to students of naval history; it is an exposure both good-natured and sternly condemnatory of the "floating hell" (a phrase borrowed by Melville from a veteran sailor) which a warship then was; it was an exposure of the military machine in its evil aspects, and of the eroding effects on the military institution and on the human character of the Articles of War. *White-Jacket* also celebrates heroism—how man in a society corrupt by nature and by structure, finds some way to assert and to fulfill his

5. The critic for *The National Era*, 25 April 1850, did say, "The book should be placed in the hands of every member of Congress."

essential manhood, whether he be Jack Chase or magnificent Old Ushant.

Had Melville written merely a faithful reflection of the Log of the *United States,* his book would today be but historical source. Because he sought out some of the meanings of his experiences, and the experiences of others, he touched truths which he would not have done had he written to the prescription of such sailor-authors as Selfridge, or Langhorne. He was an artist, not a tape recorder and a camera.

· 2 ·

Loomings
of "Loomings"

I have swam through libraries . . .

Moby-Dick, Ch. 32

The man bent over his guitar,
A shearsman of sorts.

Wallace Stevens, "The Man with the Blue Guitar"

•

WHITE-JACKET, Melville implies, was stitched together from miscellaneous patches, as had been *Mardi,* as would be *Moby-Dick.* The most significant of the "patches" utilized in the composition of *White-Jacket* were five little-known sea books. These play such an important and persistent part in the pages which now follow that a brief word about each is necessary.

The five basic books which helped Melville to structure and to fill out *White-Jacket* were:

William McNally, *Evils and Abuses in the Naval and Merchant Service Exposed: With Proposals for Their Remedy and Redress* (Boston: 1839).

Samuel Leech, *Thirty Years from Home, or A Voice from the Main Deck, being the Experience of Samuel Leech, who was for Six Years in the British and American Navies: Was Captured in The British Frigate Macedonian: Afterwards Entered the American Navy, and Was Taken in the United States Brig Syren, by the British Ship Medway* (Boston: Charles Tappan, 1843).

Nathaniel Ames, *A Mariner's Sketches* (Providence: 1831).

A British Seaman, *Life on Board a Man-of-War* (Glasgow: Blackie, Fullarton, & Co., 1829).

Henry James Mercier and William Gallop, *Life in a Man-of-War, or, Scenes in "Old Ironsides" During Her Cruise in the Pacific.* By a Fore-top-man (Philadelphia: Lydia R. Bailey, 1841). There is no author's name on the title page but the copyright was taken out by Mercier and Gallop.

All five of these books were generally useful—a phrase here, a fact there—but each had its own special kind of contribution to make to *White-Jacket.* McNally's *Evils and Abuses* was Melville's guide to procedural details within the Navy world—he furnished that body of information which enabled Melville to write in his preface: "Wherever statements are made concerning the established laws and usages of the Navy, facts have been strictly adhered to." McNally might almost be termed Melville's technical manual.

Samuel Leech's popular little book *Thirty Years from Home* supplied information and motivation to Melville for the flogging sections of *White-Jacket,* and also provided the account of the battle between the *United States* and the *Macedonian* in the War of 1812. Leech's book perhaps best fits the prefatory words of Melville: "For the hitherto unrecorded by-play of circumstances in one of two well-known naval actions referred to, the writer is indebted to seamen into whose mouths these things are put."

•

Nathaniel Ames's *A Mariner's Sketches* furnished basic material for the great climactic scene of the fall from the yard-arm, but it also supplied odds and ends of details which scholars have overlooked in the excitement of noticing the fall episode. It is quite probable that Melville was led to Ames's book by the notice in Richard Henry Dana's preface to *Two Years Before the Mast:*

> With the single exception, as I am quite confident, of Mr. Ames's entertaining, but hasty and desultory work, called *Mariner's Sketches,* all the books professing to give life at sea have been written by persons who have gained their experience as naval officers or passengers, and of these there are very few which are intended to be taken as narratives of fact.[1]

Melville's reading was apparently wider than Dana's, for he found at least four good additions to Ames. In any case, it is likely that Melville's disposition to assert a main-deck position opposed to the quarter-deck was strengthened by his friend Dana's example and by reading *A Mariner's Sketches.*

Ames's *A Mariner's Sketches* was a book that Melville obviously read with interest and used with profit. This main debt to Ames, noted long ago by Anderson, will be discussed at length later.[2]

---

1. Richard Henry Dana, *Two Years Before the Mast* (New York: Bantam Books, Inc., 1959), p. xiii. All subsequent references to Dana's book will be to this edition with page numbers parenthetically in the text.

2. Melville's full indebtedness, then, to Ames is not yet exposed. For example, a bit from Ames:

> We had an Irish family on board that amused me much. Before we were out of the Irish Channel, they began to ask, 'Sure now, an *ai'nt* we most there?' While on the passage a large *school* of porpoises played round the ship; the oldest boy ran to the after hatchway and called to his sister, 'Jasus, Molly, come up stairs and see the wild *bastes* of the *sea!*'

becomes in *Redburn:*

> The only thing that ever diverted this poor old man from his earnest search for land, was the occasional appearance of porpoises under the bows; when he would cry out at the top of his voice—'Look, look, ye divils! look at the great pigs of the s'a!'

The family's concern about being "there" is transferred by Melville to the Irish emigrants, in general, on board the *Highlander.* Also, Ames's definition: "As for

•

Most important source book of all, however, for Melville in writing *White-Jacket* was Henry Mercier's and William Gallop's *Life in a Man-of-War*. Its presence is discernible throughout *White-Jacket;* its contributions to Melville's dunderfunk, grog, and auction scenes have been analyzed by Huntress.[3] Even Mercier's title is close to Melville's prefatory remark: "The object of this work is to give some idea of the interior life in a man-of-war."

Mercier's experiences on board the frigate *Constitution*—a ship similar in construction to the *United States* (and so cousin to the *Neversink*) —were apparently the closest parallel in nautical literature to Melville's own as a navy man. The physical setting of each book was similar, the makeup of the personnel, the human structure of each ship, was the same. Mercier's *Life in a Man-of-War* was almost a chart for Melville to refer to.

Mercier was an amusing writer but a clumsy one. Stylistically naive, Mercier is almost primitive in his effects. Fond of euphemisms, quotation marks, obvious tags from Shakespeare paraded as elegant allusion, *Scenes* is mildly interesting for its awkwardness as well as for the contagious enthusiasm with which the authors rattle off their anecdotes. To compound the felony of his prose style Mercier interspersed long doggerel poems which tell in limping iambics what had already been narrated in broken-backed prose—as though two wrongs could make a right. Mercier would have benefitted from Ezra Pound's caustic dictum that "Poetry should be written at least as well as prose"; his verses lack the occasional redeeming verve of the prose.

Nevertheless, Mercier was honest if artless, informative if verbose, and some of his yarns were good enough to be retouched and retold—at least Melville thought so. Above all, Mercier knew "the facts" and was an invaluable supply store for Melville's literary tessellation.

---

hanging, or as sailors call it, 'taking a walk up Ladder lane, and down Hemp street' " appears in Chapter XVII of *Redburn* as, "When a man is hung at sea, which is always done from one of the lower yard-arms, they say he *'takes a walk up Ladder-Lane, and down Hemp-Street.'* "

3. Probably Mercier's influence carried over into *Moby-Dick;* possibly the chowder episodes at Nantucket stem from a suggestion from Mercier (p. 126): ". . . it was fish! fish! fish! every meal, three times a day; and as one of our ship's wags expressed it, 'he had eat so much *mackerel* and *perch,* he expected to see *scales* and *fins* making their appearance upon some part of his body very soon.' "

•

Life on Board a Man-of-War, by A British Seaman, has not until now been known as a significant contributor to the sewing of the jacket. From it Melville lifted several patches—odds and ends of phrases and scenes—but he looted it most entertainingly to create Jack Chase's florid "twister" about the Battle of Navarino, and to complete the third section of his concluding drama which I call the Fall from the Yard-Arm. Surely Melville had *Life on Board a Man-of-War* in mind when he mentioned drawing upon others for "illustrative scenes."

To cite these five books separately is not, eventually, to overlook the active presence of other sources, such as Richard Dana's *Two Years Before the Mast,* or *The Life and Adventures of John Nicol, Mariner;*[4] it is simply to establish their basic, more prevalent, influence on *White-Jacket.*

Although the effect of the first four of these books has already been studied in part by scholars, the subject of their influence, their operations, is far from exhausted. Close gleaning produces additional and interesting revelations. More important, studying these four books at one time to see their collective, intertwining influence on *White-Jacket,* one gains a more dynamic understanding of Melville's composition than from the unconnected, single-stranded studies of sources. One does not, as has been said, significantly study a painting in terms of one color alone. Collectively studied, placed side by side against Melville's book, these four books, along with others of lesser influence, provide an organic account of Melville's artistic strategies and struggles which, resulting in success in *White-Jacket,* shortly led to triumph in *Moby-Dick. White-Jacket* trained Melville in literary appropriation. His procedure was the practice of Shakespeare, freely to take, significantly to alter—the attitude, in our time, of Picasso, who said, "Whatever interests me, whatever I love, I wish to make my own"; he erred in adding, "I am probably describing a rare form of kleptomania."

4. It is possible that the British Seaman's reference to "John Nicol's interesting little book" may have led Melville to it. Jack Chase's florid account of the Battle of Navarino, taken primarily from the British Seaman, Melville wedged in, or filled it out with, bits from Nicol, suggesting that the two books were side by side on his writing table.

·3·

A White Duck Frock

Bart III: Your costume is seriously ill. . . . It's got to be cured. . . .
Ionesco: It's true . . . it is a little worn . . . and moth-eaten . . . I admit.

***

Bart I: Clothing is an investiture. . . .
Ionesco: I can see it's an investment.
Bart III: It's also a little investition.
Bart I: There are, as you've seen, a few simple little rules for telling whether a costume is ill or well. . . . Yours is suffering from hypertrophy of the historical function. . . . It's veridical.
Bart II: And it shouldn't be. . . .
Bart I: Your costume is just an alibi. It's shirking its responsibility!
Ionesco: I've always dressed like this!

Eugène Ionesco, Improvisation

•

WITHOUT one waste word, *White-Jacket* moves into motion. So facetious, however, is Melville's introduction to his voyage that many have missed his half-hidden meanings, misled by that very playfulness which for readers of Melville should itself be a sign of underlying seriousness, a warning to look twice. When Melville seems most simple and artless the reader does well to be most aware and artful.

The title of the book, *White-Jacket,* refers both to the narrator and to his "outlandish garment," to neglect which completely, or extensively, in favor of the propagandistic and documentary elements in the book is to miss Melville's first and most emphatic signpost to the book's essential meaning. The author's preface says, admittedly—his second signpost—that the book is about life in a man-of-war, and it is for that or in that way the book has primarily been read. Since Melville was always exact with his titles we should read them and consider them as attentively as we do the prefatory remarks. Title and preface will seem at variance unless we regard them as contrapuntal and not exclusive. The title stresses the theme of the narrator and his psychic being, synechdochized by the jacket; the preface unambiguously announces that the ship and its operations are the substance of the book. The book opens, however, with a chapter devoted exclusively to the jacket and its making, the initial sentences vivid and preparatory:

> It was not a *very* white jacket, but white enough, in all conscience, as the sequel will show.
> The way I came by it was this.
> When our frigate lay in Callao, on the coast of Peru—her last harbor in the Pacific—I found myself without a *grego,* or sailor's surtout; and as, toward the end of a three years' cruise, no pea-jackets could be had from the purser's steward; and being bound for Cape Horn, some sort of a substitute was indispensable; I employed myself, for several days, in manufacturing an outlandish garment of my own devising, to shelter me from the boisterous weather we were so soon to encounter.[1]

We must be clear about the jacket as fact before we consider it as fiction. Melville told Dana,[2] who had been interested enough in it to

1. All quotations from *White-Jacket* are referred to by the *chapter* in which they appear.
2. See Harrison Hayford, "Two New Letters of Herman Melville," *ELH,* II (March 1944), pp. 77–79; also *The Letters of Herman Melville,* p. 107.

write him about it, that it had been "a veritable jacket" which he had tossed, to his subsequent regret, into the Charles River at the end of the voyage. It was a jacket which Melville had somehow acquired for himself, and not because of the niggardliness of the Navy. Melville might have had satisfactory covering simply by appealing to the ship's purser. Anderson has shown there was no real shortage of pea jackets even after three years of voyaging.[3] It was, then, "a veritable jacket," and we may assume, though it is not necessary to do so, that it had been made as Melville described in the story—an amateur job of sewing.

But *White-Jacket*'s jacket had its origin from more than "a veritable jacket." It grew from a strong suggestion which Melville found in Mercier's *Scenes* (pp. 238–239), when, like Melville's companions, the crew of the *Constitution* are busily preparing for the homeward voyage round the Cape:

> More than ordinary preparations had been made by every one on board for doubling the Cape; and sou-westers, painted trowsers, tarpawling jackets, boots, woollen shirts, &c., met the eye at every turn; many a good warm blanket was by dint of scissors, thread and needle, transformed into comfortable drawers; many a pair of old trowsers, long before condemned as unfit for further service, was now brought forth, and patch upon patch applied to keep out the dreadful inclemency of the weather, which all thought was in store for them, for that well-written work "Two Years before the Mast" had gone the rounds of the ship; and the vivid though fearful and chilling account given there of doubling Cape Horn in the month of July, brought to our mind's eye nothing but pinnacles of ice, hail, sleet, frost, snow, adverse gales. . . .

Perhaps equally important to Melville in suggesting the clothing emphasis of his opening chapter was a scene from *Two Years Before the Mast* (pp. 182–183), of which Mercier had just reminded him, when the sailors are getting ready for rounding the Cape:

> . . . we all employed our evenings in making clothes for the passage home, and more especially for Cape Horn. As soon as supper was over and the kids cleared away, and each man had taken his smoke, we seated ourselves on our chests round the lamp, which swung from a beam, and went to work each in his own way, some making hats, others trousers, others jackets, etc., etc., and no one was idle. The boys who could not sew well enough to make

3. Charles Roberts Anderson, *Melville in the South Seas* (New York: Columbia University Press, 1939), p. 417.

their own clothes laid up grass into sinnet for the men, who sewed for them in return. Several of us clubbed together, and bought a large piece of twilled cotton, which we made into trousers and jackets, and, giving them several coats of linseed oil, laid them by for Cape Horn. I also sewed and covered a tarpaulin hat, thick, and strong enough to sit upon, and made myself a complete suit of flannel under-clothing for bad weather. Those who had no south-wester caps made them; and several of the crew got up for them-selves tarpaulin jackets and trousers, lined on the inside with flannel. Industry was the order of the day, and every one did something for himself; for we knew that as the season advanced, and we went farther south, we should have no evenings to work in.[4]

And equally important, a similar scene in Dana (p. 226) when they are getting ready for the return:

In the forenoon watches below, our forecastle looked like the workshop of what a sailor is—a Jack-at-all-trades. Thick stockings and drawers were darned and patched; mittens dragged from the bottom of the chest and mended; comforters made for the neck and ears; old flannel shirts cut up to line monkey-jackets; south-westers were lined with flannel, and a pot of paint smuggled forward to give them a coat on the outside; and everything turned to hand; so that, although two years had left us but a scanty wardrobe, yet the economy and invention which necessity teaches a sailor soon put each of us in pretty good trim for bad weather, before we had seen the last of the fine. Even the cobbler's art was not out of place. Several old shoes were very decently repaired, and with waxed ends, an awl, and the top of an old boot, I made me quite a respectable sheath for my knife.

4. *Life on Board a Man-of-War* (p. 21) also has a passage on clothing, which Melville must have seen:

"We scrambled up, one after another, in a very unseamanlike manner, and in a few minutes found ourselves standing on the quarterdeck of H. M. ship Bittern, the laughing-stock of the whole crew, who crowded on the fore-castle, and even came aft to the break of the quarterdeck, to make observa-tions on our appearance. I had the misfortune to attract most attention; and that the reader may know the reason, let him imagine, a tall young fellow, with a blue jacket made in the first style of fashion, but most wretchedly faded; trowsers in the same style and predicament; a hat broken down into a soft, shapeless mass of felt; and a pair of boots bursting with laughter at both sides. [sic] Add to this, my features were besmeared with dirt, and my whole appearance was that of a forlorn flunkey or disjaskit dandy."

•

What whiteness will you add to this whiteness?
                              Ezra Pound, *Canto LXXIV*

Melville forces us to focus on the "strange duck frock" because he makes such a fuss about it. As a phase of life aboard a man-of-war the jacket is blown up out of any reasonable proportion. The documentary literal garment need not have occupied more than a sentence, or at most, a paragraph. The literary jacket is made into three entire chapters and several significant episodes. Remembering this, we must not look at the jacket as a documentary detail, from a historical point of view, but see it as a fiction. As such it is grotesque comedy, a characteristic example of Melville's delight in the absurd. When we recognize further that the jacket used in this outlandish way was partially suggested to him by the clothes philosophy of Teufelsdrökh in Thomas Carlyle's *Sartor Resartus,* we may be receptive to an emblematic reading of the garment and of its career. It has a biography just as later, and more fully, Moby-Dick is given one.

Whether or not the tailoring metaphor had been suggested by *Sartor Resartus* little matters. What is evident is that it was deeply rooted in Melville's mind, used not only throughout *White-Jacket,* but turning up satirically—almost in burlesque—four years later in *Pierre,* in the section on "Young America in Literature." Pierre had published a sonnet called "A Tropical Summer" (for which read, of course, *Typee*), and its success brings the publishers to his door. Among them are "two young men, recently abandoning the ignoble pursuit of tailoring for the more honourable trade of the publisher (probably with an economical view of working up in books, the linen and cotton shreds of the cutter's counter . . .)" They address Pierre in a "fine needle-work hand" and the metaphor is comically extended, even farcically overworked (Book XVII, i):

'Hon. Pierre Glendinning,
     'Revered Sir,
          'The fine cut, the judicious fit of your productions fill us with amazement. The fabric is excellent—the finest broadcloth of genius. We have just started in business. Your pantaloons—productions, we mean—have never yet been collected. They should be published in the Library form. The tailors—we mean the librarians, demand it. Your fame is now in its finest nap. Now—before the gloss is off—now is the time for the library form. We have recently received an invoice of Chamois——Russia leather. The

library form should be a durable form. We respectfully offer to
dress your amazing productions in the library form. If you please,
we will transmit you a sample of the cloth——we mean a sample-
page, with a pattern of the leather. We are ready to give you one-
tenth of the profits (less discount) for the privilege of arraying
your wonderful productions in the library form:—you cashing the
seamstresses'——printer's and binder's bills on the day of publication. An answer at your earliest convenience will greatly oblige,—
   'Sir, your most obsequious servants,

                       'WONDER & WEN.'
   'P.S.—We respectfully submit the enclosed block——sheet, as
some earnest of our intentions to do every thing in your behalf
possible to any firm in the trade.
   'N.B.—If the list does not comprise all your illustrious wardrobe——works, we mean——, we shall exceedingly regret it. We
have hunted through all the drawers——magazines.
   'Sample of a coat——title for the works of Glendinning:'

Some readers may be reluctant to play with these symbolic possibilities, saying that a primrose is but a primrose, and such severity is
understandable in the light of the many ridiculous readings which
Melville's stories, *Moby-Dick* especially, have suffered. If, however, one
remembers the strong inclination to symbolism which mid-nineteenth
century writers habitually displayed; if, too, one remembers Melville's
affection for the grotesque and eccentric—the rebellious, as it were—and
if one recognizes the powerful and persistent presence of *Sartor Resartus*
in *Mardi, White-Jacket,* and *Moby-Dick*—considering all this it would
be a resistant reader who would close his mind to the airy and fantastic
possibilities of White-Jacket's white jacket.[5] Melville had seething
fancies in his brain. He was an artist seeking to find his own organic
form of expression. And now he was indulging in high-spirited mockery
at his own compositional task, his struggle with memories and books as
from each he extracted odds and ends of patches and pieced them

---

5. Cf. Henry James in *The Portrait of a Lady* (Chapter 19): "When you've
lived as long as I you'll see that every human being has his shell and that you
must take the shell into account. . . . There's no such thing as an isolated man
or woman; we're each of us made up of some cluster of appurtenances. What
shall we call our 'self?' Where does it begin? where does it end? It overflows into
everything that belongs to us—and then it flows back again. I know a large part
of myself is in the clothes I choose to wear. I've a great respect for *things!* One's
self—for other people—is one's expression of one's self; and add one's house,
one's furniture, one's garments, the books one reads, the company one keeps—
these things are all expressive."

together. It was the process described similarly by Irving in "The Art of Book-Making" from some twenty years before:

> [In the British Museum] I beheld a ragged, threadbare throng, such as may be seen plying about the great repository of cast-off clothes, Monmouth Street. Whenever they seized upon a book, by one of those incongruities common to dreams, methought it turned into a garment of foreign or antique fashion, with which they proceeded to equip themselves. I noticed, however, that no one pretended to clothe himself from any particular suit, but took a sleeve from one, a cape from another, a skirt from a third, thus decking himself out piecemeal, while some of his original rags would peep out from among his borrowed finery.

Nor was Melville alone, after Irving, in utilizing the tailor metaphor to describe literary labor, or as perhaps a version of "Clothes make the man." Compare, for instance, Hawthorne's later satiric use of clothing in "Feathertop," or, more specifically, in his description of the costumes worn by utopian dreamers of Blithedale:

> Arcadians though we were, our costume bore no resemblance to the beribboned doublets, silk breeches and stockings, and slippers fastened with artificial roses, that distinguish the pastoral people of poetry and the stage. In outward show, I humbly conceive, we looked rather like a gang of beggars, or banditti, than either a company of honest laboring-men, or a conclave of philosophers. Whatever might be our points of difference, we all of us seemed to have come to Blithedale with the one thrifty and laudable idea of wearing out our old clothes. Such garments as had an airing, whenever we strode afield! Coats with high collars and with no collars, broad-skirted or swallow-tailed, and with the waist at every point between the hip and arm-pit; pantaloons of a dozen successive epochs, and greatly defaced at the knees by the humiliations of the wearer before his lady-love,—in short, we were a living epitome of defunct fashions, and the very raggedest presentment of men who had seen better days. It was gentility in tatters.

Hawthorne and Melville knew that the costume of a man at once conceals and reveals him, and they describe the clothes of their characters for fundamental literary-psychological reasons.

•

What was that whiteness?
Truth? A pebble of quartz? For once, then, something.
                                    Robert Frost, "For Once, Then, Something"

White-Jacket gains a new glow, or glitter, when this tailor-artist metaphor is admitted as actively and intentionally operative. Other American writers before and after *White-Jacket* so used it. Emerson, when completing *Nature,* twelve years earlier, wrote in his *Journal:* "Today came to me the first proof-sheets of *Nature* to be corrected, like a new coat, full of vexations, with the first sentences of the chapters perched like mottoes aloft in small type." (Melville's vexations were of meaning, however, and not of typesetting.) And Thoreau employed the coat image for his writing at the end of the second paragraph of *Walden:* "I trust that none will stretch the seams in putting on the coat, for it may do good service to whom it fits."

Melville continues with his trope:

It was nothing more than a white duck frock, or rather shirt; which, laying on deck, I folded double at the bosom, and by then making a continuation of the slit there, opened it lengthwise— much as you would cut a leaf in the last new novel. The gash being made, a metamorphosis took place, transcending any related by Ovid. For, presto! the shirt was a coat!—a strange-looking coat, to be sure; of a Quakerish amplitude about the skirts; with an infirm, tumble-down collar; and a clumsy fullness about the wristbands; and white, yea, white as a shroud. And my shroud it afterward came very near proving, as he who reads further will find.

But, bless me, my friend, what sort of a summer jacket is this, in which to weather Cape Horn? A very tasty, and beautiful white linen garment it may have seemed; but then, people almost universally sport their linen next to their skin.

Very true; and that thought very early occurred to me; for no idea had I of scudding round Cape Horn in my shirt; for *that* would have been almost scudding under bare poles, indeed.

So, with many odds and ends of patches—old socks, old trowser-legs, and the like—I bedarned and bequilted the inside of my jacket, till it became, all over, stiff and padded, as King James's cotton-stuffed and dagger-proof doublet; and no buckram or steel hauberk stood up more stoutly.

. . . But here be it known, that I had been terribly disappointed in carrying out my original plan concerning this jacket. It had been my intention to make it thoroughly impervious, by giving it a coating of paint.

. . . Such, then, was my jacket: a well-patched, padded, and porous one; and in a dark night, gleaming white, as the White Lady of Avenel!

There is much here to echo in the mind—white, shroud, impervious, etc.—but Melville makes us *see* the jacket first of all before releasing the imagination to muse on his airier meanings. He starts as Dana had started in *Two Years Before the Mast,* where in the second paragraph the sailor's clothing is described, and Dana's "difference" in attire is mentioned. Perhaps it was Dana's paragraph which nudged Melville into focussing on the jacket, since Dana's book exerted a strong influence on Melville's life and art.

Melville liked metaphors of intricacy, metaphors of construction. In his paper on "The Art of Book-binding" he appropriately uses that craft as a metaphor of the artist and his creating a book. More memorably, in *Moby-Dick* ("The Mat-Maker," Chapter 47), he uses the construction of a mere mat as an analogue of the weaving of the Fates, and, quite probably, as an ironic account of his own attempt, just then, to construct a book in which the crude physical details of whaling might implicate the metaphysical issues which were his greatest and gravest concern. "The Mat-Maker" is a scene far greater—vaster, more varied and complex—than the opening chapter of *White-Jacket,* but in that chapter he enjoyed a trial run for his subsequent success.

•

Thus far this view of the tailoring metaphor has been general enough to be perhaps acceptable. It is more difficult and dangerous to interpret the jacket-stitching as having specific reference to specific writings, or to one specific literary struggle of Melville's. Roughly, crudely—for any symbolism, like any joke, thus explained is a deflated thing—we might explicate the jacket passage in this loose fashion: When he wrote *Mardi,* Melville had tried something new; he had felt that his literary voyage had reached a Cape Horn (always a crisis symbol for Melville), and that in this confrontation—the composition of *Mardi*—he had perforce created a special kind of literary structure. To do so he had varied his old narrative method, producing a literary form strange to readers—a gallimaufry of satire, allegory, and adventure ranging from sea depths to earth's surface to airy moon-flights. The old *Typee* structure was thus transformed into (the second two-thirds of *Mardi*) "a strange-looking coat." Remember, too, that the jacket, and so in a sense the book, were both white (the total of all colors), white representing here, as in *Moby-Dick,* the Absolute, or Truth. *Mardi* had literally introduced whiteness in its mysterious, romanticized heroine, Yillah, a literary device which almost destroyed author Melville as the white jacket ultimately nearly destroys its wearer—thus *Mardi* had proved as "white as a shroud" to Melville the professional successful writer.

Furthermore, *Mardi,* like the jacket, was compiled (in the manner of the narrator piecing together the odds and ends of papers from the zodiac bags in *Sartor*) from shreds and patches—from Sir Thomas Browne, Carlyle, Rabelais, Shakespeare, the Bible, and Frederick Debell Bennett, among others. These shreds and patches of allusion, however, could not constitute a sound narrative, being, as they were, inorganic, artistically unfunctional. *Mardi* was, he seems to say in conclusion, an attempt to grasp the "truth of things" (Tell the Truth, and go to the soup-kitchens," Melville wrote to Duyckinck) with a Truth figure, Yillah, as unreal and ghostly as that of Sir Walter Scott's *Guy Mannering* with its unconvincing ghost of The White Lady of Avenel.

Quickly it must be admitted—meeting an obvious objection of the reader (of this and of *White-Jacket*)—that such a specific interpretation may sound lunatic, and the indulgence in particularity is fraught with grave danger—the interpreter's own destruction. What is urged here is that this interpretation is a capricious possibility worthy of consideration because of the playful habits which Melville himself elsewhere engaged in. Our peril is nonetheless grave, since a symbolic meaning should not be made into an allegorical equation, a fault to which over-particularity is liable.

•

These are not things transformed.
Yet we are shaken by them as if they were.
We reason about them with a later reason.
          Wallace Stevens, "Notes toward a Supreme Fiction"

Captain Ahab urged the pursuit: "But yet a little lower layer." A more properly symbolic reading of the jacket throughout Melville's book as a significant theme in *White-Jacket* does not imply that it is a fully achieved one. Not at all. It rather insists that Melville's theme is developed but tentatively, that timidity made him mute.

Only six chapters out of the book's 94 deal primarily with the white jacket, although it appears in several others, popping up like a jack-in-the-box to startle and amuse. This disproportionate emphasis on life in a man-of-war to the neglect of the jacket explains why the jacket theme goes unnoticed for much of the book, but it *is* there persistently and repetitively enough to warrant straining our ears to trace its melody, its meaning.

When this thesis was first stated openly in 1949,[6] it was proffered as a corrective to the single view of *White-Jacket* as only a realistic book, a *roman à clef,* a piece of harsh propaganda. The materialist view has dominated since 1850, although even then some critics sensed a secondary meaning. The reviewer in *Bentley's Miscellany* suggested that the jacket of the title "assumes a sort of personal interest, from the part it plays, and from the importance of its multifarious functions," but he did not follow up this clue, nor did subsequent readers do more than hint such a possibility without ever exploring it. Charles Anderson perceived that Melville had invented a symbol "to unify an otherwise disjointed narrative," but he limited too much the meaning of the symbol, particularizing it "autobiographically as a coat-of-arms for the Gansevoort-Melville sense of family pride; though ostensibly mixing with the seamen as a common tar, Melville sets himself apart as a sheep from among goats, securely cloaked in the aristocratic tatters of his White Jacket." This, possibly, but also much more. Symbols, said Emerson, are fluxional.

The jacket as symbol had appeared earlier in an even more scattered and unexploited way, in *Redburn,* and the jacket of *White-Jacket* is a retailored item from the opening words of *Redburn:*

> "Wellingborough, as you are going to sea, suppose you take this shooting-jacket of mine along; it's just the thing—take it, it will save the expense of another. You see, it's quite warm; fine long skirts, stout horn buttons, and plenty of pockets."

Later appearances, and they are frequent, of this old shooting-jacket demand that it be seen not only as a comic object, a recurrent joke, but also as a grotesque symbol. On every occasion when the venturing Redburn feels inadequate in a social situation he protectively draws his jacket about him half-defiantly, retreatingly. No big scenes are made out of the life of Redburn's shooting-jacket; however, in *White-Jacket,*

6. Howard P. Vincent, *"White-Jacket:* An Essay in Interpretation," *New England Quarterly,* XXII (September 1949), pp. 304–315.

written immediately following *Redburn* (and during the same summer), Melville again used a jacket prominently, hence significantly, giving it a more active, dramatic life, foreshadowing its powers and its fate almost as if it were a person, as it is indeed a character in the book.

It might be suggested (for it cannot be proved) that Melville began *White-Jacket* without this jacket theme, and that he had gone far before it occurred to him that the *Redburn* jacket with which he had played so casually and loosely might be made to serve symbolically—a specific physical fact to be enlarged, allowing him timidly, gropingly, to touch on a deeper theme, one dominant in his writing and made unforgettably fast in the world's imagination by the opening sentence of *Moby-Dick,* "Call me Ishmael."

It follows from this suggestion that Melville must have had difficulties incorporating the jacket story with the documentary line, and there are places where his attempts to sew them together show clearly, although in general his tailoring has not been much noticed. Further, this entrance of his moral or psychological symbol late in his book's construction is similar to what happened in the composition of *Moby-Dick* when, well along in the whaling voyage, Moby Dick himself swam into the book and had to be taken care of.[7]

If this suggestion is accepted, it is then easy to see that Melville had little difficulty in enlarging *White-Jacket* from a pure documentary to something more. His naval voyage was so freely organized, so unarticulated from chapter to chapter, or sometimes from section to section, that it was easy to insert his new jacket chapters into such a loose structure. Of the six main jacket chapters, three were strategically placed at the beginning (1), the middle (47), and the end (92), and the other three (9, 10, 17) were fitted into the earlier half without any special disruption—indeed they helped fill out, as with "The Jacket aloft," what would otherwise have been skimpy and uncompleted sections. Admittedly whether or not Melville so came, as we have suggested, to this discovery of the jacket as an actor and a symbol, and hence as plot, is conjectural, but such a hypothesis helps to explain the otherwise digressive and conspicuous character of the jacket chapters.

One of the most important themes of both *Redburn* and *White-Jacket* is rejection—the inevitable, the necessary, rejection entailed by the

7. See Howard P. Vincent, *The Trying-Out of Moby-Dick* (Boston: Houghton Mifflin, 1949), p. 48, where it is suggested that the White Whale was made part of the book late in its writing, in the spring of 1851.

process of growing up. In London on Christmas Day 1849, Melville bought a copy of *The Auto-Biography of Goethe; Truth and Poetry, From My Own Life; The Concluding Books* (Volume II); *Also Letters from Switzerland, and Travels in Italy* (London, 1849) in which he "emphatically" scored Goethe's words, p. 37.[8]

> For a time we may grow up under the protection of parents and relatives; we may lean for a while upon our brothers and sisters and friends, be supported by acquaintances, and made happy by those we love, but in the end man is always driven back upon himself, and it seems as if the Divinity had taken a position towards men so as not always to respond to their reverence, trust, and love, at least not in the precise moment of need.

Redburn dealt with the young boy's separation from brothers and sisters and friends; *White-Jacket* shows man finally driven back upon himself, which will be the great theme developed in Ishmael's adventures as a whaleman.

The rhetorical reduction of Melville's symbolical meaning to a vulgar paraphrase is now made apologetically, but with the hope that it will lead the reader back to Melville's book. *White-Jacket* proudly stitches his comic jacket, expecting magic powers from it.

Encased in this crudely contrived garment patched up from wishful thinking, childhood dreams, escapist hopes, and aristocratic pretensions, White-Jacket in his isolated retreat high in the main-top hopes that he will be protected from the storms which rage around Cape Horn (evil, the heedless, destroying world). This withdrawal recalls Father Mapple's into his pulpit in the Whaleman's Chapel in *Moby-Dick,* at which Ishmael inquired: "Can it be, then, that by that act of physical isolation, he signifies his spiritual withdrawal for the time, from all outward worldly ties and connections?" White-Jacket's isolation, however, results not from any deep desire to know himself through contemplation but rather from his refusal to participate in the ordinary life of humanity. Though he achieves a delusory protection from the cold and the storm, he finds his jacket inadequate and must, in time, abandon it or be destroyed by it.

The jacket is also a symbol of pseudo self-sufficiency, of what

8. Jay Leyda, *The Melville Log* (New York: Harcourt, Brace, 1951), Vol. I, p. 354. The other markings listed by Leyda are interesting, *e.g.,* p. 38: "I clearly felt that a creation of importance could be produced only when its author isolated himself."

Hawthorne, writing about Peter Goldthwaite's jacket, called "windy schemes and empty hopes."[9] In a long account "Of the Pockets that were in the Jacket" (Chapter 9), Melville describes the jacket in a labyrinth metaphor similar to his subsequent description in "I and My Chimney" of the old Arrowhead chimney; both jacket and chimney represent, among other things, striking but slightly differing symbols of the Self: "my jacket, like an old castle, was full of winding stairs, and mysterious closets, crypts, and cabinets; and like a confidential writing-desk, abounded in snug little out-of-the-way lairs and hiding-places, for the storage of valuables." Every want seemed taken care of; its proud owner says, "I fairly hugged myself, and reveled in my jacket; till alas! a long rain put me out of conceit of it." Other experiences put him further out of conceit with it, and these will be seen in due course.

In any case, in the opening chapter Melville has ironically dramatized not so much White-Jacket's psychic sorrows as his own authorial one. He has portrayed the sailor as tailor as author, thus admitting the patchwork character of *writing* itself, but especially the structuring of a book, or books, made up in good part from diverse literary and experiential "sources."

Comic self-deprecation is the effect of Chapter 1. The author is seldom an actor in his book but on those few occasions his acting is important—at the beginning and at the end, with a few stage entrances strategically spotted throughout. In Chapter 2 White-Jacket the actor withdraws for the most part and White-Jacket assumes his role as narrator.

•

Earlier it was suggested that possibly the first chapter of *White-Jacket* had been added late in the composition of the book, when the idea of using the jacket thematically and structurally occurred to Melville. It might, of course, be argued the other way, that Melville started with the jacket but found that he needed a large world of daily life on board a man-of-war to build up a solid book. Which way it happened may not

9. "Peter Goldthwaite's Treasure," *The Novels and Tales of Nathaniel Haw-thorne,* edited and with an introduction by Norman Holmes Pearson (New York: The Modern Library, 1937), p. 997: "His upper garment was a mixture surtout, wofully faded, and patched with newer stuff on each elbow; beneath this he wore a threadbare black coat. . . . He was the perfect picture of a man who had fed on windy schemes and empty hopes."

be proved, but Melville's method, as with *Moby-Dick,* was generally to start from a realistic world. In any case, Chapter 1 of *White-Jacket* is totally different from the opening chapters of other sea narratives of its kind, while the second chapter is, on the other hand, much like the openings of books by his contemporaries—especially of Mercier's *Scenes.*

The vivacity of Chapter 1, introducing the jacket, prepares the reader to be receptive to the ship world in which that jacket is to function. The man-of-war with its anchors and rigging, its capstans and cannons, becomes the solid, central concern of the chapter, of the book—the ship as sheer fact.

·4·

The Beginning
of the Voyage

"HOMEWARD-BOUND" (Chapter 2) is an immediate example of the very patchwork process which Melville had just described in his opening comic introduction. It is made up from two sections in Mercier's *Scenes*, the first when Mercier's ship leaves America, the second when the ship prepares for the home voyage: two embarkations from which Melville constructs one.

Both Melville and Mercier convey the excitement of the sailors at the prospect of mere action, but also at the prospect of home. Both show the alacrity and pleasure with which the crews ready the ship for sailing. In both is the picture of the disorderly order of a sailing, multiplicity becoming unity. "All," wrote Mercier, "was now a scene of life and bustle." And Melville enacts the excitement:

> We were all arrayed in our best, and our bravest; like strips of blue sky, lay the pure blue collars of our frocks upon our shoulders; and our pumps were so springy and playful, that we danced up and down as we dined.

This is in part Mercier's "scene rife with bustle and liveliness." Melville's style is not yet fully controlled, but he is trying to make his rhythms appropriate to the excited emotions described, especially in the anapestic dance of the alliterative dentals. It is an excess also seen later in this chapter, where he wrote:

> More rural than naval were the sounds [of the animals on deck]; continually reminding each mother's son of the old paternal homestead in the green old clime; the old arching elms; the hill where we gambolled; and down by the barley banks of the stream where we bathed.

Certainly these sentences do not lag even though they may be a bit too bouncy. Also far sprightlier, or more vivid, than Mercier is that simile of the blue jackets "like strips of blue sky." It is over-writing but the sort of try in which Melville soon succeeds.

Melville's short chapter of but two pages tightens and tidies up Mercier's sprawling pages, the contrast apparent in the following representative parallels:

Melville (Chapter 2)	Mercier (pp. 24–25)
	All was now a scene of life and bustle. Carpenters shipping their capstan bars—tierers and holders getting their hook-ropes and chain-hooks in readiness—the indefatigable topmen passing the nippers around the chain —quarter gunners and idlers stretching the messenger along
"All hands up anchor!" When that order was given, how we sprang to the bars, and	—the marines too with buoyant spirits rendering all the assistance in their power towards

heaved round that capstan;
every man a Goliath, every
tendon a hawser!—round and
round—round, round it spun
like a sphere, keeping time with
our feet to the time of the fifer,
till the cable was straight up
and down, and the ship with
her nose in the water.

"Heave and pall! unship
your bars, and make sail!"
It was done:—bar-men,
nipper-men, tierers, veerers,
idlers and all, scrambled up the
ladder to the braces and halyards; while like monkeys in
Palm-trees, the sail-loosers ran
out on those broad boughs, our
yards; and down fell the sails
like white clouds from the ether
—top-sails, top-gallants, and
royals; and away we ran with
the halyards, till every sheet was
distended.

"Once more to the bars!"

"Heave, my hearties, heave
hard!"
With a jerk and a yerk, we
broke ground; and up to our
bows came several thousand
pounds of old iron, in the shape
of our ponderous anchor.

weighing our ponderous anchor
—in fact every one throughout
the ship, young and old, officers
as well as men, might be perceived hurrying to and fro on
every deck, their countenances
plainly intimating that it was
the general wish to see "Old
Ironsides" once more "cleaving
her foamy track."
"Man the bars" now sono-
rously resounded from the
speaking trumpet of our first
lieutenant. The word was electric. Each one was at his station
in a moment; the fifer thrilled
[sic] off two or three notes to
show that his instrument was in
complete order for the occasion
—the after-guard stationed at
the capstan bars, took up their
positions with distended arms,
to give the greater force to their
first movement—the mizentop-
men seated themselves comfort-
ably upon deck close to the
messenger, blessing their stars
for having such a sinecure. . . .
The order to "heave round" was
now given; the fifer made the
gun deck re-echo with the
lively and applicable tune of
"off she goes," the men at the
bars kept unerring time with
their feet, as they made the
capstan obey the impulse of
their vigorous nerves, the incessant clink of the chain was
heard, as it flew through the
hawsehole with a quickness
scarcely to be equalled, and in
as short a time as can well be
imagined our ponderous anchor
was short apeak.

> "All hands make sail," was
> now thrillingly proclaimed by
> the boatswain and his mates,
> and a scene rife with bustle
> and liveliness immediately took
> place . . . [details of each
> type of activity]
>   The heavy sails, as if by
> magic, now burst from the
> *gaskets* that had held them in
> such secure and graceful folds,
> and as the merry notes of the
> shrill fife re-echoed amongst
> the adjacent hills, sail after sail
> was made, the anchor was calted
> and fished, the yards were
> trimmed to the wind; our old
> frigate began to feel its influ-
> ence—and she was soon "walk-
> ing the waters like a thing of
> life," leaving the happy shores
> of Columbia in the distance.

Mercier's passage—one of the better ones in his book, surprisingly uncluttered with euphemisms and cutely quoted words—has been concentrated by Melville into a dramatic action, much shorter than Mercier and therefore more effective. Less is more.

Most of Melville's chapter was the setting forth of the ship on her voyage, but the concluding words suddenly swing to White-Jacket himself:

> Where was White-Jacket then?
> White-Jacket was where he belonged. It was White-Jacket that loosed that main-royal, so far up aloft there, it looks like a white albatross' wing. It was White-Jacket that was taken for an albatross himself, as he flew out on the giddy yard-arm!

This is a tacked-on bit, a quick stitching by Melville so that the first two chapters may be connected more smoothly, rather than depending simply on the implied presence of the narrator—just as the very opening, and no more, of Chapter 3 is another similarly intentioned stitching, really unnecessary to the documentary materials which follow it: "Having just designated the place where White-Jacket belonged, it must needs be related how White-Jacket came to belong there."

Chapter 3, "A Glance at the principal Divisions, into which a Man-of-war's Crew is divided," is intended also not so much to convey information as pure impression or effect. The confusion of the sailing becomes, understandably, the confusion of the novice sailor as he tries to find himself amid the shouting and scurrying. With speed the chapter ranges throughout the ship, from the top-man down to the " 'holders,' who burrow, like rabbits in warrens, among the water-tanks, casks, and cables. . . . They may circumnavigate the world fifty times, and they see about as much of it as Jonah did in the whale's belly. They are a lazy, lumpish, torpid set; and when going ashore after a long cruise, come out into the day like terrapins from their caves, or bears in the spring, from tree-trunks." These sentences, like the entire chapter, are in the vigorous manner of *Moby-Dick*—even to the verbal anticipation of "this terraqueous globe." In five packed pages, the dense accumulation of facts, similes, and allusions makes for an admirably clear picture of outer and inner confusion. The last four paragraphs of the chapter are strikingly in the vein of *Moby-Dick,* and although they do not have the range of such a chapter as "The Whiteness of the Whale," they have similar cadences, similar felicities; they employ similar devices, such as the catalogue of names, the rhetorical questions, the directive and connective words like "Consider," "Mark him," and the summarizing sentence which pins the great variety together. "Study, then, your mathematics, and cultivate all your memories, oh ye! who think of cruising in men-of-war," Melville writes in *White-Jacket,* having just detailed chaos worse confounded, and in *Moby-Dick* (Chapter 42) he will question us after opening to us a more profound chaos and complexity, the whiteness of the whale and of the moral universe: "Wonder ye then at the fiery hunt?"

·5·

A Pair of Jacks

ONE of the distinguishing merits of *White-Jacket* is its informal portrait gallery hung with sketches of sailors and officers, most of them having the quick directness of a Delacroix drawing, the sitter's individuality seized in a paragraph or a short chapter. In many of them, such as Captain Claret, Cadwallader Cuticle, Old Combustibles, Mad Jack, or Selvagee, a single trait, almost a humor, is trapped and treated to the exclusion of others. Melville's eye for salient detail, for the physical or psychological peculiarity, the significant gesture even, is as developed and as competent as when, shortly, he created Queequeg or Stubb in *Moby-Dick*. In *Moby-Dick,* however, the characters are not just portraits but actors created to sustain a coherent and developing action, whereas in *White-Jacket* they are but incidental parts of the overall subject, life in a man-of-war. Single scenes are built around them, but no plot.

Brilliant as the portraits are, they must be looked upon, especially those of the officers, as semi-fictions and not photographic facts. Anderson seems to have done most of what can or need be done to show the extent to which Melville described the actual officers of the *United States*. He found that it was discernibly little. Melville himself tried scrupulously to hide the real people; when Richard Henry Dana asked about them, he refused to write down the originating names:

> Will you excuse me from telling you—or rather from putting on pen-&-ink record over my name, the real names of the individuals who officered the frigate. I am very loath to do so, because I have never indulged in any ill-will or disrespect for them, personally; & shrink from any thing that approaches to a personal identification of them with characters that were only intended to furnish samples of a tribe—character[s], also, which possess some not wholly complimentary traits. If you think it worth knowing,—I will tell you all, when I next have the pleasure of seeing you face to face.[1]

We must, then, respect Melville's cloaking, a concealment amounting to fundamental alteration in order to make individuals "samples of a tribe."

Melville's mirrors distorted like those in a fun fair. His was the method of caricature, whereby a single trait is exaggerated out of normal proportion, and, presto, a person who in actuality is complex is reduced to metonymy. As pseudo-realistic, prototypical officers they are vividly set off, painted with a vigorous brush, but as particular portraits for hanging as memorials in the Naval Institute—no. Melville's is not the distortion of a Picasso, but it is certainly not the realism of a Sargent.

For one thing Melville would have known the senior officers only from a distance. The quarter-deck and the main-deck were different and divided worlds. Also, Melville painted his portraits five years after his own experiences. He could only use his few scraps of memory as starting points for fictional portraits. Take Captain Claret. As his name indicates, he is a type and not a portrait. Perhaps Captain Armstrong,[2]

1. *The Letters of Herman Melville,* edited by Merrell R. Davis and William H. Gilman (New Haven: Yale University Press, 1960), p. 107.

2. Charles Roberts Anderson, *Melville in the South Seas* (New York: Columbia University Press, 1939), pp. 362–363, discusses the identification as a possibility (evidence of Armstrong's drunkenness on one gala occasion being the chief link), although Harrison Robertson's copy of *White-Jacket* has a note reading: "Capt. James Armstrong is described as 'Capt. Claret.'" However, the chief actions of "Captain Claret" are those taken from Melville's literary rather than his experiential sources—just as with "Mad Jack," whom we next study.

under whom Melville had served, was given to intemperance, but Captain Claret's arrogance, brutality, and pigheadedness seem more to have derived from what Melville had read and known about other captains and from his need for a contrasting abstraction than from the real Captain Armstrong of the frigate *United States,* and the big scenes in which he is prominent were, as we shall see, not logbook events from Melville's firsthand experience, but were each from some one of Melville's various sources. The ill-will and disrespect which are so strong in *White-Jacket* were surely not always, if ever, feelings held by Melville towards his own officers.

How extensive and how fictional Melville's transformations of actuality were may be seen in his shaping of two of his heroic figures, Jack Chase and "Mad Jack."[3] Not a novel, *White-Jacket* has neither a strong central hero around whom a continuous and developing action is built, nor consequently any similar sort of villain. It has, rather, a set of people known from a voyage, not from a plot. There are in *White-Jacket* men of heroic stature and men of villainous actions but only as part of the institution which they serve—the military machine—and the functions they fulfill. If there be a single novelistic hero, involving any sustained though ghostly action, it then must be White-Jacket, but he is the unheroic hero, who, like you and me (and that is Melville's point), is able proleptically to quote Prufrock: "I am not a hero, nor was meant to be."

One figure, however, remains ineffaceable in the memory of readers even as it remained ineffaceable in the memory of Melville. He enters (Chapter 4) with a fanfare:

> First and foremost was Jack Chase, our noble First Captain of the Top. He was a Briton, and a true-blue; tall and well-knit, with a clear open eye, a fine broad brow, and an abounding nut-brown beard. No man ever had a better heart or a bolder. He was loved by the seamen and admired by the officers; and even when the Captain spoke to him, it was with a slight air of respect. Jack was a frank and charming man.

This "figure of romantic panache," as Ronald Mason has characterized him, lights up the pages of *White-Jacket* like a corposant. Flamboyant and rhetorical, he seems at times like an epitome of the handsome tar from a Dibdin song, from a Cooper novel, or from a Hollywood film. He is that, but he is much more; he is, said William Plomer, "a central

---

3. His *third,* Ushant, will be discussed later.

figure in the Melvillean mythology." William Ellery Sedgwick wrote that "All that is affirmative and radical and warm-blooded about *White-Jacket* centers upon the hero of the book."[4]

Before we establish Jack Chase as a historical fact we should recognize that he is partly literary convention, the handsome sailor of tradition. Of all the handsome sailors from song and story since Smollett's day who might have modeled for Melville's character, the most likely must have been Thompson, from his friend Richard Henry Dana's *Two Years Before the Mast* (pp. 65–66):

> One of them I shall always remember as the best specimen of the thoroughbred English sailor that I ever saw. He had been to sea from a boy, having served a regular apprenticeship of seven years, as English sailors are obliged to do, and was then about four or five and twenty. He was tall; but you only perceived it when he was standing by the side of others, for the great breadth of his shoulders and chest made him appear but little above the middle height. His chest was as deep as it was wide, his arm like that of Hercules, and his hand "the fist of a tar—every hair a rope-yarn." With all this, he had one of the pleasantest smiles I ever saw. His cheeks were of a handsome brown, his teeth brilliantly white, and his hair, of a raven black, waved in loose curls over all his head and fine open forehead; and his eyes he might have sold to a duchess at the price of diamonds, for their brilliancy. As for their colour, every change of position and light seemed to give them a new hue; but their prevailing colour was black, or nearly so. Take him with his well-varnished black tarpaulin stuck upon the back of his head, his long locks coming down almost into his eyes, his white duck trousers and shirt, blue jacket, and black kerchief, tied loosely round his neck, and he was a fine specimen of manly beauty.
>
> . . . He was fond of reading, and we lent him most of the books which we had in the forecastle, which he read and returned to us the next time we fell in with him. He had a good deal of information, and his captain said he was a perfect seaman, and worth his weight in gold on board a vessel, in fair weather and in foul. His strength must have been great, and he had the sight of a vulture. It is strange that one should be so minute in the description of an unknown, outcast sailor, whom one may never see again and whom no one may care to hear about; yet so it is. Some persons we see under no remarkable circumstances, but whom, for

4. William Ellery Sedgwick, *Herman Melville: The Tragedy of Mind* (Cambridge: Harvard University Press, 1944), p. 70.

some reason or other, we never forget. He called himself Bill
Jackson; and I know no one of all my accidental acquaintances to
whom I would more gladly give a shake of the hand than to him.
Whoever falls in with him will find a handsome, hearty fellow,
and a good shipmate.

Melville knew Dana's book well, he knew the sea writings of Smollett,
Dibdin, Marryat, and Cooper, and he knew Jack Chase. Around the
actual man John J. Chase spreads the aura of sentiment, a compound of
personal attraction and of literary and theatrical tradition.

The actual Jack Chase may be sketchily traced behind the Melville
creation. This is both fortunate and surprising. Of all people, the forecastle sailor is the one most likely to have as his epitaph, "Here lies one
whose name was writ in water," except that he has the irony of never
having even this bleak appropriate memorial entered on the books. By
sheer chance enough of Jack Chase's activities have been traced to shape
a small biography, and so to correct, or to refocus, Melville's account,
tacitly accepted by most readers as being straightforward fact.

John J. Chase was born in London in 1790. When Melville met him in
August 1843, Chase was fifty-three years old. Although Melville can-
nily gives him no age he nevertheless creates the image of a somewhat
younger, though experienced, man. Furthermore, knowing the year of
Jack Chase's birth serves to gloss Melville's dedication of *Billy Budd:*

Dedicated
to
Jack Chase
Englishman
Wherever that great heart may now be
Here on Earth or harbored in Paradise
Captain of the Maintop
in the year 1843
in the U. S. Frigate
United States

Certainly Jack Chase could not have been "Here on earth" when *Billy
Budd* was completed, for he would have been 101 years old. He was
alive only in Melville's memory.

Earliest located record of any sort for Jack Chase was his enlistment at
Malta in the British Navy, 23 March 1826, on the *Brisk,*[5] where he was

5. Muster Book of the *Brisk,* Admiralty 37/7368.

listed (No. 54) as age 37, born in London, and rated as an able-bodied seaman. Since the *Brisk* was over her complement, Chase was two days later transferred to the *Sybille*.[6] He was entered in its books for various small purchases (one pound sixteen shillings for slops [clothing], one shilling, fourpence for soap), and was listed as being in the ship's hospital at Malta on 29 March 1826. His monthly payment was one pound, one shilling, eightpence. Chase served out this cruise of the *Sybille,* and was paid off with the rest of the crew at Portsmouth, November 1826. Between this date and his later service in the United States Navy in 1839 is a blank. Melville's story of Jack Chase's valiant service at the Battle of Navarino is—as we shall later see—fiction,[7] and thus confuses the literal record.

Earliest American naval record for John J. Chase was his signing for service as a Seaman on board the *Consort,* 1 March 1839. He was soon promoted to Boatswain's Mate, 4 April 1839, serving in that capacity until his transfer a month later, 26 May 1839, to the *St. Louis:* "Received from U.S. Packet Brig Consort the following: John J. Chase." One month later, 29 June, the *St. Louis* sailed from New York for the Pacific Ocean, stopping at Rio de Janeiro on 9 September and arriving at Callao, Peru, on 12 January 1840. Eleven months later the logbook of the *St. Louis* reported, 18 November 1840: "All the men returned who went on Liberty yesterday, except John Bates, James Egan, G. Barrett, F. Gold, George Nixon, John Chase." Chase had thus deserted the United States Navy to serve—so Melville says—in the Peruvian Navy in her War of Independence. He left behind him a pay accumulation of $348.67.

Most of what we know about this desertion and about Chase's subsequent return unpunished to the United States Navy is the racy report given in *White-Jacket.* First, however, the solid fact of record seen in the log of the *United States;* the entries may be barer than old bones, but they are unassailable evidence:

18 May, 1842.   Commodore Jones visited the Peruvian ship [*Tungay*].

19 May   Peruvian Minister of Marine visits ship [*United States*].

22 May   Peruvian Admiral visits ship.

6. Muster Book of the *Sybille,* Admiralty 37/6999.

7. Muster Book of the *Asia,* Admiralty 37/7302, has no Jack Chase entered, nor is the name of Jack Chase to be found in the Muster Books of the other British ships engaged in the Battle of Navarino.

29 May   Received on board John J. Chase, a deserter from the U.S.S. St. Louis with a particular request to Com. Jones, from the Peruvian Admiral (in whose service he had shipped), that he might be pardoned, which was complied with by Com. Jones.

Here are indeed the elements of drama, in the ceremonial visits between the ships, in the implied pressures and resistances, in the ultimate yielding. Melville exploits the extraordinary events (Chapter 5) by the rhetorical flourishes with which he fills out, with literary license, the echoing spaces between the logbook lines:

> Here, I must frankly tell a story about Jack, which, as touching his honor and integrity, I am sure, will not work against him, in any charitable man's estimation. On this present cruise of the frigate Neversink, Jack had deserted; and after a certain interval, had been captured.
>
> But with what purpose had he deserted? To avoid naval discipline? to riot in some abandoned seaport? for love of some worthless signorita? Not at all. He abandoned the frigate from far higher and nobler, nay, glorious motives. Though bowing to naval discipline afloat; yet ashore, he was a stickler for the Rights of Man, and the liberties of the world. He went to draw a partisan blade in the civil commotions of Peru; and befriend, heart and soul, what he deemed the cause of the Right.
>
> At the time, his disappearance excited the utmost astonishment among the officers, who had little suspected him of any such conduct as deserting.
>
> "What? Jack, my great man of the main-top, gone!" cried the Captain: "I'll not believe it."
>
> "Jack Chase cut and run!" cried a sentimental middy. "It must have been all for love, then; the signoritas have turned his head."
>
> "Jack Chase not to be found?" cried a growling old sheet-anchor-man, one of your malicious prophets of past events: "I thought so; I know'd it; I could have sworn it—just the chap to make sail on the sly. I always s'pected him."
>
> Months passed away, and nothing was heard of Jack; till at last, the frigate came to anchor on the coast, alongside of a Peruvian sloop of war.
>
> Bravely clad in the Peruvian uniform, and with a fine, mixed martial and naval step, a tall, striking figure of a long-bearded officer was descried, promenading the Quarter-deck of the

stranger; and superintending the salutes, which are exchanged between national vessels on these occasions.

This fine officer touched his laced hat most courteously to our Captain, who, after returning the compliment, stared at him, rather impolitely, through his spy-glass.

"By Heaven!" he cried at last—"it is he—he can't disguise his walk—that's his beard; I'd know him in Cochin China.—Man the first cutter there! Lieutenant Blink, go on board that sloop of war, and fetch me yon officer."

All hands were aghast—What? when a piping-hot peace was between the United States and Peru, to send an armed body on board a Peruvian sloop of war, and seize one of its officers, in broad daylight?—Monstrous infraction of the Law of Nations! What would Vattel say?

But Captain Claret must be obeyed. So off went the cutter, every man armed to the teeth, the lieutenant commanding having secret instructions, and the midshipmen attending looking ominously wise, though, in truth, they could not tell what was coming.

Gaining the sloop of war, the lieutenant was received with the customary honors; but by this time the tall, bearded officer had disappeared from the Quarter-deck. The Lieutenant now inquired for the Peruvian Captain; and being shown into the cabin, made known to him, that on board his vessel was a person belonging to the United States Ship Neversink; and his orders were, to have that person delivered up instanter.

The foreign captain curled his mustache in astonishment and indignation; he hinted something about beating to quarters, and chastising this piece of Yankee insolence.

But resting one gloved hand upon the table, and playing with his sword-knot, the Lieutenant, with a bland firmness, repeated his demand. At last, the whole case being so plainly made out, and the person in question being so accurately described, even to a mole on his cheek, there remained nothing but immediate compliance.

So the fine-looking, bearded officer, who had so courteously doffed his chapeau to our Captain, but disappeared upon the arrival of the Lieutenant, was summoned into the cabin, before his superior, who addressed him thus:—

"Don John, this gentleman declares, that of right you belong to the frigate Neversink. Is it so?"

"It is even so, Don Sereno," said Jack Chase, proudly folding his gold-laced coat-sleeves across his chest—"and as there is no resisting the frigate, I comply.—Lieutenant Blink, I am ready. Adieu! Don Sereno, and Madre de Dios protect you! You have been a most gentlemanly friend and captain to me. I hope you will yet thrash your beggarly foes."

With that he turned; and entering the cutter, was pulled back to the frigate, and stepped up to Captain Claret, where that gentleman stood on the quarter-deck.

"Your servant, my fine Don," said the Captain, ironically lifting his chapeau, but regarding Jack at the same time with a look of intense displeasure.

"Your most devoted and penitent Captain of the Main-top, sir; and one who, in his very humility of contrition is yet proud to call Captain Claret his commander," said Jack, making a glorious bow, and then tragically flinging overboard his Peruvian sword.

"Reinstate him at once," shouted Captain Claret—"and now, sir, to your duty; and discharge that well to the end of the cruise, and you will hear no more of your having run away."

So Jack went forward among crowds of admiring tars, who swore by his nut-brown beard, which had amazingly lengthened and spread during his absence. They divided his laced hat and coat among them; and on their shoulders, carried him in triumph along the gun-deck.

Only the discovery of further records, in Peru or Washington, could precisely verify or correct Melville's version. Meantime, the reader will be wise to accept it but wisely remember the terse log entries. He will remember, too, that it is well to suspect Melvillean deception when confronted with such a rhetorical floodtide. That such an attitude is prudent is proved by finding that one striking element in Melville's version, the spy-glass discovery of Chase, was undoubtedly suggested to him by a passage in *Thirty Years from Home,* from which Melville took so much else. Leech wrote (pp. 75–76):

We had on board a colored man whose name was Nugent, who possessed a remarkably fine person, was very intelligent, exceedingly polite in his manners, and easy in his address. He soon grew weary of the caprices of our officers, and ran away. He was taken, however, in rather a curious manner. The officers frequently walked the deck with their spy-glasses. As one of them was spending a few leisure moments in looking at the surrounding shipping, what should appear within the field of his glass, but the person of the fugitive Nugent on the deck of an American vessel! Upon this, a boat was despatched [sic], which soon returned with the crestfallen deserter, who was unceremoniously thrown into irons. By some fortunate chance, however, he escaped a flogging.

Deserter Jack Chase was extraordinarily pardoned and entered on the Muster Roll as Number 573.[8] Within a month, on 19 July 1842, he was promoted to Captain of the Maintop, where he served, and where we see him in the book, for the rest of the voyage. His extraordinary pardon and his flattering promotion are substantive affirmations of the basic truth (Chase as hero) of Melville's portrait.

Jack Chase's striking personality is highlighted several times in vivid scenes. Was it real or was it rhetorical? We can never know, but we can notice to our surprise that the scenes in which that personality is set are ones borrowed by Melville from his books. The arraignment of White-Jacket, the liberty granted to the crew at Rio, and the Battle of Navarino are three striking glorifications of Jack Chase, but they are events which Melville conveniently found elsewhere than in memory to serve as a foil for his heroic friend. These actions, then, are not part of the biography of John J. Chase; they are, rather, a part of the reputation of *Neversink*'s Jack Chase.

One instance of Melville's search for an appropriate setting for Chase occurs early in *White-Jacket*. In the British Seaman's *Life on Board a Man-of-War* (pp. 83–84), a tar named Jack Burgess vexes his mates by his too-frequent reference to his former service on board the famous frigate *Tremendous:*

> "Well, well, Jack," said a wag of the name of Smith, "I hope it is not again going to be, 'When I was aboard *The Tremendous.*'"
> "None of your bloody jaw," retorted Burgess, "many things I seed in *The Tremendous* before you knew the difference 'twixt a gun and marlin-spike." "Come, some, Jack, get on," said several more of them. . . . "Well, d'ye see, when I was on board—d——— me! what are you laughing at, Smith? Do you think I was coming out with '*The Tremendous*' again?"

8. Rear Admiral Thomas O. Selfridge's criticism of the Chase section reads: "He early introduces us to his beau ideal of a sailor Jack Chase, an Englishman, who had served in His, or Her Majesty's service, & was a Captain of the Neversink's Maintop; between whom and himself quite an intimacy existed—This character is too overdrawn for a reality—The slang uttered by Jack Chase to Tubbs the whaler savours of any thing but the gentleman, a title which the author is of opinion could be deservedly applied to his friend—
"The clemency shown towards Jack Chase, after his recapture as a deserter, is not in accordance with experience & usage—" Charles R. Anderson, "A Reply to Herman Melville's *White-Jacket* by Rear-Admiral Thomas O. Selfridge, Sr.," *American Literature,* VII (May 1935), pp. 127–128.

Although Burgess' habit is referred to in four other places, this small scene suggested to Melville one of similar scope and point, giving Jack Chase the occasion for a bit of fore-top wit (Chapter 4):

> His whole demeanor was in strong contrast to that of one of the Captains of the fore-top. This man, though a good seaman, furnished an example of those insufferable Britons, who, while preferring other countries to their own as places of residence; still, overflow with all the pompousness of national and individual vanity combined. "When I was on board the Audacious"—for a long time, was almost the invariable exordium to the fore-top Captain's most cursory remarks. It is often the custom of men-of-war's-men, when they deem any thing to be going on wrong aboard ship, to refer to *last cruise,* when of course every thing was done *ship-shape and Bristol fashion.* And by referring to the *Audacious*—an expressive name by the way—the fore-top Captain meant a ship in the English navy, in which he had had the honor of serving. So continual were his allusions to this craft with the amiable name, that at last, the *Audacious* was voted a bore by his shipmates. And one hot afternoon, during a calm, when the fore-top Captain, like many others, was standing still and yawning on the spar-deck; Jack Chase, his own countryman, came up to him, and pointing at his open mouth, politely inquired, whether that was the way they caught *flies* in Her Britannic Majesty's ship, the *Audacious?* After that, we heard no more of the craft.

From this, and later patchwork, we shall see that Jack Chase of the *Neversink* is altered from "reality" as much as any other portraits in the book.

•

Until recently the story of Jack Chase was uncritically held to be "true." (As was *White-Jacket* itself.) Then Charles Anderson turned up some of the records to verify some of that truth, strengthening the conviction that the Chase story must be all "true." The present study may confuse more than clarify the neat conclusions of those who want it all one way or the other. What makes *White-Jacket* interesting is, however, this blend of fable and fact which was Melville's special recipe. Melville does not contradict the evidence of logbooks and muster rolls; he simply embroiders on them. Let us use a rule: when Chase's language and actions become extravagantly flamboyant (remember, though, that much of this is not so much sheer sound as it is Melvillean irony), Melville is then reworking something he has read and which is therefore not, as related to Chase, "real." This rule operated in the fly-in-the-mouth scene; it operated in the spy-glass discovery touch; it will operate in several more instances, as it now operates in the lively Chapter 23 on "Theatricals in a Man-of-war."

"Theatricals in a Man-of-war" (Chapter 23) is one of those episodes which puzzled and troubled Melville's sailor readers, upsetting them because their log memories told them that no such theatricals had actually occurred on board the frigate *United States* on its South Seas cruise. Harrison Robertson wrote in his copy of the book, "Fiction." What they did not see was that the theatricals take place on board the *Neversink* and constitute, therefore, a pseudo-fact, having validity as a characteristic, or representative, event, and not a literal fact of life aboard the *United States*.

The theatricals did, in a sense, take place in a somewhat different way, but on board the frigate *Constitution,* if we may accept Mercier's narrative as essentially literal. Two chapters of Mercier's *Scenes* are Melville's indispensable source. To dramatize the Mercier material and to strengthen his delineation of Jack Chase, Melville made Chase the star performer in the theatricals. John J. Chase actually existed, but as this present study will show, what we really know about him from *White-Jacket* is very little, so completely has Melville wrapped him round with actions taken from other books.

Melville's alteration and embroidery of Mercier's two sections on ship theatricals is considerable. *Scenes,* for example, describes in two different places two different performances: "Aquatic Theatricals" (pp. 118–124), and "Fourth of July in a Yankee Frigate," (pp. 218–229). From these two long accounts Melville took the essential details for the single performance which takes place on the *Neversink.*

Appropriately the play is given as a Fouth of July diversion. Now in Mercier the Fourth of July had first been celebrated with a "skylarking," a ship custom in which normal discipline is suspended, the grog ration increased, and time given over to drunken revelry—dances, wrestling, fights. The orgy is described in several pages of *Scenes;* Melville summarizes it in 400 words as common naval practice, concluding, almost primly, "But from scenes like these the Neversink was happily delivered. Besides that she was now approaching a most perilous part of the ocean [Cape Horn]—which would have made it madness to intoxicate the sailors—her complete destitution of *grog,* even for ordinary consumption, was an obstacle altogether insuperable, even had the Captain felt disposed to indulge his man-of-war's men by the most copious libations." Thus Melville tied his theatre fiction to his earlier grog fiction in Chapter 15, both taken from *Scenes.*

Melville had no similar ship memories to associate with what he read in Mercier. The log of the *United States* has no record of shipboard theatricals during Melville's service. Melville adopts the fiction that Captain Claret, having formerly refused shipboard theatricals in the harbor at Callao, Peru, was now disposed to allow them as a substitute for skylarking:

> Now, some weeks prior to the Neversink's sailing from home— nearly three years before the time here spoken of—some of the seamen had clubbed together, and made up a considerable purse, for the purpose of purchasing a theatrical outfit; having in view to diversify the monotony of lying in foreign harbors for weeks together, by an occasional display on the boards—though if ever there was a continual theatre in the world, playing by night and by day, and without intervals between the acts, a man-of-war is that theatre, and her planks are the *boards* indeed.

This passage is an interesting weaving. The "considerable purse" raised by the sailors was taken from two such funds in *Scenes,* the first (p. 118):

> At the commencement of our cruise the entire ship's company came forward, with all a sailor's frank generosity, and subscribed something like two hundred and fifty dollars towards the theatrical fund.

and, later (p. 122):

> so taken were our old sea-dogs with the theatrical *mania,* that they again set a subscription on foot, and replenished the funds with two or three hundred dollars more.

The metaphor of the ship as a stage was Melville's development of the reminder in *Scenes:* "But Shakespeare says that 'all the world's a stage.'" The bad pun on "ruffian" which Melville puts in Captain Claret's mouth was made from a simple statement in *Scenes* (p. 121)

that the dramatic troupe on board the *Constitution* "by particular request
of the officers . . . again came forth with the Ruffian Boy."

The best addition, perhaps, which Melville made to the materials
from Mercier was the parody playbill announcing the *Neversink* performance: "a broadside of staring capitals . . . found tacked against
the main-mast on the gun-deck. It was as if a Drury-Lane bill had been
posted upon the London monument." It was the expansion of a simple
hint in Mercier (p. 124):

> During the whole cruise, our Thespians "trod the boards" with
> untiring energy; and the morning preceding a performance, crowds
> might be seen around the main-topsail-sheet bitts on the main
> deck, eagerly conning over the *dramatis personae,* which in large
> written characters stared them in the face, with as much *gusto* as
> the play-goer on *terra firma* would a flaming bill of fare of the
> Park or Bowery; and plenty of willing tars were always ready to
> volunteer their services, to *rig up* in the neatest style possible, our
> acquatic theatre.

The extravagance of the handbill was admirably in keeping with the
tone of the entire scene as Melville reworked it, and above all as he
centered it on hero Jack Chase, so that the flourishes of the playbill are
appropriate to the panache (partly creating it) of the sailor-poet-actor
whose name comically dominates the bill, who gaily dominates the play
itself. Even the idea of using Chase in this way was quite probably
suggested to Melville by the fore-top-man who spoke the prologue for
the performances on board the *Constitution* (p. 119):

> As soon as the company were all assembled the tinkling of the
> prompter's bell was heard; in another moment the curtain was
> gently raised, and all awaited in breathless anxiety to see how the
> affair was about to commence; one of our fore-top-men now
> stepped out, tastily rigged *a la mariner;* he was greeted with a
> round of applause; and after making his obeisance to the impatient
> audience, who were staring at him as if they would pierce him to
> the very soul, delivered the following address, which he had previ-
> ously *manufactured for the* occasion[.]

One hundred pages later Mercier brings "our fore-top poet" again to
recite a prologue. From these hints Melville produced his own fore-top
actor and poet, Jack Chase.

The "uncommon attraction" advertised in this parody poster was *The*

CAPE HORN THEATRE.

Grand Celebration of the Fourth of July.
DAY PERFORMANCE.
UNCOMMON ATTRACTION.

THE OLD WAGON PAID OFF!
JACK CHASE........PERCY ROYAL-MAST.
STARS OF THE FIRST MAGNITUDE.
For this time only,
THE TRUE YANKEE SAILOR.

The managers of the Cape Horn Theatre beg leave to inform the inhabitants of the Pacific and Southern Oceans that, on the afternoon of the Fourth of July, 184–, they will have the honor to present the admired drama of

THE OLD WAGON PAID OFF!

Commodore Bougee......*Tom Brown, of the Fore-top.*
Captain Spy-glass.......*Ned Brace, of the After-Guard.*
Commodore's Cockswain..*Joe Bunk, of the Launch.*
Old Luff...............*Quarter-master Coffin.*
Mayor.................*Seafull, of the Forecastle.*
PERCY ROYAL-MAST.....JACK CHASE.
Mrs. Lovelorn..........*Long-locks, of the After-Guard.*
Toddy Moll............*Frank Jones.*
Gin and Sugar Sall......*Dick Dash.*
Sailors, Marines, Bar-keepers, Crimps, Aldermen, Police-officers, Soldiers, Landsmen generally.

Long live the Commodore! ‖ Admission Free.

To conclude with the much-admired song by Dibdin, altered to suit all American Tars, entitled

THE TRUE YANKEE SAILOR.
True Yankee Sailor (in costume), Patrick Flinegan, Captain of the Head.

Old Wagon Paid Off, Melville's simple variation of Mercier's play,
"Old Ironsides paid off." "The Old Wagon" was the nickname of the
Frigate *United States.* Jack Chase carries off the leading role of Percy
Royal-Mast; when he "rescues fifteen oppressed sailors from the watch-
house, in the teeth of a posse of constables, the audience leaped to their
feet, overturned the capstan bars, and to a man hurled their hats on the
stage in a delirium of delight. . . . The commotion was now terrific;
all discipline seemed gone for ever." The officers became so alarmed that
they ordered the drum beaten to call the men to quarters, and, just in
time to furl sails against a coming storm, order was restored. Alas, a
salacious promise in the handbill was not fulfilled: "the sailors never
recovered from the disappointment of not having the *'True Yankee
Sailor'* sung by the Irish Captain of the Head." Now the frolic was
ended: "an old sailor touched my shoulder, and said, 'See, White-
Jacket, all round they [the officers] have *shipped their quarter-deck
faces* again. But this is the way.' "

•

We see Jack Chase several more times as we move through *White-
Jacket,* but only once does he show up in history outside, and after, the
events narrated by Melville. After parting at Boston in October 1844
when the crew of the *United States* was paid off, Herman Melville and
Jack Chase apparently never met again. Chase, however, continued, for a
time at least, to serve in the United States Navy. A marginal notation in
my first edition of *White-Jacket,* written beside the name of Jack Chase,
reads: "Now serving on board the Constitution in the Mediterranean."
The muster roll and the log for the 1850/1851 cruise of the *Constitution* verify this note. Chase's name is also entered in the medical record
for treatment both for dysentery and boils, inglorious sufferings for a
hero who thus proves himself to be of the same frailty as ordinary men.
But the most significant, even startling, record of Chase's activity in
connection with the *Constitution* is exposed in the log entry for 12 July
1850:

and Jno. J. Chase Cap. F: C, disrated to sea from 7th July (the
time his liberty expired), for breaking his liberty 52 hours—disobedience of orders and being brought off by the Police—reported
and confined by Lt. Rowan—rated Joseph Bennett (Qr. Gunner)
Cap. of F. C, from 7th July vice Jno. J. Chase disrated to Sea.

The unflawed, unflogged Jack Chase of the *Neversink* was, during his service aboard the *Constitution,* flawed and almost flogged—saved from that brutality only by his rating. In other words, at the very moment when *White-Jacket* was being reviewed by the press of England and America and when Jack Chase was parading as the handsome sailor in a book savagely attacking the penal practices of the United States Navy, especially flogging, John J. Chase himself came close to undergoing that inhumane treatment. It is this kind of irony—life commenting thus on literature—that is to recur on the publication of *Moby-Dick,* when, as if for a publicity stunt, a sperm whale sank the *Ann Alexander* in the South Pacific. "Ye Gods," Melville could have said, "What a commentator is this *Constitution* Log Book!" Biographically, the rest is silence, pending the discovery of further records. Jack Chase's mythical service at the Battle of Navarino in 1828, and his rescue of White-Jacket as told by Melville, are fables which will be discussed later.

•

Jack Chase is the heroic sailor of the main-deck. His quarter-deck counterpart is Mad Jack, one of the *Neversink* lieutenants. Mad Jack is a flawed hero indeed, much given to drink and to vile tempers, but a man for a crisis. He appears in but two actions, but both are critical and in each he is magnificent.

We know little or nothing about his prototype, if prototype there was. However born in Melville's mind, Mad Jack aroused Duyckinck's admiration in the *Literary World:* "Chaucer could not have seen him with brighter eyes." It has been said that he was modeled from Lieutenant Avery[9] on board the *United States,* and the ups and downs of that man's record suggest that he might possibly be the "source." Lieutenant Percival, too, has been suggested for the role. However this may be, it really doesn't matter because the two actions of which Mad Jack is the hero are ones which happened elsewhere, to other men, in books read and used by Melville. Mad Jack appears briefly but strongly; his "reality" is emphatic because of Melville's admiration for his

9. See Charles Roberts Anderson, *Melville in the South Seas* (New York: Columbia University Press, 1939), pp. 363–365, for a discussion of Lieutenant Latham B. Avery as the prototype for "Mad Jack." Here, as possibly with Captain Claret-from Captain Armstrong, Melville has probably taken the physical, actual officer as a point of departure, and to this remembered form has added actions from literary sources. Avery was No. 69 on the *United States'* Muster Roll.

courage, his decisiveness in danger. To define the manliness of Mad Jack, Melville created a contrasting character, described at length and with satiric sneers, in Lieutenant Selvagee. Of Selvagee no prototype has been nor can be reasonably nominated from the *United States* Muster Roll. His name itself is a metonymy, a selvagee being (Chapter 8):

> a slender, tapering, unstranded piece of rope; prepared with much solicitude; peculiarly flexible; and wreathes and serpentines round the cable and messenger like an elegantly modeled garter-snake round the twisted stalks of a vine. Indeed, *Selvagee* is the exact type and symbol of a tall, genteel, limber, spiralizing exquisite. So much for the derivation of the name which the sailors applied to the Lieutenant.

Not that Selvagee was incompetent—"Theoretically he understood his profession; but the mere theory of seamanship forms but the thousandth part of what makes a seaman. You cannot save a ship by working out a problem in the cabin; the deck is the field of action." Selvagee, like Cassio, or like Tybalt, worked from the book. Mad Jack worked from a sense of the situation. Selvagee, then, represents the head, the calculated and unspontaneous response, in contrast to the heart and the instinctively right intuitive action, ready when it counted, of Mad Jack. Here he is:

> With this gentleman of cravats and curling irons, how strongly contrasts the man who was born in a gale! For in some time of tempest—off Cape Horn or Hatteras—*Mad Jack* must have entered the world—such things have been—not with a silver spoon, but with a speaking-trumpet in his mouth; wrapped up in a caul, as in a main-sail. . . .
> Mad Jack is in his saddle on the sea. *That* is his home; he would not care much, if another Flood came and overflowed the dry land; for what would it do but float his good ship higher and higher and carry his proud nation's flag round the globe, over the very capitals of all hostile states! Then would masts surmount spires; and all mankind, like the Chinese boatmen in Canton River, live in flotillas and fleets, and find their food in the sea.

Interestingly, this passage not only portrays Mad Jack; it anticipates an even greater passage in *Moby-Dick* in its tidal rhythm, its strong stresses: the closing lines on Nantucket, where in similar images—the Chinese afloat, Noah's flood, the terraqueous world—Melville honors not just one great sailor in particular, like Mad Jack, but the greatest of all sailors, the Nantucket whaleman. Familiar though the words are, it is well to print them again to set them against their first draft:

> The Nantucketer, he alone resides and riots on the sea; he alone, in Bible language, goes down to it in ships; to and fro ploughing it as his own special plantation. *There* is his home; *there* lies his business, which a Noah's flood would not interrupt, though it overwhelmed all the millions in China. He lives on the sea, as prairie cocks in the prairie; he hides among the waves, he climbs them as chamois hunters climb the Alps. For years he knows not the land; so that when he comes to it at last, it smells like another world, more strangely than the moon would to an Earthsman. With the landless gull, that at sunset folds her wings and is rocked to sleep between billows; so at nightfall, the Nantucketer, out of sight of land, furls his sails, and lays him to his rest, while under his very pillow rush herds of walruses and whales.

In *White-Jacket* Mad Jack twice averts disaster. Paradoxically and ironically, because he *is* such a good officer he supports Melville's implied thesis that most officers are scarcely to be trusted—he is the exception. His first dramatic appearance saves the very ship itself, but before this exploit may be described, we should notice the prior encounter of the *Neversink* with the *Sultan,* for this passage (Chapter 26), too, anticipates greater episodes in *Moby-Dick,* and is in effect first draft for them.

> Ere the calm had yet left us, a sail had been discerned from the fore-top-mast-head, at a great distance, probably three leagues or more. At first it was a mere speck,[10] altogether out of sight from the deck. By the force of attraction, or something else equally inscrutable, two ships in a calm, and equally affected by the currents, will always approximate, more or less. Though there was not a breath of wind, it was not a great while before the strange sail was descried from our bulwarks; gradually, it drew still nearer.
> What was she, and whence? There is no object which so excites interest and conjecture, and, at the same time, baffles both, as a sail, seen as a mere speck on these remote seas off Cape Horn.
> A breeze! a breeze! for lo! the stranger is now perceptibly near-

10. This is, of course, an echo from Coleridge's "Rime of the Ancient Mariner," the coming-on of the spectre ship of Life-in-Death. For other Coleridge echoes in the Cape chapters of *White-Jacket,* see below, pp. 80–82.

ing the frigate; the officer's spy-glass pronounces her a full-rigged ship, with all sail set, and coming right down to us, though in our own vicinity the calm still reigns.

She is bringing the wind with her. Hurrah! Ay, there it is! Behold how mincingly it creeps over the sea, just ruffling and crisping it.

Our top-men were at once sent aloft to loose the sails, and presently they faintly began to distend. As yet we hardly had steerage-way. Toward sunset the stranger bore down before the wind, a complete pyramid of canvass. Never before, I venture to say, was Cape Horn so audaciously insulted. Stun'-sails alow and aloft; royals, moon-sails, and every thing else. She glided under our stern, within hailing distance, and the signal-quarter-master ran up our ensign to the gaff.

"Ship ahoy!" cried the Lieutenant of the Watch, through his trumpet.

"Halloa!" bawled an old fellow in a green jacket, clapping one hand to his mouth, while he held on with the other to the mizzen-shrouds.

"What ship's that?"

"The Sultan, Indiaman, from New York, and bound to Callao and Canton, sixty days out, all well. What frigate's that?"

"The United States ship Neversink, homeward bound."

"Hurrah! hurrah! hurrah!" yelled our enthusiastic countryman, transported with patriotism.

By this time the Sultan had swept past, but the Lieutenant of the Watch could not withhold a parting admonition.

"D'ye hear? You'd better take in some of your flying-kites there. Look out for Cape Horn!"

But the friendly advice was lost in the now increasing wind. With a suddenness by no means unusual in these latitudes, the light breeze soon became a succession of sharp squalls, and our sail-proud braggadocio of an Indiaman was observed to let every thing go by the run, his t'-gallant stun'-sails and flying-jib taking quick leave of the spars; the flying-jib was swept into the air, rolled together for a few minutes, and tossed about in the squalls like a foot-ball. But the wind played no such pranks with the more prudently managed canvass of the Neversink, though before many hours it was stirring times with us.

The Neversink has been warned of peril; in disregarding the warning she is almost destroyed, saved only by miracle and by the command of Mad Jack. Such a situation of disregarding warning, of ships' meeting, is a carefully worked out pattern in Moby-Dick, the nine important meetings in which the *Pequod* is warned against the white whale, not one of which is respected by the willful captain. Captain Claret can be equated in no other way than this with Captain Ahab, that he too will not listen to prudence, and it is only through his imprudent lieutenant, alcoholic and choleric Mad Jack, that he survives. Ahab had no such corrective; sane, sober Starbuck could not rise to the heroic defiance of Mad Jack. Again *White-Jacket* served *Moby-Dick* as training exercise. Mad Jack's saving act, contrary to the orders of the befuddled Captain Claret, follows immediately as the storms mentioned by the *Sultan* strike the *Neversink* and are about to overturn her:

In a sudden gale, or when a large quantity of sail is suddenly to be furled, it is the custom for the First Lieutenant to take the trumpet from whoever happens then to be officer of the deck. But Mad Jack had the trumpet that watch; nor did the First Lieutenant now seek to wrest it from his hands. Every eye was upon him, as if we had chosen him from among us all, to decide this battle with the elements, by single combat with the spirit of the Cape; for Mad Jack was the saving genius of the ship, and so proved himself that night. I owe this right hand, that is this moment flying over my sheet, and all my present being to Mad Jack. The ship's bows were now butting, battering, ramming, and thundering over and upon the head seas, and with a horrible wallowing sound our whole hull was rolling in the trough of the foam. The gale came athwart the deck, and every sail seemed bursting with its wild breath.

All the quarter-masters, and several of the forecastle-men, were swarming round the double-wheel on the quarter-deck. Some jumping up and down, with their hands upon the spokes; for the whole helm and galvanized keel were fiercely feverish, with the life imparted to them by the tempest.

"Hard *up* the helm!" shouted Captain Claret, bursting from his cabin like a ghost in his night-dress.

"Damn you!" raged Mad Jack to the quarter-masters; "hard *down*—hard *down*, I say, and be damned to you!"

Contrary orders! but Mad Jack's were obeyed. His object was to throw the ship into the wind, so as the better to admit of close-reefing the top-sails. But though the halyards were let go, it was impossible to clew down the yards, owing to the enormous horizontal strain on the canvass. It now blew a hurricane. The spray flew over the ship in floods. The gigantic masts seemed about to snap under the world-wide strain of the three entire top-sails.

"Clew down! clew down!" shouted Mad Jack, husky with

excitement, and in a frenzy, beating his trumpet against one of the shrouds. But, owing to the slant of the ship, the thing could not be done. It was obvious that before many minutes something must go—either sails, rigging, or sticks; perhaps the hull itself, and all hands.

Presently a voice from the top exclaimed that there was a rent in the main-top-sail. And instantly we heard a report like two or three muskets discharged together; the vast sail was rent up and down like the Vail of the Temple. This saved the main-mast; for the yard was now clewed down with comparative ease, and the top-men laid out to stow the shattered canvass. Soon, the two remaining top-sails were also clewed down and close reefed.

Above all the roar of the tempest and the shouts of the crew, was heard the dismal tolling of the ship's bell—almost as large as that of a village church—which the violent rolling of the ship was occasioning. Imagination can not conceive the horror of such a sound in a night-tempest at sea.

"Stop that ghost!" roared Mad Jack; "away, one of you, and wrench off the clapper!"

But no sooner was this ghost gagged, than a still more appalling sound was heard, the rolling to and fro of the heavy shot, which, on the gun-deck, had broken loose from the gun-racks, and converted that part of the ship into an immense bowling-alley. Some hands were sent down to secure them; but it was as much as their lives were worth. Several were maimed; and the midshipmen who were ordered to see the duty performed reported it impossible, until the storm abated.

The elements of this experience seem to have been suggested to Melville by a long passage in *Scenes* (p. 261) where the ship is saved by the tearing of the great sail:

The cry of "all hands shorten sail," brought the ship's company on deck, and the confusion became general. "If she comes to the wind, or parts the wheel-ropes," cried our boatswain, "we'll have a woful tale to tell to-morrow morning." But an all-bounteous Providence interfered, she paid off; and at that moment the fore-sail with the report of a loud clap of thunder, was split to shreds; which occurrence had it taken place some seconds before, ere the ship began to feel her helm and pay off, nothing could have saved her from broaching to; and the consequences, God only knows how dreadful they might have been. By the time we got the fore-top-sail furled, and the fragments of the foresail secured on the yard, the fierceness of the squall relaxed; but it still blew a gale, and whilst endeavouring to get our top-sails reefed and a fore-storm staysail in readiness to set, another deafening report told but too plainly the infuriated tempest had made more ravages; and upon looking aloft there was the three-reefed maintop-sail, which up to this time had powerfully withstood the wrath of the maddened elements, literally split to pieces, the heavy canvass streaming in the air like a gossamer, and defying like an enraged tiger the most determined to dare approach it.

I must not fail to give praise where it is due; our first lieutenant remained firm at his post, giving his orders with that determined coolness, which plainly proved to even those who were not otherwise prepossessed in his favour, that he was an officer in whom implicit confidence might be placed in extreme danger[.]

There is no countermanded order, but Mad Jack may have been suggested by Mercier's "first lieutenant [who] remained at his post, giving his orders with that determined coolness. . . ."[11]

The rest of Melville's chapter portraying nature's storm and man's coolness, "The Pitch of the Cape," tells of the crew's later, futile attempt to furl the great flapping sail, with the ship heeled at a sharp angle, the poles covered with ice—a time when, fear at last transcended, "You become identified with the tempest; your insignificance is lost in the riot of the stormy universe around." It is marine writing of the highest excellence, worthy of *Moby-Dick* itself—indeed, the chapter ending on a symbolic note in which the intense physical experience becomes a kind of parable:

But, sailor or landsman, there is some sort of a Cape Horn for all. Boys! beware of it; prepare for it in time. Gray-beards! thank God it is passed. And ye lucky livers, to whom, by some rare fatality, your Cape Horns are placid as Lake Lemans, flatter not yourselves that good luck is judgment and discretion; for all the yolk in your eggs, you might have foundered and gone down, had the Spirit of the Cape said the word.

Melville's salty and monster-infested marine world found its inevitable and eloquent correspondence in his spiritual universe. In such a universe, most memorably described in *Moby-Dick,* men are heightened, made heroic or villainous, on a scale permitting such confrontations or retreats from Nature.

11. It might even be that the *Sultan* episode, just discussed, was suggested by the meeting of the *Constitution* with the *Sarah.*

Mad Jack will appear, as we shall soon see, once again to save the Captain from his folly. His defiance is not uncommon in sea literature; it is, indeed, a built-in situation from sea-life, and hence in sea memoirs and novels, as, for example, Starbuck in *Moby-Dick* down to the central situation of *The Caine Mutiny*.

·6·

The Search
for Significant Themes

JACK CHASE was introduced in Chapters 4 and 5, Mad Jack in Chapter 8. In between, the other officers were presented in quick sketches, each introduction emphasizing the hierarchic structure of the *Neversink,* its microcosmic role: "For a ship is a bit of terra firma cut off from the main; it is a state in itself; and the captain is its king. . . . He is lord and master of the sun" (Chapter 6). Melville, that is, is slowly finding his center or his strongest subject, gathering himself together for his subsequent full-throated assault on autocratic tyranny. For the moment, however, mere information and good-natured mockery govern these introductions.

At times the comedy is broad. "Breakfast, Dinner, and Supper" (Chapter 7) pokes fun at the class structure as shown by the different feeding times of these naval animals; it is a satire of the problems of a ship's mess, and rising to his conclusion, Melville sees the enervating effects in comically exaggerated consequences, appealing for help to high authority:

> Mr. Secretary of the Navy, in the name of *the people* [the for-gotten sailor], you should interpose in this matter. Many a time have I, a main-top-man, found myself actually faint of a tempestu-ous morning watch, when all my energies were demanded—owing to this miserable, unphilosophical mode of allotting the govern-ment meals at sea.

This parody appeal does more than merely lighten the early section of the book; it prepares the reader for the passionate appeals on funda-mental human issues which later give *White-Jacket* its propagandistic power.

Food for Melville was a frequent, favorite subject for humor. This very chapter is almost an early draft of those scenes in *Moby-Dick* (Chapter 33, "The Specksynder," and Chapter 34, "The Cabin Table") when Ahab and his mates go through their daily ritual dance of status— their descent to the cabin to dine, one following the other, representing their descent in official and human rank.

•

The mess is crowded, the decks are crowded—the *Neversink* is a crowded world where privacy is at a premium, where the individual soul has difficulty finding itself, protecting itself. It is from and for such a theme that Melville reintroduces the jacket in "Of the Pockets that were in the Jacket" (Chapter 9). In that crowded world will the jacket, altered to the purpose, give him self-sufficiency?

> Now, in sketching the preliminary plan, and laying out the foundation of that memorable white jacket of mine, I had had an earnest eye to all these inconveniences, and resolved to avoid them. I proposed, that not only should my jacket keep me warm, but that it should also be so constructed as to contain a shirt or two, a pair of trowsers, and divers knickknacks—sewing utensils, books, bis-cuits, and the like. With this object, I had accordingly provided it with a great variety of pockets, pantries, clothes-presses, and cupboards.

The more intricate the jacket becomes the less effectively it serves. It is now labyrinthine to futility and to comic excess. What has happened in Melville's treatment of the jacket as theme is that he has muted and muffled the implications of the jacket as artistic problem, as book, and has brought forward the other symbolism, the jacket as self-sufficiency and psychological security, to make that theme predominate for the rest of his narrative. The jacket-as-book, which was the emphasis of the first chapter, is now the jacket-as-self; but this is not an outright displacement, it is obligato and echo. After all, an author's book is a significant part of himself; his sequence of books is a series of reports on himself as much as it is upon the physical worlds they pretend objectively to mirror. White-Jacket as author is not entirely lost in the subsequent comedy of White-Jacket as maturing mind—itself a subject almost lost beneath the man-of-war materiality.

Chapter 9, however, giving nothing by way of information concerning life on board a man-of-war, simply tells in comic terms of the ineffectuality of pockets, and of jackets in general. "So, in the end, I masoned up my lockers and pantries; and save the two used for mittens, the white jacket ever after was pocketless."

•

The crowded *Neversink* versus the individual's privacy threads its way as theme through the two subsequent chapters, "From Pockets to Pickpockets" (Chapter 10) and "The Pursuit of Poetry under Difficulties" (Chapter 11). Himself a poet, Melville creates one for the ship, perhaps even remembers one.

A source study of such detail as this book might seem to imply that very little, almost nothing, in *White-Jacket* is from Melville's own direct experience, but is material taken and transformed from books, from the "sources." Such an implication would be directly opposite from the view of the early sailor-reader—that *White-Jacket* was straightforward Melville autobiography. Surely, and certainly, there is a middle ground. Actuality keeps breaking into our *White-Jacket*, taking us from the library to the deck of the *United States* itself, or to Melville's memory of it.

Such an instance seems to occur in Chapter 11, "The Pursuit of Poetry under Difficulties." Melville is making the general point that the ship is a crowded microcosm and that privacy is at a premium under such conditions. How in a crowded world does one find, and then maintain, one's self-reliance, the virtue so insisted on by Emerson? One way, Melville implies, is through authorship, but he makes comedy of the idea by describing the difficulties of a ship-poet, "Lemsford, the gun-deck bard," who finds that the writing and the preservation of poetry amid eyes both prying and hostile is difficult to a laughable degree.

Melville has much fun with Lemsford and his dilemma both here and later in Chapter 45, and Lemsford is prominent enough to suggest a "source" in fact or in fiction. Three nominations have been made from the *United States* Muster Roll: George W. Wallace, George W. Weir, and Ephraim Curtiss Hine.

Charles R. Anderson[1] proposed the first two names when he dis-covered inserted in the log of the *United States* a manuscript of verses "Respectfully Inscribed to J. J. C. by his sincere Friend G. W. W." "J. J. C." was easy to identify because the only one with those initials in the Muster Roll was John J. Chase. Indeed, who else more deserved the honor of a dedication than Jack Chase! Anderson found two "G. W. W."s, and since no further evidence was available whereby to distinguish between them, both were possibilities. The inscribed verses were not original but were simply a transcript of lines by Felicia Hemans.

Years later a more probable candidate was nominated by Harrison Hayford,[2] who brought forward a good argument for Ephraim Curtiss Hine, number 339 on the Muster Roll. Hine served on board the *United States* eleven of the fourteen months of Melville's own service, and one year before the actual writing of *White-Jacket*, Ephraim C. Hine pub-lished *The Haunted Barque, and Other Poems* (Auburn and New York: M. H. Newman & Co., 1848), verses dealing primarily with scenes visited during his *United States* cruise. His prefatory remarks contain some illuminating sentences:

> Most of the following poems were composed at sea, while the Author was attached to an American Frigate cruising in the Pacific Ocean, to while away the tedious hours—the monotony and ennui of life on board a ship of war. The kind partiality of his friends, and his own belief that some of the pieces possess merit, induce him to lay them before the public. With these few remarks the Author rests his defence, and sensible that the work must stand or fall on its own merit, commits it to the indulgence of his readers.

1. Charles Roberts Anderson, *Melville in the South Seas* (New York: Co-lumbia University Press, 1939), p. 367.
2. "The Sailor Poet of *White-Jacket*," *Boston Public Library Quarterly*, III (July 1951), pp. 221–228.

Two points from these words should be developed. First, it is possible that Hine's reference to "the monotony and ennui of life on board a ship of war" suggested to Melville his use of Lemsford's poetics in Chapter 45, "Publishing Poetry in a Man-of-war," especially in a section devoted to ways of passing time while the *Neversink* is in the harbor at Rio. Hine's "monotony" becomes an amusing and unmonotonous chapter in Melville's monotony section.[3]

The second point is Hine's mention of the disastrous "public" reception of his poems. Lemsford's "public reception" of his shipboard poetry was even more disastrous, for they were shot from the cannon where he had hidden them, his verses coming out with a bang and not a whimper—Hine's the opposite!—in each case a calamity for the poor author. This may have suggested the nice distinction which Jack Chase forces from the poet when, referring to his previous and much-criticized book of poems, Lemsford says, in Chapter 45:

> "Blast them, Jack, what they call the public is a monster, like the idol we saw in Owhyhee, with the head of a jackass, the body of a baboon, and the tail of a scorpion!"
> "I don't like that," said Jack; "when I'm ashore, I myself am part of the public."
> "Your pardon, Jack; you are not. You are then a part of the people, just as you are aboard the frigate here. The public is one thing, Jack, and the people another."
> "You are right," said Jack; "right as this leg. Virgil, you are a trump; you are a jewel, my boy. The public and the people! Ay, ay, my lads, let us hate the one and cleave to the other."

Hayford has assembled the arguments tellingly, and it is wise, other evidence lacking, to accept his conclusion:

> Allowing for Melville's characteristic humorous heightening, Lemsford's original was evidently a dedicated if facile poet. Upon these grounds E. Curtiss Hine qualifies as the original of Lems-

---

3. Early in Mercier (pp. 27ff.) there is a social gathering of sailors on board ship, including "Some sons of poetry and romance . . . imbibing the balmy influence of the weather on the *booms*"; however, it is impossible to determine how such bits attracted Melville's attention and so furnished inspiration for adaptation and development of such a casual item.

ford; and, in any case, as an exemplar of the gun-deck poets of whose tribe Melville made Lemsford the representative.[4]

One other possibility might be lightly entertained: that Melville had himself in mind and may have been mocking poetic ardors of his own. Yoomy in *Mardi* is evidence not only that Melville himself wrote poetry during the 1840's, but also that he could laugh at his own, and others', poetizing. This is not to say that Melville, a poet *manqué,* went out in sympathy and identification, as well as with mockery, to his gun-deck poet and friend. Melville altered the characters and personalities of his old friends from the *United States,* but apparently his sketches of Nord, Williams, and Lemsford are affectionate personal memories not much disguised.

Structurally, *White-Jacket* is built as a documentary and not as a novel; the narrator serves more as guide than as creator; he leads us around the man-of-war to show us its life—both "its" life as a ship and the living within the ship. Being an imaginative man, he makes his descriptions vivid, and when he has the chance—he also creates the chances!—he likes to tell a story. Always, however, as he is telling us, we can remember that others have told him, and that generally he is writing out of that unbeatable combination of personal experience, reading for verification and stimulation, and fictive imagination. "Originality," as a scientist paradoxically wrote, "comes from reading." Now as we move about the *Neversink's* world, we will see that it is in good part stitched together with patches, mainly from Mercier and, especially in the examples to follow, Samuel Leech.

Like Mercier, Leech makes much of the various divisions on a man-of-war. On pages 39–45, in particular, he discusses the watches, the stations, the crowdedness and the discomfort; each paragraph from *Thirty Years from Home* becomes a chapter in *White-Jacket,* many of them dramatic scenes. Leech's words (p. 39), which served him almost as a topic sentence for his pages, might well serve Melville for his chapters:

A vessel of war contains a little community of human beings, isolated, for the time being, from the rest of mankind. This

---

4. Hayford, *op. cit.,* p. 227. Hayford discovered a short novel by Hine: *Orlando Melville or the Victims of the Press-Gang, A Tale of the Sea* (Boston: 1848). Orlando Melville and his Irish companion are impressed on board *H. M. S. Macedonian* and fight against the *United States.* There is also a flogging, and also framed-up charges against the Irishman, but Hayford concludes that "the resemblances to anything in *White-Jacket* or *Billy Budd* are slight."

community is governed by laws peculiar to itself; it is arranged and divided in a manner suitable to its circumstances. Hence, when its members first come together, each one is assigned his respective station and duty.

Most of this had been expository help to Melville. Rambling though the chapters may be, they are tactfully diversified, shifting from dramatic scenes to comic interludes to informative lectures at the will of the narrator. Certainly it is for comic relief primarily that Chapter 14, "A Drought in a Man-of-war," was adapted from Mercier's *Scenes*.[5] Telling of the crew's woe at the absence of grog, the episode is not in the *United States* log.[6] The chapter adds very little to our knowledge about "life in a man-of-war" except to show the sailor's fondness for grog; it is, rather, a comic interlude, alleviating the monotony of too much straightforward exposition.

Information and humor are well blended in Melville's succeeding Chapter 15, "A Salt-Junk Club in a Man-of-war." Here Melville returns to the ship's mess—Melville may be trusted to bring up frequently the subject of food—the problems of food supplies, of cooking, of sociality in the mess. From the fifth chapter of John Nicol's *Life and Adventures* (p. 74), Melville took the name of the Negro cook, "Coffee," and also the good-natured character of the Negroes on shipboard with their dances and songs. Melville lifts the text of one song from Nicol (p. 72):

> I lost my shoe in an old canoe,
> Johnio! come Winum so;
> I lost my boot in a pilot boat,
> Johnio! come Winum so.

and to these lines, from some source unknown, he adds two more lines to complete the stanza:

> Den rub-a-dub de copper, oh!
> Oh! copper rub-a-dub-a-oh.

5. Even explaining why the grog scene, out of Mercier, was introduced at this point, to give dramatic life to dull fact. See Keith Huntress, "Melville's Use of a Source for *White-Jacket*," *American Literature*, XVII (1945), 66–74.

6. See Anderson, pp. 396–398.

What is important about the chapter is Melville's introduction of the rejection theme: White-Jacket has difficulty getting into a mess because of the sailors' dislike of the white jacket:

> Somehow, there had never been a very cordial feeling between this mess and me; all along they had nourished a prejudice against my white jacket. They must have harbored the silly fancy that in it I gave myself airs, and wore it in order to look consequential. . . .

White-Jacket tucks up his jacket and withdraws from the mess. It is only through the intercession of Jack Chase that he is able to find acceptance in any other place. The episode, extended to several pages, should be read rather than paraphrased. The germ of this scene of rejection was Leech's *Thirty Years from Home* (pp. 36–37), and was related to the "divisions" section of his book, guide for Melville.

> The morning after my arrival, I was put into a "mess." The crew of a man of war is divided into little communities of about eight, called *"messes."* These eat and drink together, and are, as it were, so many families. The mess to which I was introduced, was composed of your genuine, weather-beaten, old tars. But for one of its members, it would have suited me very well; this one, a real gruff old "bull-dog," named Hudson, took into his head to hate me at first sight. He treated me with so much abuse and unkindness, that my messmates soon advised me to change my mess, a privilege which is wisely allowed, and which tends very much to the good fellowship of a ship's crew; for if there are disagreeable men among them, they can in this way be got rid of; it is no unfrequent case to find a few, who have been spurned from all the messes in the ship, obliged to mess by themselves.

Hudson becomes in Melville a "little, oily fellow, who had once kept an oyster-cellar ashore; he bore me a grudge" and the short anecdote of Leech's expands dramatically and comically, ironically, and even gets caught in the folds of the shroudlike jacket.

·

The factual fullness of *White-Jacket* is employed for various effects— for simple information, for humor, for satire, for moral indignation. "General Training in a Man-of-war," Chapter 16, is Melville's first instance of moral concern. Leech's *Thirty Years from Home* was the essential source but the moral horror which Melville introduces is his own.

A man-of-war is not ultimately a cruise-ship, although recruitment posters might suggest this. It is an instrument of destruction; this being so, men must learn to kill.

> As the specific object for which a man-of-war is built and put into commission is to fight and fire off cannon, it is, of course, deemed indispensable that the crew should be duly instructed in the art and mystery involved.

There are the preliminaries to battle, and there is the mock battle, both primarily out of Leech's pages. Take, for example, his account of the beat to quarters (p. 41):

> Stations are also assigned at the guns, to the whole crew. When at sea, the drummer beats to quarters every night. This beat, by which the men are summoned to quarters, is a regular tune. I have often heard the words sung which belong to it; this is the chorus:
>
> > "Hearts of oak are our ship, jolly tars are our men.
> > We always are ready, steady, boys, steady,
> > To fight and to conquer again and again."
> > At the roll of the evening drum, all hands hurry to the guns.

Melville follows this closely:

> The summons is given by the ship's drummer, who strikes a peculiar beat—short, broken, rolling, shuffling—like the sound made by the march into battle of iron-heeled grenadiers. It is a regular tune, with a fine song composed to it; the words of the chorus, being most artistically arranged, may give some idea of the air:
> > "Hearts of oak. . . ."

As the sham battle, or war game, continues, White-Jacket's imagination dwells more and more on the "vast difference—if you sound them—between a reality and a sham," and several paragraphs take on an intensity appropriate to a "real" battle. The reason for this intensity is apparent when one sees that in describing the exercise Melville has taken material from Leech's vivid account of a real battle. Leech served him all

the way through the chapter. Even Leech's "station at the fifth gun"
turns up in Melville: "The carronade at which I was stationed was
known as 'Gun No. 5,' on the First Lieutenant's quarter-bill." Melville
will towards the end of *White-Jacket* describe two actual naval battles,
and for one of these he will use much of this present material from
Leech. Leech's account, however, was a long one, sufficiently full for
Melville to extract sections of it for the exercises and still have plenty
left for the real battle later. His image of the amputation scenes below
decks, the shattered masts and yards, the freely flowing rivers of blood—
all comes straight from the pages (142–147) of *Thirty Years from
Home*. Even though deeply indebted to Leech, Melville's scene, ending
with the terrible roll call, is something far beyond Leech's skill:

> *Then,* when all was over, and all hands would be piped to take
> down the hammocks from the exposed nettings (where they play
> the part of the cotton bales at New Orleans), we might find bits of
> broken shot, iron bolts, and bullets in our blankets. And, while
> smeared with blood like butchers, the surgeon and his mates would
> be amputating arms and legs on the berth-deck, an underling of
> the carpenter's gang would be new-legging and arming the broken
> chairs and tables in the Commodore's cabin; while the rest of his
> *squad* would be *splicing* and *fishing* the shattered masts and
> yards. . . .
>   *Then,* upon mustering the men, and calling the quarter-bills by
> the light of a battle-lantern, many a wounded seaman, with his
> arm in a sling, would answer for some poor shipmate who could
> never more make answer for himself:
>   "Tom Brown?"
>   "Killed, sir."
>   "Jack Jewel?"
>   "Killed, sir."
>   "Joe Hardy?"
>   "Killed, sir."
>   And opposite all these poor fellows' names, down would go on
> the quarter-bills the bloody marks of red ink—a murderer's fluid,
> fitly used on these occasions.

This striking roll call, however, is not in Leech but another favorite
Melville source: the British Seaman's *Life on Board a Man-of-War* (p.
171):

> The Purser then began to call the names; a dead silence reigned
> over the deck.

The names had been called for a little, and the answer was, "Here," till one didn't answer. "He's killed, sir," said one; "Mark him off, Mr. Andrews," said the Captain. Thus it went on, every two or three names that were called being answered by the words, "Killed," or "Wounded."

Melville's heightening of the Leech–British Seaman sources is a savage spurt of the *saeva indignatio* which blazes through the last third of *White-Jacket*. Melville is beginning to find significant subjects, both here and in the two chapters which follow.

•

The rhetorical intensity of "The Jacket aloft," Chapter 19, tapers off towards the end of the chapter into the comedy of the paint-quest and of White-Jacket's rejection, but that very comedy itself is unusual, almost forced, an embarrassed laugh with which to pass off the emotionalism just displayed. In any case, as if aware of his discordant intensity, Melville follows with three chapters as ordinary as might be imagined—the sleeping and cleaning practices on board a crowded ship; he turns from the disturbing symbolic world of the jacket to the trivialities of the main-deck. It is a story of physical discomfort and of gripes and grumbles; but it is also an attack on sadistic tyranny, the subject which becomes increasingly important throughout *White-Jacket*.

The third of the three washing chapters, Chapter 22, "Wash-day, and House-cleaning in a Man-of-war," is an account of holy-stoning. Now it may be that Melville himself actually had had to holy-stone the decks of the *United States,* so that memory gave momentum to his attack on the custom, but as so often happened, Melville also wrote from at least one other account. Seldom mentioned in sailor narratives, holy-stoning *was* described by four of Melville's sources—once by the British Seaman,[7] twice by Mercier, but more vividly by Dana and by Leech; it is from the latter two that Melville adopted his description.

7. P. 28: "On reaching deck, I got a holy-stone* placed in my hand, and was told to lend a hand in scrubbing the boards. It was a cold January morning; a strong sharp east wind was blowing at the time; we were obliged to go on our knees on the wet decks, and my fingers soon got so benumbed that they could scarcely hold the stone. While engaged in this comfortless occupation (which lasted for two hours), I could not help thinking how preferable. . . ."

* *Holy-stones* are smooth sand-stones, and are rubbed on the deck after it is wet and sanded, which makes the deck appear, when dry, of a beautiful white.

Dana (p. 142)   Leech (pp. 83–84)

The head pump was then rigged, and the decks washed down by the second and third mates; the chief mate walking the quarter-deck and keeping a general supervision, but not deigning to touch a bucket or a brush. Inside and out, fore and aft, upper deck and between-decks, steerage and forecastle, rail, bulkwarks, and water-ways, were washed, scrubbed, and scraped with brooms and canvas, and the decks were wet and sanded all over, and then holy-stoned. The holystone is a large soft stone, smooth on the bottom, with long ropes attached to each end, by which the crew keep it sliding fore and aft over the wet sanded decks. Smaller handstones, which the sailors call "prayerbooks," are used to scrub in among the crevices and narrow places where the large holystone will not go. An hour or two we were kept at this work, when the head pump was manned, and all the sand washed off the decks and sides. Then came swabs and squilgees; and after the decks were dry, each one went to his particular morning job.

By holy-stoning, I mean cleaning them with stones, which are used for this purpose in men of war. These stones are, some of them, large, with a ring at each end with a rope attached, by which it is pulled backwards and forwards on the wet decks. These large stones are called holy bibles; the smaller hand ones are also called holy-stones, or prayer-books, their shape being something like a book. After the decks are well rubbed with these stones, they are wiped dry with swabs made of rope-yarns. By this means the utmost cleanliness is preserved in the ship.

Thus for the description, but Melville had not brought up the subject of holy-stoning as a mere encyclopedic fact. He wanted to use it to attack the officers for their tyranny—the main-deck and its eternal opposition to the quarter-deck. Accepting, as Melville did, that on shipboard over-cleanliness was next to ungodliness, Melville saw how routine was made the cover for sadistic authority:

Melville (Chapter 22)

Leech (pp. 100–101)

Then on all three decks the operation of holy-stoning begins, so called from the queer name bestowed upon the principal instruments employed. These are ponderous flat stones with long ropes at each end, by which the stones are slidden about, to and fro, over the wet and sanded decks; a most wearisome, dog-like, galley-slave employment. For the by-ways and corners about the masts and guns, smaller stones are used, called *prayer-books;* inasmuch as the devout operator has to down with them on his knees. . . .

In the Neversink, as in other national ships, the business of *holy-stoning* the decks was often prolonged, by way of punishment to the men, particularly of a raw, cold morning. This is one of the punishments which a lieutenant of the watch may easily inflict upon the crew, without infringing the statute which places the power of punishment solely in the hands of the Captain.

The abhorrence which men-of-war's-men have for this protracted *holy-stoning* in cold, comfortless weather—with their bare feet exposed to the splashing inundations—is shown in a strange story, rife among them, curiously tinctured with their proverbial superstitions.

The First Lieutenant of an English sloop of war, a severe

The most disagreeable duty in the ship was that of holy-stoning the decks on cold, frosty mornings. Our movements were never more elastic than when at this really severe task. As usual, it gave occasion to a variety of forecastle yarns about cold stations. Among these was one which was attested by many witnesses, and there can be no doubt of its truth.

A British frigate was once stationed in a cold climate. The first lieutenant was a complete tyrant, delighting in everything that caused the crew to suffer. Among other things, he took especial care to make the work of holy-stoning as painful as possible, by forcing them to continue at it much longer than was necessary. Although he had no watch on deck, he would contrive to be up in season to annoy the men with his hated presence. One morning, the weather being unusally [sic] severe, the men sprang to their task with unwonted agility, and contrived to finish it before the appearance of their persecutor. To their vexation, however, just as they had completed their work, he bounced on deck, with a peremptory order to wash the decks all over a second time.

The men dropped on their knees with the holy-stones, and prayed, as the tyrant went below, that he might never come on deck again alive. Whether disciplinarian, was uncommonly particular concerning the whiteness of the quarter-deck. One bitter winter morning at sea, when the crew had washed that part of the vessel, as usual, and put away their holy-stones, this officer came on deck, and after inspecting it, ordered the *holy-stones* and *prayer-books* up again. Once more slipping off the shoes from their frosted feet, and rolling up their trowsers, the crew kneeled down to their task; and in that suppliant posture, silently invoked a curse upon their tyrant; praying, as he went below, that he might never more come out of the ward-room alive. The prayer seemed answered; for being shortly after visited with a paralytic stroke at his breakfast-table, the First Lieutenant next morning was carried out of the ward-room feet foremost, dead. As they dropped him over the side—so goes the story—the marine sentry at the gangway turned his back upon the corpse.

God heard the cry of the oppressed crew, or whether it was the action of the ordinary natural laws, the reader must determine for himself; but when the lieutenant again appeared on deck, he was brought up "feet foremost," to be buried. He was taken sick that morning: his disease baffled the skill of the surgeon, and in a few days he was a corpse. The opinion that he died a monument of the divine displeasure against cruel, hard-hearted men of power, and of disregard for the miseries and tears of the oppressed poor, is at least worthy of serious consideration.

Dana and Leech had provided Melville with his description of holy-stoning; Leech supplied the illustrative anecdote; but it was William McNally who gave him the theme itself as he described the "harrassing and unnecessary" work imposed on sailors by petty tyrants. Melville's simple statement:

Among all men-of-war's-men, it is a maxim that over-neat vessels are Tartars to the crew; and perhaps it may be safely laid down that, when you see such a ship, some sort of tyranny is not very far off.

is really a distillation of several hints from McNally, this one especially (p. 98):

the most harrassing and unnecessary work was done on board that ship; every handspike, crow-bar, and belaying-pin was scoured bright; the iron straps of snatch blocks, iron travellers round the masts, linchpins of the guns, ringbolts in the deck, trainbolts in the gun carriages, iron rail round the forecastle, and the iron straps of the cat blocks were all kept as bright as silver; and many hundreds of floggings did keeping these bright occasion; which was entirely out of order and as such was laughed at by the rest of the officers on the station.

Anyhow, Melville has now described the ship sufficiently to use it as the setting for some action, to add narration to description—although of course the categories are not discrete—so that he next uses his art to describe the passage of Cape Horn, able to compete with, as well as to use, not merely Ames and Mercier, but, most daringly, Richard Henry Dana.

·7·

The Ship as Fact,
Fiction, and Symbol

I N Honolulu 17 August 1843 Herman Melville became a crew member of the United States Frigate *United States,* entered in the Muster Roll as Number 572 for a term of either three years or the "cruize." Fourteen months later, on 14 October 1844, the crew was paid off at Boston, and Herman Melville was released. After instructions from his brother Gansevoort to shave and make himself presentable, he returned to his mother's home in Lansingburgh, near Albany, soon to drift into the career of professional authorship.

That fateful—because it in time helped to create Melville's book—year's cruise has been closely studied by Charles R. Anderson.[1] It should

1. *Melville in the South Seas* (New York: 1939), pp. 361–394.

be stressed here, however, that the *United States* was then an ancient vessel with an honorable history. Built at a cost of nearly $300,000, she was launched at Philadelphia on 10 July 1797. She was built under the Act of 1796 and was a sister ship to the *Constellation*.[2] One of her crew succinctly described and praised her:

> The United States Frigate United States is a fine Single banked Frigate, measuring 178 [175] feet from the Knight heads to the Tafrail, 45 [43.6] feet moulded beam, and 29 feet from her Kelson to Spar Deck; mounting 20 thirty two's and 2 twenty four pounders on Spar Deck, and 30 twenty four pounders on Gun Deck; and of 1750 tuns. She was built in Philadelphia, Pa., in 1797 and has always been considered the fastest sailor in the American Navy.[3]

Her moment of greatness was her defeat and capture of the British ship *Macedonian,* 12 October 1812, to be discussed later. When Melville signed on the *United States* she was near the end of her long career. There is fateful if fanciful symbolism discernible here: Melville set out for the South Seas on a ship just born, the *Acushnet,* and returned on a ship just concluding its career. Even the names are appropriate: the first for Ishmael-Melville seeking fulfillment of romantic dream in a primitive world, and the second, a White-Jacket–Melville returning to a codified world, a "real" world, to become an American author. As Melville said, from his twenty-fifth year he dated his life, a birthday which, literally, he observed on board the man-of-war nearing its home port.

·

The *Pequod* is of course the flagship of Melville's fictional fleet. At first for Melville the ship was but a ship, unsymbolic and realistic. So for the *Julia* and the *Dolly* in *Typee* and *Omoo*—good honest whaling craft. The war canoes in *Mardi* carrying a set of allegorical characters among the allegorical islands were never genuine war canoes,

2. F. S. Hill, *Twenty-Six Historic Ships* (New York and London: 1903), pp. 199–201.
3. Charles Roberts Anderson, ed., *Journal of a Cruise to the Pacific Ocean, 1842–1844, in the Frigate United States,* with notes on Herman Melville (Durham: 1937), p. [20]. The author of this abstract of the cruise is unidentified.

really described, *felt,* and used as such, but only convenient transporta-
tion for the strange seekers of the even stranger Yillah. Although realistic in contrast to the *Mardi* stage-craft, the *Highlander* in *Redburn* is
no more than a transatlantic sailing ship, although more than the
previous ships she is used as an arena of human struggle, a container of
human varieties constituting a limited world. She is not, however, a
microcosm. With *White-Jacket* and the *Neversink,* Melville finally
found his symbolic ship in the solidly materialistic man-of-war, and
from this creation it was but a step to the *Pequod* world, a United
Nations, or, as Melville put it (remembering his Carlyle), "an Anachar-
sis Clootz deputation of nations." The ship as a microcosm then first
fully appears in *White-Jacket.* As Evert Duyckinck wrote in *The
Literary World,* 16 March 1850, "To Melville the ship is a new world,
now first conquered. No man has so occupied it."

Modeled mainly on the frigate *United States,* but, literarily, modeled also on Mercier's memory of the *Constitution,* White-Jacket's
Neversink has a splendid actuality. *White-Jacket* is a solidly realistic
book. As an account of a nineteenth-century man-of-war under sail it is
the classic book on the subject, just as *Moby-Dick* is the Bible for
students of whales and whaling, authentic in its facts and vivid in its
historic realism. It is an *informed* and not merely a studied realism,
achieved by Melville's memories of the *thing* and by his reading to
corroborate or to correct those memories.

The ship is a microcosm. . . .

So stereotyped has this image become we may fail, as Duyckinck did
not, to perceive its freshness and force when Melville used it, and so
deny him his proper priority. Perhaps he was encouraged to use it from
reading Jacques' "All the world's a stage" quoted in *Scenes* (Mercier
had a decided tendency to drag out the obvious literary tags.). Melville's
logic might be that if Shakespeare the actor could use his metier, the
stage, as a microcosm, why shouldn't he, mariner Melville, use the ship
likewise? "If ever there was a continual theatre in the world, playing by
night and by day, and without intervals between the acts, a man-of-war
is that theatre, and her planks are the *boards* indeed." Melville, like
Shakespeare, was writing from a long literary convention, but then no
author may use the metaphors of sun, sea, stars, moon, woods without
the same weight on his back. Such archetypal symbols are always old and
only in the hands of an original author do they become new. The ship as
a microcosm traces back, no doubt, to the ark, and comes to us through
the ship-of-fools motif of the Middle Ages and the Renaissance. In
America, however, the microcosmic nature of America, the melting pot,

made Melville's use of the metaphor fresh and significant. It had almost been phrased four years before, in Autumn 1845, in Emerson's *Journal:* "so in this continent,—asylum of all nations,—the European tribes,—of the Africans, and of the Polynesians,—will construct a new race, a new religion, a new state. . . ." all of which is, of course, an echo from Crevecoeur.

In any case, what gives Melville's metaphor life as against the deadliness of a cliché, is the surrounding and full physical sense of the ship.

The specific suggestion[4] for the metaphor came to Melville from two passages in Mercier's *Scenes* (p. 129):

> The crew of a Yankee man-of-war, presents as curious an amalgamation of Adam's descendants as can be well imagined—amongst them, you may perceive mechanics of every sort—from the unsophisticated tippling son of Crispin, to the loquacious wit-cracking setter of types—from the sinewy iron-framed son of Vulcan, to the cadaverous pale-faced maker of muffins and crumpets—from the prodigal, broken down blower of glass, to the rough-spun slayer of sheep and oxen. The articled clerk, tired of wielding his "gray goose-quill"—the fashionable black-leg, completely "done up"—the quibbling pettifogger, whose chicanery had become odious to the public—the hero of the sock and buskin, whose benefits had produced but "a beggarly account of empty boxes"—the ignorant quack, whose multitudinous hyperbole in the columns of the daily papers, could not procure him a single patient of respectability—as well as the little gad-fly of fashion, pursued by hungry and remorseless creditors—fly to the confines of a man-of-war in their several difficulties; and here, in the friendly society of the rough, unpolished sons of Neptune, and amidst the unceasing turmoil of nautical life, forget in some measure the disquietudes and perplexities that assailed them on shore.

and on p. 200:

> Well, say what you will, a Yankee man-of-war is a curious place. Some writers expatiate in glowing terms upon the scenes to be met

4. What is meant by "suggestion" includes the idea, so memorably stated by T. S. Eliot, that the poet's mind in creative activity combines strange objects or ideas to make new wholes. Or as Emerson put it in his *Journal,* 1837(?), "The art of writing consists in putting two things together that are unlike and that belong together, like a horse and cart."

with in a small watering-place, amongst itinerant violin-players, broken down dancing-masters, hard-run black-legs, and pert little misses in their teens—pshaw! take a tight Yankee frigate such as "Old Ironsides," place her on a foreign station, and you will see more diversity of character develope [sic] itself—you will see more real scenes enacted to the life amongst the curious medley by which she is manned, in one short week, than the naval novelists, Marryatt or Chamier, could dish up for the public palate in a twelvemonth.

Working from these statements, Melville created Chapter 18 of *White-Jacket,* "A Man-of-war Full as a Nut." He radically improved the wording of his source, however, just as, indeed, he developed its metaphorical sense. Mercier makes a statement to the effect that a ship is a cosmos but he does not *use* the trope. His *Constitution* is limitedly realistic. Read Melville's words to see the contrast in style and in meaning.

Indeed, from a frigate's crew might be culled out men of all callings and vocations, from a backslidden parson to a broken-down comedian. The Navy is the asylum for the perverse, the home of the unfortunate. Here the sons of adversity meet the children of calamity, and here the children of calamity meet the offspring of sin. Bankrupt brokers, boot-blacks, blacklegs, and blacksmiths here assemble together; and castaway tinkers, watch-makers, quill-drivers, cobblers, doctors, farmers, and lawyers compare past experiences and talk of old times. Wrecked on a desert shore, a man-of-war's crew could quickly found an Alexandria by themselves, and fill it with all the things which go to make up a capital.

Melville's care with his sentences in his adaptation bespeaks his concern for the meaning. His opening sentence is nicely balanced in both sound—rhythm and alliteration—and sense; the next sentence balances two rhythmical phrases, while the third sentence is closely interlocked by word repetitions that enhance the wit. If the next sentence—"Bankrupt brokers . . ."—seems overly alliterative, especially in its first clause, remember that its intent is to suggest a long catalogue so that the effect of the successive "b" words is appropriately that of a roll-call.

The second half of the chapter develops four picturesque and apt semi-Homeric similes, reinforcing what Melville has already stated. The ship is (1) "a city afloat," (2) "a garrisoned town, like Quebec," (3) "like the lodging houses in Paris," and (4) like "a three-story house in a suspicious part of town." The aptness and pleasantness of the tropes conceal the fact that Melville is hammering home his single point.

Two of these images Melville used again. The "city afloat"—Leech's "floating city"—was implicit in creating the *Pequod* (which, if not a city, was at least a village), and later, the *Fidèle* in *The Confidence-Man*. The Quebec simile Melville reused to describe Father Mapple in his pulpit, "impregnable in his little Quebec."

In this short chapter of less than 500 words, Melville carefully set forth some of his basic metaphors, thus formally and separately announcing it was a programmatic act of recognition, a making explicit that which will subsequently be implicit. The image was especially apt, of course, for a crowded man-of-war, with its variety of men, of professions, of activities, and with its hierarchy, its undemocratic structure, a feudal world in contradiction of the democratic world for which it acted as agent, as instrument. When, soon, the *Pequod* sails, she will be more genuinely a general world, a floating cosmopolis, although she too will become ironically and destructively subservient to the will of a tyrant—Melville goes from feudalism to fascism. Melville's original metaphor —or at least the way his use of it gave it new freshness—was felt by at least one reviewer, Henry F. Chorley, writing for *The Athenaeum*: "We cannot recall another novelist or sketcher who has given the poetry of the Ship—her voyages and her crew—in a manner at all resembling his." Later, Melville complained of the difficulty of getting "poetry from blubber" but here he had learned to get poetry from oaken timbers. The poetry in *White-Jacket* is much more muted than that in *Moby-Dick,* but *White-Jacket* has, to borrow a phrase from Thoreau, "a right materialistic treatment which delights everyone."

Since the ship as a whole becomes an active symbol in Melville, it is likely, almost inevitably, that special parts of the ship are also symbolic. "A Man-of-war Full as a Nut" had succinctly and poetically described the ship as a microcosm, a *world*-enclosure. It is certainly no accident that immediately following this, in Chapter 19, "The Jacket aloft," Melville counterpointed his social symbol with a private one. The appropriate place on the ship for symbolic self-enclosure was the mast-head, to which White-Jacket retreated, far above the deck, dreamily to stare into space. The contrapuntal play of the social and the private themes in *White-Jacket* has been neglected whereas the "socialities" and the "isolatoes" in *Moby-Dick* have been much discussed. Unheeded, too, has been the striking resemblance between the mast-head meanings of *White-Jacket* and those of "The Mast-Head" (Chapter 35) in *Moby-*

Dick. Different in many details, they are twins in spirit, in essential meaning, and both come from the same active sensibility, from the same exaltation and delight in the act of mast-head-sitting.

Evidence of Melville's personal pleasure in life aloft abounds in his books, but it is in his journals as well. When travelling as a passenger to England in the fall of 1849 (the manuscript of *White-Jacket* in his valise), he wrote: "Spent the entire morning in the main-top with Adler & Dr. Taylor," or nine days later, "Ran about aloft a good deal." The conversations engaged in during these lofty moments were metaphysical and philosophical.

With this evidence we may take as essentially personal the feeling toward the main-top as conveyed in his books from *Redburn* (1849) to *Billy Budd* (1891).

In *Redburn,* the first ascent of the rigging and the terror-delight at height, space, and motion are expressed with a power and vividness new to Melville, in Chapter 16, "At Dead of Night He is Sent up to Loose the Main-Skysail." Eight chapters later, "He Begins to Hop about in the Rigging like a Saint Jago's Monkey," Redburn sums up his feeling: "There was a wild delirium about it; a fine rushing of the blood about the heart; and a glad thrilling, and throbbing of the whole system. . . ."

As has been said and as we shall several times see, life aloft plays a considerable part in *White-Jacket.* Much of the action—the Shenley episode, the fall of Bungs, the flashbacks to Navarino and to the War of 1812, the fall of White-Jacket from the mast-head—and much of the book's inner meaning are there. Jack Chase was Captain of the Fore-top, and White-Jacket held it a high honor to be of the "club" which gathered aloft to enjoy the socialities of sea songs and sailor yarns.

The special significance of the top for White-Jacket is first stated forthrightly in Chapter 19:

Again must I call attention to my white jacket, which about this time came near being the death of me.

I am of a meditative humor, and at sea used often to mount aloft at night, and, seating myself on one of the upper yards, tuck my jacket about me and give loose to reflection. In some ships in which I have done this, the sailors used to fancy that I must be studying astronomy—which, indeed, to some extent, was the case —and that my object in mounting aloft was to get a nearer view of the stars, supposing me, of course, to be short-sighted. A very silly conceit of theirs, some may say, but not so silly after all; for surely

the advantage of getting nearer an object by two hundred feet is
not to be underrated. Then, to study the stars upon the wide,
boundless sea, is divine as it was to the Chaldean Magi, who observed their revolutions from the plains.

And it is a very fine feeling, and one that fuses us into the
universe of things, and makes us a part of the All, to think that,
wherever we ocean-wanderers rove, we have still the same glorious
old stars to keep us company; that they still shine onward and on,
forever beautiful and bright, and luring us, by every ray, to die and
be glorified with them.

While these connections are being made, it is well to relate the fusion-in-
the-universe sort of thing also with a familiar passage from one of
Melville's letters, written to Hawthorne when *Moby-Dick* was almost
ready for the press:

In reading some of Goethe's sayings, so worshipped by his vo-
taries, I came across this, *"Live in the all."* That is to say, your
separate identity is but a wretched one,—good; but get out of
yourself, spread and expand yourself, and bring to yourself the
tinglings of life that are felt in the flowers and the woods, that are
felt in the planets Saturn and Venus, and the Fixed Stars. What
nonsense! Here is a fellow with a raging toothache. "My dear
boy," Goethe says to him, "you are sorely afflicted with that tooth;
but you must *live in the all,* and then you will be happy!" As with
all great genius, there is an immense deal of flummery in Goethe,
and in proportion to my own contact with him, a monstrous deal
of it in me.

Having said this much, Melville ironically qualified his words in a
postscript:

This "all" feeling, though, there is some truth in. You must often
have felt it, lying in the grass on a warm summer's day. Your legs
seem to send out shoots into the earth. Your hair feels like leaves
upon your head. This is the *all* feeling. But what plays the mis-
chief with the truth is that men will insist upon the universal
application of a temporary feeling or opinion.

Such a passage goes far to illuminate Melville's enchanted dreamer
passages in his novels, the postscript above all showing a sensibility able
poetically to sympathize (not necessarily to accept) with that which his

mind told him to resist, a man sensitively balanced between idealism and realism. Melville is always contrasted with Emerson by writers, but he himself admitted to attraction to as well as repulsion from the Emersonian school of thought, and his momentary absorption into the All is at once a discerning criticism of and a susceptibility to the wise passivity of the Romantics.

·8·

The Initiation
of Cape Horn

And now there came both mist and snow,
And it grew wondrous cold:
And ice, mast-high, came floating by,
As green as emerald.
                    Coleridge, "The Rime of the Ancient Mariner"

IN *White-Jacket* there is surprisingly little about the actual voyage
itself. Perhaps for two reasons: (1) very little actually happened outside
normal routine on Melville's own trip, and (2) his subject is life *on
board* a man-of-war. Melville, however, extends his own remembered
normal routine to include episodes from others' cruises; and he uses the

limitation of "life on board a man-of-war" with equal freedom. This recognized, still there is in *White-Jacket* very little about the actual sea and the ship's passage through it.

One important exception to this is the four chapter sequence about Cape Horn. The passage of the Cape could, as Melville reminds us, often be routine—attended with less hardship, than a passage undertaken from the Atlantic—but it could be, and was, just as often sheer hell for ships and men.[1] It was for its terrors and not for its serenities that Cape Horn had become a symbol for storm and stress, as much an initiation experience for a sailor as killing an Indian was for Natty Bumppo. From the Cape Horn passage Melville constructed one of his longest unified sections, running to four chapters (24–27) as the *Neversink* rounds the Cape, and two more chapters as she edges away from it. In quality, too, as well as quantity, this section bulks large in Melville's book.

As the Ancient Mariner's ship moved towards the challenge of the Cape, she had a tutelary angel protecting her, granting her fair winds. The *Neversink* has in its turn the spirit of Coleridge to give it grace, and the great lines of the "Rime of the Ancient Mariner" irradiate the seamanly chapters of Melville. Melville's opening paragraph to Chapter 24, "Introductory to Cape Horn," emphatically echoes the familiar poetic lines quoted at the head of this chapter. "And now, through drizzling fogs and vapors, and under damp, double-reefed top-sails, our wet-decked frigate drew nearer and nearer to the squally Cape." Such a sentence is a palpable derivation, and in the subsequent chapters there are other equally undisguised echoes, to such an extent that one asserts and happily accepts this tutelary attendance of the poet as an enlarging element in the documentary prose. Melville has sought Coleridge's aid partly because the Cape passage has assumed mythic significance to him, giving a new dimension to otherwise prosy materials, allying now his chapter, on the Cape experience, with the great initiation myths of western literature, as in the short second paragraph:

> Who has not heard of it? Cape Horn, Cape Horn—a *horn* indeed, that has tossed many a good ship. Was the descent of

1. Melville's own trip around the Cape, returning home, was neither placid nor eventfully perilous or stormy. See log of the *United States* for the latter half of July 1844. Cape Horn has always been to navigators the epitome of the confrontation of peril, and for a modern example of such a confrontation, see Sir Francis Chichester, *Gipsy Moth Circles the World* (London and New York: 1968), Chapter 14, pp. 172–190. One would give much to see Melville's marginal comments on such pages.

Orpheus, Ulysses, or Dante into Hell, one whit more hardy and sublime than the first navigator's weathering of that terrible Cape?

Or, Melville implies, of any navigator's first weathering of "that terrible Cape," or of any life-navigator confronting his own personal psychological-spiritual cape. It is the confrontation theme thus sewn into Melville's chapters which partly explains their heightened meaning, their super-Mercier, almost super-Dana, effect.

Coleridge's influence is strong in the third paragraph; one needs not quote the poetic lines to discern their presence in Melville's prose:

> Turned on her heel by a fierce West Wind, many an outward-bound ship has been driven across the Southern Ocean to the Cape of Good Hope—*that* way to seek a passage to the Pacific. And that stormy Cape, I doubt not, has sent many a fine craft to the bottom, and told no tales. At those ends of the earth are no chronicles. What signify the broken spars and shrouds that, *day after day,*[2] are *driven* before the *prows* of more fortunate vessels? or the *tall masts,* imbedded in *icebergs,* that are found *floating by?* They but hint the old story—of ships that have sailed from their ports, and never more have been heard of.

This is this sort of borrowing, undisguised and openly allusive, which gives resonance to the borrower's work.

Although "Introductory to Cape Horn" is introductory in trying sketchily to give the history of the Cape, it is introductory in that the first half is a semi-lyric address to the "squally," the "terrible," the "stormy," the "Impracticable Cape!" A poetic sense of the menace, and yet the majesty, of the sea sings through the paragraphs—which is why, perhaps, he summoned the guiding genius of Coleridge. There was another and more immediate genius at hand; "But if you want the best idea of Cape Horn, get my friend Dana's unmatchable 'Two Years Before the Mast.' But you can read, and so you must have read it. His chapters describing Cape Horn must have been written with an icicle."

Melville's praise is merited, and Dana's famous fifth chapter is the second tutelary spirit to Melville's section. There is, however, a third writer helping Melville, and that is the reliable if prosy Mercier, whose words on the Cape, already quoted on page 49, perhaps suggested, besides Cape clothing, Melville's remarkable tribute to Dana's style.

Of Dana's two Cape chapters, 5 and 32, it was the first which most

---

2. These and following editorial italics are to point up for the forgetful reader the Coleridgean language.

aided Melville. It is a remarkably fine piece of writing, so fine and so famous that Melville consciously tried to avoid any apparent direct borrowing from it. If Melville made no (or at best few) verbally discernible borrowings from Dana for the four-chapter Cape section, the spirit of his friend's writing hovers over his pages, as he was quick to acknowledge. His tribute is a recognition that Dana's account is archetypal, the *fons et origo* for all subsequent writers, that Dana had appropriated as *his* the Cape, just as Cezanne appropriated Mont Sainte Victoire to make it difficult for subsequent painters to sketch.

Melville's second Cape chapter, "The Dog-days off Cape Horn," is a gallimaufry of sources, a literary patchwork.

Melville is conscious of his patchwork method of composition as he writes: "I endeavoured to amend these misfortunes by sewing a sort of canvas ruffle, by way of a continuation or supplement to the original work, and by doing the same with the wristbands." Here the literary metaphor is blended with the clothing one, belated evidence that the previously discussed opening jacket chapter was probably an extended metaphor of Melville's writing method.

> Colder and colder; we are drawing nigh to the Cape. Now gregoes, pea jackets, monkey jackets, reefing jackets, storm jackets, oil jackets, paint jackets, round jackets, short jackets, long jackets, and all manner of jackets, are the order of the day, not excepting the immortal white jacket, which begins to be sturdily buttoned up to the throat, and pulled down vigorously at the skirts, to bring them well over the loins.

The repetition of "jacket" is more than a mere nursery-rhyme incantation; it is a tacit admission of the inadequacy of ordinary prose, of mere travel documentary, to embrace significant experience; it implies that as experience grows—both in an individual and in a tribe—the old modes of arraying it must be discarded, new ones discovered. That the jacket has, too, a psychological symbolism, not separate from the literary one, must be kept in mind. The thread of Melville's theme weaves through seven short paragraphs on the jacket, the fifth and sixth being perhaps the most suggestive:

> I endeavored to amend these misfortunes by sewing a sort of canvass ruffle round the skirts, by way of a continuation or supplement to the original work, and by doing the same with the wristbands.

This is the time for oil-skin suits, dread-naughts, tarred trowsers and overalls, sea-boots, comforters, mittens, woolen socks, Guernsey frocks, Havre skirts, buffalo-robe shirts, and moose-skin drawers. Every man's jacket is his wigwam, and every man's hat his caboose.

"Dog-days off Cape Horn" was itself a twist on the customary Cape account, which conventionally described the furious storms. Melville both varies and extends his narrative by preceding, and hence contrasting, his subsequent storm with this freezing calm which descended (imaginatively only, since it is not recorded in the log of the *United States*) on the *Neversink*. The calm is, perhaps, an eccentric variant of Coleridge's deadly one in the "Rime of the Ancient Mariner," placed by Melville in a man-of-war setting devoid of supernatural mumbo-jumbo. The cold which numbs the crew is a kind of joke:

Colder, and colder, and colder, till at last we spoke a fleet of icebergs bound North. After that, it was one incessant *"cold snap,"* that almost snapped off our fingers and toes. Cold! It was cold as *Blue Flujin,* where sailors say fire freezes.

but the joke may be there partly as a sign of embarrassment on Melville's part, at having lifted his patch from Nathaniel Ames' *A Mariner's Sketches* (p. 193),[3] which makes much of the cold, referring to "that part of the world generally known to sailors by the name of 'Blue Flujin' where it is said fire freezes." Even in such a short snippet, however, one notices the Melville touches which excuse the bad pun: the repetitions of "Colder" to intensify the effect, the witty nautical image of speaking ship-bergs, and the placement of Ames's metaphor at the end, the better to frame its novelty and humor.

The unusual calm gives Melville a chance (or the chance gave us the calm) to sew in another patch from Mercier's *Scenes.* The *Neversink* crew, made idle, are threatened with freezing from their inactivity. To relieve them of boredom and to exercise them, the order is given: *"D'ye hear there, fore and aft! all hands skylark!' "* The effect of this order on the spirits of the men is electric. What is perhaps more interesting, just now, is that Melville took this scene from Mercier's chapter on Theatricals (pp. 218ff.), economically and more effectively to use it here. The

---

3. Ames also complains (p. 194) about the difficulty of washing and scrubbing clothes in a snowstorm, without shoes and stockings. If Dana suggested the element of terror, Ames perhaps suggested that of discomfort.

skylarking in *Scenes* takes place on the Fourth of July and is a drunken debauch; Melville's skylarking is an energetic, helpful warming-up brawl: "It was a Babel here, a Bedlam there, and a Pandemonium every where. The Theatricals were nothing compared with it." Melville's description, starting with this amusing blend of "Old MacDonald had a farm" and Book II of *Paradise Lost,* omits the intoxication and stresses the sheer energy and the "din," which "frightened the sea-fowl, that flew by with accelerated wing."

Chapter 27, "Some Thoughts growing out of Mad Jack's Counter-manding his Superior's Order," has been discussed earlier, but the con-sequences, which are the latter half of the chapter, merit attention. Mad Jack's action for Melville "invites the question, Are there incompetent officers in the American navy?" After all, Melville pessimistically tells us, "the trumpets of one victory drown the muffled drums of a thousand defeats." How many ciphers are there in a navy, made significant by but one numeral—that a Nelson or a Jones—or, by implication, and on a lesser scale, by a Mad Jack able to maintain his temperance. Melville says with considerable cynicism: "And if all the men who, since the beginning of the world, have mainly contributed to the warlike successes or reverses of nations, were now mustered together, we should be amazed to behold but a handful of heroes."

To answer his own question about incompetence in navies, Melville cites the example of Lord Collingwood who was deemed so indispen-sable by the Admiralty to the English Mediterranean Fleet that despite the availability of a hundred other admirals, not one was deemed worthy or adequate to fill his place so that his request for furlough—he a sick man—was denied. The Navy, Melville says, is filled with Paper Jacks, men untried at sea, unknowing of ships. His detailed indictment of the personnel inadequacies of the American Navy is taken freely and in quantity from William McNally's *Evils and Abuses,* the entire first chapter of which is an exposure of the harsh treatment of Navy personnel.

Chapter 28, "Edging Away," is both an edging away from Cape Horn and Melville's edging away from the intensities of the four pre-ceding Cape chapters. As if aware that he has written rather richly, Melville admits that he has used a rhetoric beyond the facts of his memory, as seen in the *United States* log:

> It is worth mentioning here that, in nineteen cases out of twenty, a passage from the Pacific round the Cape is almost sure to be much shorter, and attended with less hardship, than a passage under-taken from the Atlantic.

Nevertheless, Melville himself for a moment is in the poetic-symbolic mood, writing: "We rolled and rolled on our way, like the world in its orbit, shipping green seas on both sides, until the old frigate dipped and went into it like a diving-bell." We come back to prosaic realities, discomforts, through food, with the difficulties the men face in eating in a rolling sea:

Melville (Chapter 28)   Mercier (pp. 77–78)

In fair weather, the ship's company messed on the gun-deck; but as this was now flooded almost continually, we were obliged to take our meals upon the berth-deck, the next one below. One day, the messes of the starboard-watch were seated here at dinner; forming little groups, twelve or fifteen men in each, reclining about the beef-kids and their pots and pans; when all of a sudden the ship was seized with such a paroxysm of rolling that, in a single instant, every thing on the berth-deck—pots, kids, sailors, pieces of beef, bread-bags, clothes-bags, and barges —were tossed indiscriminately from side to side. It was impossible to stay one's self; there was nothing but the bare deck to cling to, which was slippery with the contents of the kids, and heaving under us as if there were a volcano in the frigate's hold. While we were yet sliding in uproarious crowds—all seated—the windows of the deck opened, and floods of brine descended, simultaneously with a violent lee-roll. The shower was hailed by the reckless tars with a hurricane of yells; al-

One day in particular, our frigate under close-reefed storm-sails laboured dreadfully, rolling almost her spar-deck guns under—dinner was piped, and our lads were huddled together around their several messes, endeavouring as they best could to transmit the contents of a pan well filled with bean-soup to the inner man. Each one as he received his *quantum,* placed himself in some solid and secure position to commence his meal, taking advantage of the interval between every roll of the ship to bring a portion of the delicious liquid to his impatient lips; a fellow on the forward part of the deck, sung out lustily, "look out for your beans;" the words were scarcely uttered, than, before any body could make a second preparation, she gave one of the most tremendous rolls I think I ever experienced; I actually thought she would never *right* again; my eyes, what a scene now presented itself— away went simultaneously with one movement—in one confused mass, kettles of hot-water —baskets of small biscuit— pans of soup—pots—kettles—

though, for an instant, I really imagined we were about being swamped in the sea, such volumes of water came cascading down.

frying pans—gridirons—and all the *etceteras* of the galley; here might be seen a poor fellow struggling amidst a heap of clothes-bags—spit boxes—pots—pans and spoons, endeavouring to regain his feet, which the well-greased slippery deck almost rendered an impossibility; further along, you might observe two or three marines well besmeared with soup, trying with rueful countenances to gain possession of the *paraphernalia* of their mess chest, which, as well as themselves had been tumbled into the main-hold at the first onset, with but little ceremony. In the midst of the uproar, the *bon-mot* and *repartee* flew round with rapidity, (for at what time will not Jack enjoy his joke,) and though many lost their dinners on the occasion, and several got sore heads and pummeled ribs from the effects of their falls, yet all with one accord joined in the laughter that this affair occasioned.

The poetic feeling will not, however, completely leave Melville, and immediately following as he describes the *Neversink*'s passage along Staten Land, with the "fair, free wind," the glaciers, and the albatross, he blends his Coleridgean-infused description with a Miltonic adaptation: "High, towering in their own turbaned snows, the far-inland pinnacles loomed up, like the border of some other world. Flashing walls and crystal battlements, like the diamond watch-towers along heaven's furthest frontier."

The chapter closes with the incomprehension of snow and hail by Wooloo, the Captain's Polynesian servant. He ridiculously fails to understand the qualities and mutability of snow, and makes himself comic by his unadaptation to this new, different world. Melville's commentary, closing the chapter, is:

> In our man-of-war, this semi-savage, wandering about the gun-deck in his barbaric robe, seemed a being from some other sphere. His tastes were our abominations: ours his. Our creed he rejected: his we. We thought him a loon: he fancied us fools. Had the case been reversed; had we been Polynesians and he an American, our mutual opinion of each other would still have remained the same. A fact proving that neither was wrong, but both right.

What is perhaps most valuable about the Wooloo episode is that it undoubtedly supplied the comedy of Queequeg at the Spouter Inn in *Moby-Dick*. Melville was reluctant to leave the Cape behind; it had become for him an experience of important symbolic meaning which he clearly found it difficult to drop. Nor had the mere passage around the Cape, with its comical as well as heroic circumstances, exhausted *his* potential literary use of that voyage. There remained the jacket, itself a symbol of psychological infantilism, to be woven into the Cape passage. And so it is, to distinguish and separate its owner from his fellow sailors, to bring on him, through his prominence, extra and onerous tasks. He is unable to swap it; it stays with him to trouble more than to assist.

·9·

Flogging
on the *Neversink*

A good indignation brings out all one's powers.
                    Ralph Waldo Emerson, *Journals*

A DISH of Dunderfunk," Chapter 32, was little more than a competent rewriting of Mercier's episode, and in fact up to this time *White-Jacket* itself has been a book which, had it so continued, would be not much more important than a Mercier, a Leech, or an Ames. Melville's powers had not yet been brought out; it is through a stout indignation that this release was effected—in the very next chapter.

"If you begin the day with a laugh, you may, nevertheless, end it with a sob and a sigh." This sentence opening Chapter 33, "A Flogging," suddenly transfers us from the comic world of food to that of brutality and blood; it is a transition to a heartless world not met with before in Melville save for two or three scenes just completed in *Redburn*.

The scene is rapidly set:

> Among the many who were exceedingly diverted with the scene between the Down Easter and the Lieutenant, none laughed more heartily than John, Peter, Mark, and Antone—four sailors of the starboard-watch. The same evening these four found themselves prisoners in the "brig," with a sentry standing over them. They were charged with violating a well-known law of the ship—having been engaged in one of those tangled, general fights sometimes occurring among sailors. They had nothing to anticipate but a flogging, at the captain's pleasure.

The sardonic reversal of situation is intensified by the irony of "nothing," which operates somewhat in the way of Jonathan Swift's savage sentence: "Last week I saw a woman flayed, and you will hardly believe how much it altered her appearance for the worse." Slyly sardonic, too, is Melville's "the captain's pleasure."

Surprisingly, except for Dana's celebrated fifteenth chapter, "Flogging," this terrible subject had not, until *White-Jacket*, been adequately dealt with in literature. This lack was Melville's literary luck, an opportunity shrewdly seized. It was, apparently, Dana's moral stance which strengthened Melville's resolution to propagandize against the evil of flogging. Dana wrote (p. 81):

> I had no real apprehension that the captain would lay a hand on me; but I thought of our situation, living under a tyranny, with an ungoverned, swaggering fellow administering it; of the character of the country we were in; the length of the voyage; the uncertainty attending our return to America; and then, if we should return, the prospect of obtaining justice and satisfaction for these poor men; and I vowed that, if God should ever give me the means, I would do something to redress the grievances and relieve the sufferings of that class of beings with whom my lot had so long been cast.

It is possible, too, to see in this passage the germ of a later episode, White-Jacket's narrow escape from flogging, in the sentence: "I had no real apprehension that the captain would lay a hand on me," for Melville's episode dramatizes the question which is implied by Dana's statement: "What *would* one do in such a contingency?"

Melville, however, needed no *Two Years Before the Mast* to launch his attack; he had his own sickening memories of 163 floggings witnessed on board the *United States* between the day of his enlistment on 17 August 1843 and the day of his dismissal in October 1844. On the first day of his own service aboard the *United States,* Melville had witnessed floggings of four men, listed tersely in the ship's log: "John Hall, twelve lashes for striking sentry on post; George Clark, twelve lashes for smuggling liquor; Joseph Stanley, apprentice, twelve lashes with the kittens for fighting; William Ewing, six for provoking language." The next day three more men were flogged: George Davis, William Steward, and Antonio Guavella—twelve lashes each for drunkenness. For a former resident of the Typee Valley, and of Hawaiian lotus land, this was an ironic commencement for a return to civilization.

Melville needed no books for the arousal of passionate anger, but he needed them, or used them, for the framing of his attack. Chief literary source for his first account of a flogging was Samuel Leech's *Thirty Years from Home*. Leech, too, had a reforming purpose like Dana's, saying (p. vi) : "If this work should, in any degree, stir up the public mind to amend the condition of seamen, I shall feel gratified, and fully repaid for the labor of placing these facts on record." Leech's greatest discernible success was his effect on Melville, but that was much.

Melville's and Leech's flogging episodes are long, but since almost no one today has read Leech and since too few have read *White-Jacket,* the two accounts are printed at length so that one may study Melville's method of appropriation. Leech (pp. 48–51) :

> Short as was the period between weighing anchor off Gravesend and our arrival at Spithead, it gave opportunity for one of those occurrences which are a disgrace to the naval service of any nation, and a degradation to our common humanity, which the public opinion of the civilized world should frown out of existence: I allude to the brutal practice of flogging.
>
> A poor fellow had fallen into the very sailor-like offence of getting drunk. For this the captain sentenced him to the punishment of four dozen lashes. He was first placed in *irons* all night: the irons used for this purpose were shackles fitting round the ankles, through the ends of which was passed an iron bar some ten or twelve feet in length: it was thus long because it was no unfrequent case for half a dozen men to be ironed at once. A padlock at the end of the bar held the prisoner securely. Thus placed in

"duress vile," he was guarded by a marine until the captain bade the first lieutenant prepare the hands to witness the punishment. Upon this the lieutenant transmitted the order to the master at arms. He then ordered the grating or hatch full of square holes to be rigged: it was placed accordingly between the main and spar decks, not far from the mainmast.

While these preparations were going on, the officers were dressing themselves in full uniform and arming themselves with their dirks: *the[1] prisoner's messmates carried him his best clothes, to make him appear in as decent a manner as possible. This is always done, in the hope of moving the feelings of the captain favorably towards the prisoner.*

This done, the hoarse, dreaded cry of "All hands ahoy to witness punishment!" from the lips of the boatswain, peals along the ship as mournfully as the notes of a funeral knell. At this signal the officers muster on the spar deck, the men on the main deck. Next came the prisoner; guarded by a marine on one side and the master at arms on the other, he was marched up to the grating. His *back was made bare and his shirt laid loosely upon his back;* the two quarter-masters proceeded to seize him up; that is, they tied his hands and feet with spun-yarns, called the seizings, to the grating. The boatswain's mates, whose office it is to flog on board a man of war, stood ready with their dreadful weapon of punishment, the cat-o'-nine-tails. This instrument of torture was composed of nine cords, a quarter of an inch round and about two feet long, the ends whipt with fine twine. To these cords was affixed a stock, two feet in length, covered with red baize. The reader may be sure that it is a most formidable instrument in the hands of a strong, skilful man. Indeed, any man who should whip his horse with it would commit an outrage on humanity, which the moral feeling of any community would not tolerate; he would be prosecuted for cruelty; yet it is used to whip MEN on board ships of war!

The boatswain's mate is ready, with coat off and whip in hand. The captain gives the word. Carefully spreading the cords with fingers of his left hand, the executioner throws the cat over his right shoulder; it is brought down upon the now uncovered herculean shoulders of the MAN. His flesh creeps—it reddens as if blushing at the indignity; the sufferer groans; lash follows lash, until the first mate, wearied with the cruel employment, gives place to a second. Now two dozen of these dreadful lashes have been inflicted: the lacerated back looks inhuman; it resembles

1. Italics mine throughout passage to indicate Melville's most direct borrowing.

roasted meat burnt nearly black before a scorching fire; yet still the
lashes fall; the captain continues merciless. Vain are the cries and
prayers of the wretched man. "I would not forgive the Saviour,"
was the blasphemous reply of one of these naval demi-gods, or
rather demi-fiends, to a plea for mercy. The executioners keep on.
Four dozen strokes have cut up his flesh and robbed him of all self-
respect; there he hangs, a pitied, self-despised, groaning, bleeding
wretch; and now the captain cries, forbear! His shirt is thrown over
his shoulders; the seizings are loosed; he is led away, staining his
path with red drops of blood, and the hands, "piped down" by the
boatswain, sullenly return to their duties.

and now Melville:

If you begin the day with a laugh, you may, nevertheless, end it
with a sob and a sigh.

Among the many who were exceedingly diverted with the scene
between the Down Easter and the Lieutenant, none laughed more
heartily than John, Peter, Mark, and Antone—four sailors of the
starboard-watch. The same evening these four found themselves
prisoners in the "brig," with a sentry standing over them. They
were charged with violating a well-known law of the ship—
having been engaged in one of those tangled, general fights sometimes occurring among sailors. They had nothing to anticipate but
a flogging, at the captain's pleasure.

Toward evening of the next day, they were startled by the dread
summons of the boatswain and his mates at the principal hatchway—a summons that ever sends a shudder through every manly
heart in a frigate:

"All hands witness punishment, ahoy!"

The hoarseness of the cry, its unrelenting prolongation, its being
caught up at different points, and sent through the lowermost
depths of the ship; all this produces a most dismal effect upon
every heart not calloused by long habituation to it.

However much you may desire to absent yourself from the scene
that ensues, yet behold it you must; or, at least, stand near it you
must; for the regulations enjoin the attendance of the entire ship's
company, from the corpulent Captain himself to the smallest boy
who strikes the bell.

"All hands witness punishment, ahoy!"

To the sensitive seaman that summons sounds like a doom. He
knows that the same law which impels it—the same law by which
the culprits of the day must suffer; that by that very law he also is
liable at any time to be judged and condemned. And the inevi-

tableness of his own presence at the scene; the strong arm that drags him in view of the scourge, and holds him there till all is over; forcing upon his loathing eye and soul the sufferings and groans of men who have familiarly consorted with him, eaten with him, battled out watches with him—men of his own type and badge—all this conveys a terrible hint of the omnipotent authority under which he lives. Indeed, to such a man the naval summons to witness punishment carries a thrill, somewhat akin to what we may impute to the quick and the dead, when they shall hear the Last Trump, that is to bid them all arise in their ranks, and behold the final penalties inflicted upon the sinners of our race.

But it must not be imagined that to all men-of-war's-men this summons conveys such poignant emotions; but it is hard to decide whether one should be glad or sad that this is not the case; whether it is grateful to know that so much pain is avoided, or whether it is far sadder to think that, either from constitutional hard-heartedness or the multiplied searings of habit, hundreds of men-of-war's-men have been made proof against the sense of degradation, pity, and shame.

As if in sympathy with the scene to be enacted, the sun, which the day previous had merrily flashed upon the tin pan of the disconsolate Down Easter, was now setting over the dreary waters, veiling itself in vapors. The wind blew hoarsely in the cordage; the seas broke heavily against the bows; and the frigate, staggering under whole top-sails, strained as in agony on her way.

"All hands witness punishment, ahoy!"

At the summons the crew crowded round the main-mast; multitudes eager to obtain a good place on the booms, to overlook the scene; many laughing and chatting, others canvassing the case of the culprits; some maintaining sad, anxious countenances, or carrying a suppressed indignation in their eyes; a few purposely keeping behind to avoid looking on; in short, among five hundred men, there was every possible shade of character.

All the officers—midshipmen included—stood together in a group on the starboard side of the main-mast; the First Lieutenant in advance, and the surgeon, whose special duty it is to be present at such times, standing close by his side.

Presently the Captain came forward from his cabin, and stood in the centre of this solemn group, with a small paper in his hand. That paper was the daily report of offences, regularly laid upon his table every morning or evening, like the day's journal placed by a bachelor's napkin at breakfast.

"Master-at-arms, bring up the prisoners," he said.

A few moments elapsed, during which the Captain, now clothed in his most dreadful attributes, fixed his eyes severely upon the crew, when suddenly a lane formed through the crowd of seamen, and the prisoners advanced—the master-at-arms, rattan in hand, on one side, and an armed marine on the other—and took up their stations at the mast.

"You John, you Peter, you Mark, you Antone," said the Captain, "were yesterday found fighting on the gun-deck. Have you any thing to say?"

Mark and Antone, two steady, middle-aged men, whom I had often admired for their sobriety, replied that they did not strike the first blow; that they had submitted to much before they had yielded to their passions; but as they acknowledged that they had at last defended themselves, their excuse was overruled.

John—a brutal bully, who, it seems, was the real author of the disturbance—was about entering into a long extenuation, when he was cut short by being made to confess, irrespective of circumstances, that he had been in the fray.

Peter, a handsome lad about nineteen years old, belonging to the mizzen-top, looked pale and tremulous. He was a great favorite in his part of the ship, and especially in his own mess, principally composed of lads of his own age. That morning two of his young mess-mates had gone to his bag, taken out his best clothes, and, obtaining the permission of the marine sentry at the "brig," had handed them to him, to be put on against being summoned to the mast. This was done to propitiate the Captain, as most captains love to see a tidy sailor. But it would not do. To all his supplications the Captain turned a deaf ear. Peter declared that he had been struck twice before he had returned a blow. "No matter," said the Captain, "you struck at last, instead of reporting the case to an officer. I allow no man to fight on board here but myself. *I* do the fighting."

"Now, men," he added, "you all admit the charge; you know the penalty. Strip! Quarter-masters, are the gratings rigged?"

The gratings are square frames of barred wood-work, sometimes placed over the hatch-ways. One of these squares was now laid on the deck, close to the ship's bulwarks, and while the remaining preparations were being made, the master-at-arms assisted the prisoners in removing their jackets and shirts. This done, their shirts were loosely thrown over their shoulders.

At a sign from the Captain, John, with a shameless leer, advanced, and stood passively upon the grating, while the bareheaded old quarter-master, with gray hair streaming in the wind, bound his feet to the cross-bars, and, stretching out his arms over his head, secured them to the hammock-nettings above. He then retreated a little space, standing silent.

Meanwhile, the boatswain stood solemnly on the other side, with a green bag in his hand, from which taking four instruments of punishment, he gave one to each of his mates; for a fresh "cat," applied by a fresh hand, is the ceremonious privilege accorded to every man-of-war culprit.

At another sign from the Captain, the master-at-arms, stepping up, removed the shirt from the prisoner. At this juncture a wave broke against the ship's side, and dashed the spray over his exposed back. But though the air was piercing cold, and the water drenched him, John stood still, without a shudder.

The Captain's finger was now lifted, and the first boatswain's-mate advanced, combing out the nine tails of his *cat* with his hand, and then, sweeping them round his neck, brought them with the whole force of his body upon the mark. Again, and again, and again; and at every blow, higher and higher rose the long, purple bars on the prisoner's back. But he only bowed over his head, and stood still. Meantime, some of the crew whispered among themselves in applause of their ship-mate's nerve; but the greater part were breathlessly silent as the keen scourge hissed through the wintery air, and fell with a cutting, wiry sound upon the mark. One dozen lashes being applied, the man was taken down, and went among the crew with a smile, saying, "D——n me! it's nothing when you're used to it! Who wants to fight?"

The next was Antone, the Portuguese. At every blow he surged from side to side, pouring out a torrent of involuntary blasphemies. Never before had he been heard to curse. When cut down, he went among the men, swearing to have the life of the Captain. Of course, this was unheard by the officers.

Mark, the third prisoner, only cringed and coughed under his punishment. He had some pulmonary complaint. He was off duty for several days after the flogging; but this was partly to be imputed to his extreme mental misery. It was his first scourging, and he felt the insult more than the injury. He became silent and sullen for the rest of the cruise.

The fourth and last was Peter, the mizzen-top lad. He had often boasted that he had never been degraded at the gangway. The day before his cheek had worn its usual red, but now no ghost was whiter. As he was being secured to the gratings, and the shudderings and creepings of his dazzlingly white back were revealed, he turned round his head imploringly; but his weeping entreaties and vows of contrition were of no avail. "I would not forgive God Almighty!" cried the Captain. The fourth boatswain's-mate ad-

vanced, and at the first blow, the boy, shouting *"My God! Oh! my
God!"* writhed and leaped so as to displace the gratings, and
scatter the nine tails of the scourge all over his person. At the next
blow he howled, leaped, and raged in unendurable torture.

"What are you stopping for, boatswain's-mate?" cried the Captain. "Lay on!" and the whole dozen was applied.

"I don't care what happens to me now!" wept Peter, going
among the crew, with blood-shot eyes; as he put on his shirt. "I
have been flogged once, and they may do it again, if they will. Let
them look out for me now!"

"Pipe down!" cried the Captain, and the crew slowly dispersed.

Let us have the charity to believe them—as we do—when some
Captains in the Navy say, that the thing of all others most repul-
sive to them, in the routine of what they consider their duty, is the
administration of corporal punishment upon the crew; for, surely,
not to feel scarified to the quick at these scenes would argue a man
but a beast.

You see a human being, stripped like a slave; scourged worse
than a hound. And for what? For things not essentially criminal,
but only made so by arbitrary laws.

It was brave of Melville to borrow from such a strong passage as
Leech's; it showed a confidence in his ability to absorb and to master
Leech's account. For one thing, he dramatized the flogging more,
shaping much of it into active dialogue as against authorial description—it is an enactment and not just a narration. Melville, too, makes
nature correspond to the human occasion:

As if in sympathy with the scene to be enacted, the sun, which the
day previous had merrily flashed upon the tin pan of the disconsolate Down Easter, was now setting over the dreary waters,
veiling itself in vapors. The wind blew hoarsely in the cordage;
the seas broke heavily against the bows; and the frigate, staggering
under whole top-sails, strained as in agony on her way.

The agony of the ship and the fury of the sea is a strong objective
correlative for the human agony of both victims and witnesses, the sort
of consonance which Melville later establishes in the opening paragraphs of *Benito Cereno,* or in the black sea on which Captain Vere
gazes during the trial of Billy Budd.

A further refinement by Melville is the triple repetition of "All hands
witness punishment, ahoy!," "its unrelenting prolongation" suggested

by the very repetition, giving it both solemnity and the terror of the trumpets of the Day of Judgment—so Melville himself states: "To the sensitive seaman that summons sounds like a doom."

Melville's skill, further, is in the sharpening of sentences and images, such as Leech's:

> His flesh creeps—it reddens as if blushing at the indignity; the sufferer groans; lash follows lash; until the first mate, wearied with the cruel employment, gives place to a second.

Melville physically intensifies and emotionally extends this to read: "Again, and again, and again; and at every blow, higher and higher rose the long, purple bars on the prisoner's back."

Melville's skill betrays itself in the way the witnessing crew participate empathically in the horror and the degradation. All share in the shame. "You see a human being, stripped like a slave; scourged worse than a hound.[2] And for what? For things not essentially criminal, but only made so by arbitrary laws."

•

> Where's the great rage of a rocking heart, the high rare true dangerous indignation? Let me proceed more slowly.
> Theodore Roethke, "O, Thou Opening, O"

Melville's dramatic scene of flogging is, in effect, a scream against an act which words must always fail adequately to describe. Nevertheless, screams are no substitute for sustained arguments at the bar of justice, for which facts must be assembled, assorted, and given rhetorical life. The support to his scream was the substance of Melville's next three chapters, "Some of the Evil Effects of Flogging" (34), "Flogging not Lawful" (35), and, finally, "Flogging not Necessary" (36). For these chapters Melville needed all of his adroitness in argument to accompany and to control his turbulence of feeling.

Melville's chain rods to slow his furious reaction were two sources especially—Leech, of course, whose example had been largely responsible for the description of flogging; and McNally, whose details while less undramatic were useful in developing a "thesis."

2. Cf. McNally, p. 130: "flogged like a dog."

The change in tone between the flogging chapter and the subsequent expository chapters is considerable, as if Melville consciously saw the wisdom of contrast as a rhetorical weapon. He begins almost pedantically, in Chapter 34:

> There are incidental considerations touching this matter of flogging, which exaggerate the evil into a great enormity. Many illustrations might be given, but let us be content with a few.

This does not mean that Melville's passion is spent; it is only momentarily muted, for, just as he often does in *Moby-Dick,* Melville coolly proceeds with a series of "illustrations," the calm before the rage; for two pages, then, he follows, or uses, hints from Leech and McNally, recharging his emotional batteries in preparation for the concluding denunciation of the chapter. For two thirds of the chapter Melville moves from illustration to illustration, from fact to fact. To the critical bloodhound trailing his literary course he seems to take a series of little leaps like a man crossing an ice pack, his floes being, variously, Leech, McNally, and Ames. His first leap is to Leech. Several sailors inadvertently offend an officer, and are told that they will be flogged next day (pp. 258–259):

> With this consolatory information we returned to our station, without the least inclination to sleep again for that watch. With a sort of philosophic desperation, I laughed and said, "Dick, which would you rather do—have your grog stopped awhile, or take a flogging?"
>
> Dick was very fond of his grog; so he replied, "Oh, I had rather they would stop my wind than my grog, and would sooner be flogged by considerable than lose that." I question, however, if he had been left to choose between grog and whip at the gangway, whether he would not have altered his tone in favor of his grog. Still, his answer shows, how strongly sailors are attached to their beloved rum. I am happy to know that this regard is dying away, and that temperance is doing something among sailors.

Melville flattens this anecdote to a statement:

> It is one of the most common punishments for very trivial offences in the Navy, to "stop" a seaman's *grog* for a day or a week. And as most seamen so cling to their *grog,* the loss of it is generally

deemed by them a very serious penalty. You will sometimes hear them say, "I would rather have my wind *stopped* than my *grog!*"[3]

Melville proceeds, in the next paragraph, to speak further of grog stopping:

> But there are some sober seamen that would much rather draw the money for it, instead of the grog itself, as provided by law; but they are too often deterred from this by the thought of receiving a scourging for some inconsiderable offence, as a substitute for the stopping of their spirits. This is a most serious obstacle to the cause of temperance in the Navy.

Now, however, it is not Leech supplying him but McNally (p. 43):[4]

> On board of several vessels in the navy many men have been induced by their commanders voluntarily to relinquish their spirits, and a great inducement for them to do so was to have the money paid to them for it. But that is not always done, and sometimes if any thing goes wrong aloft the topmen are called down and those who do not draw their grog are whipped, while others who do, have it stopped; so the former to save his back, draws his grog again.

McNally's passage is part of a temperance argument, more extended than Leech's, but Melville uses the information to expose not intemperance or the evils of giving out grog but as an example of the indiscriminate and unjust use of flogging; this he pursues through a long paragraph, drawing freely on another section of McNally (Chapter 10) to denounce the whimsical and unauthorized use of the *cat*, the *colt*, or "a bit of *ratlin-stuff.*" Once again parallel passages will demonstrate how, in expository materials, Melville adapts his source:

Melville (Chapter 34)	McNally (pp. 87–89)
But, in many cases, even the reluctant drawing of his grog	At that time there was a custom in the service, (directly

3. This passage is adapted from a section more concerned with temperance than with flogging, and is 200 pages removed from Leech's flogging account quoted above. This is a mere detail, but it shows Melville's collecting and filing mind.

4. Somewhat similar material is in Ames, pp. 198–199.

can not exempt a prudent seaman from ignominy; for besides the formal administering
of the *"cat"* at the gangway for
petty offences, he is liable to the
"colt," or rope's-end, a bit of
ratlin-stuff, indiscriminately
applied—without stripping
the victim—at any time, and in
any part of the ship, at the
merest wink from the Captain.
By an express order of that officer, most boatswain's mates
carry the "colt" coiled in their
hats, in readiness to be administered at a minute's warning
upon any offender. This was the
custom in the Neversink. And
until so recent a period as the
administration of President
Polk, when the historian Ban-
croft, Secretary of the Navy,
officially interposed, it was an
almost universal thing for the
officers of the watch, at their
own discretion, to inflict chas-
tisement upon a sailor, and this,
too, in the face of the ordinance
restricting the power of flogging
solely to Captains and Courts
Martial. Nor was it a thing
unknown for a Lieutenant, in
a sudden outburst of passion,
perhaps inflamed by brandy, or
smarting under the sense of
being disliked or hated by the
seamen, to order a whole watch
of two hundred and fifty men,
at dead of night, to undergo
the indignity of the "colt."

contrary to law,) whereby any
officer of the deck could inflict
punishment; but for the credit
of the navy it must be told, that
this has very seldom been the
case of late years, for few captains will allow it, at the present
day, to be done on board of
their vessels. This was not
punishment with the cat, which
the law directs to be the instrument of punishment, but with
what is termed "colt:" this is a
piece of eighteen-thread ratline,
or one-inch rope, and generally
has one or two hard twine
whippings upon each end.
Twelve lashes with this, over a
thin frock or shirt, gave greater
pain and bruised the flesh more
than the cat would have done;
and it was with this instrument
that the deck officers of the
Fairfield punished the men, and
there was no limit to the number of lashes, but just as many
as it might please the officer to
order—sometimes one, and at
other times as many as three
dozen. Such punishment frequently brought the blood
through the shirt, and often
left the flesh black for two or
three weeks, and then yellow
for as many more, before it
healed perfectly.

Punishment on board that
vessel was not always inflicted
in the face of day; many cruel
deed has the pale moon witnessed upon her deck. This was
directly contrary to the law,
which only vests captains with
power to punish, and then not

McNally (pp. 87–89)

exceeding twelve lashes for any one offence. There is no single offence but what two or more may be made of it, if such is the captain's wish. Drunkenness, for instance, is drunkenness, disobedience of orders— very likely, neglect of duty, insolence, and insubordination; for when liquor is in, wit is out, and the offences which a man may then commit will subject him to three or four dozen lashes. I will relate some occurrences, which took place after I left the Fairfield, as I knew them to be. One night, while the ship was on her way from Smyrna to Mahon, it fell calm, and the officer of the deck, Lieut. H——r, ordered the forecastle men and fore top men to man the fore clue garnets and buntlines, and stand by to haul up the foresail. The word was given, and the sail hauled up, but not so quickly as he wished it to be. The yards were braced sharp up, and, as there was no wind, the fore tack and sheet blocks caught in the lee fore rigging, on the ratlines, and a man had to clear them. Nothing, however, would be taken as an excuse, and he flogged the whole watch of the forecastle and fore top men, giving them one dozen each, and ordered them forward to set the sail again. It was set, and they were ordered to man the clue garnets and buntlines, to haul it up again. The lee clue caught in the rigging as before, and he flogged them all again. Once more the sail was set, and hauled up with the same results; in fact, it was a moral impossibility to run the lee clue right up, as the heavy blocks would catch in the rigging; and the men were flogged three times, in less than one hour. There were eleven men in the fore top, and twelve on the forecastle, making twenty-three men, punished with three dozen lashes each, for no offence under the face of heaven. Eight bells (midnight) were struck, and before the tyrant was relieved by another officer, he ordered one of the midshipmen to tell the purser's steward to stop their grog for twenty-four hours. This caitiff, this monster, however, did not long survive the act. His wicked, abominable soul, tempted him, after the ship arrived in port, to propose the commission of a crime for which there is no punishment prescribed in the naval code of laws—it being too unnatural for the legislators of our country ever to think of. On this horrible affair being reported to the captain, he was suspended; and finding that no human being could ever again countenance him, he shot himself, in his

state room. The sentinel, when   was huddled into the grave by
his remains passed over the lar-   a single officer and boat's crew.
board gangway, turned his back.   A fit end for tyrants!
No funeral note was heard. He

Two more passages from McNally (pp. 98 and 128) carry Melville
through two more paragraphs. Then, after a bit from Ames, Melville
mounts to his passionate denunciation of flogging as a violation of the
sacredness of the human soul, concluding:

> Join hands with me, then; and, in the name of that Being in whose
> image the flogged sailor is made, let us demand of Legislators, by
> what right they dare profane what God himself accounts sacred.

This direct assault on senatorial responsibility strengthens the story that
a copy of *White-Jacket* was placed on every congressman's desk and that
it was largely responsible for the passage of the bill abolishing flogging
in the United States Navy. However that may be, the bill passed against
the opinions of experts. A file of 83 letters collected by the Navy for
"evidence" in their fight to retain flogging shows that 80 of the captains
categorically predicted the collapse of the Navy with the passage of the
bill. What was the counterweight to this heartless expertise? It may not
be provable, but it is attractive to believe that tradition is right, and that
White-Jacket helped to persuade the legislators against the intelligence
and logic of the officers. Anyhow, flogging abolished, Melville happily
wrote to Duyckinck on 6 October 1850, "I am offering up devout
jubilations for the abolition of the flogging law."

Melville was a master of the art of dramatically constructing the
chapter. We have just seen how he built a chapter from a quiet opening
to a climactic peroration. Most of the chapters in *White-Jacket* and
Moby-Dick are as carefully self-contained. But not exclusively, for again
and again Melville pairs chapter with chapter, not in the sense of a
flowing from one to the other but as companions. This is his "doublet"
practice, which is especially striking in *Moby-Dick*.[5]

The flogging sequence is itself a larger unit of four chapters, but each
has its own emphatic development, its own independence. Having risen
to the emotional rhetoric with which he concluded "Some of the Evil

5. See H. P. Vincent, *The Trying-Out of Moby-Dick*, pp. 299ff.

Effects of Flogging" (34), Melville in "Flogging not Lawful" (35) once again begins with quieted voice, with casual manner: "It is next to idle, at the present day, merely to denounce an iniquity. Be ours, then, a different task."

In effect this is a tacit recognition that the ending of his previous chapter *had* been denunciation; it is also an implicit promise that now he will be judicial and proceed coolly, logically—a promise which even Melville would find, later, impossible long to observe; the amassing of argument stirs the author to the very emotions intended for his readers, so that by the end of this forthcoming chapter the passionate voice is again exhorting if not directly denouncing.

Ours, too, is a different task in tracing Melville's sources through the sections of his argument. He does not make it easy for the reader—as he sometimes does with narration—by taking big, juicy chunks of action or bright bits of poetic language from his sources. Writing argument he is more interested in finding "illustration"—the factual material to support his "thesis." There is in such borrowing, naturally, little or no poetic enhancement; one stares at stolen bricks rather than at stolen jade.

Melville presses his indictment hard as he reminds us that the Articles of War, and Navy disciplinary practices, are against the genius of the American Constitution: in allowing "irresponsibility in a judge, un-limited discretionary authority in an executive, and the union of an irresponsible judge and an unlimited executive in one person." The Articles of War simply do not specify misdemeanors for which flogging is the punishment, and the Captain is at once legislator, judge, and executive. Habeas corpus is suspended, the sailor is a virtual slave. Melville's picture is a far cry from the jolly-tar tradition of fiction, but it is one which he has adapted from McNally's indictment. For once McNally's own prose strengthens in emotion (p. 129):

> Oh, Americans, to what are you coming! the blood of your ancestors is turned to water in your veins. Those who exclaim loudest against slavery, had better turn their attention to objects of suffering, and benevolence at home, before they look for them abroad, hundreds of whom will be found to stand as much in need of their assistance, and emancipation from the yoke of tyranny and oppression, as the swarthy sons and daughters of Africa. . . .
> No judge can order a lash to be inflicted on a citizen or alien, yet the master of a merchant vessel can be the accuser, the judge, and

the executor of his own sentence; seize to the rigging and flog any seaman who may have, even through ignorance, violated any of his orders; that person may have received honorable scars in defence of your country and rights, and yet he may be flogged like a dog.

To see how McNally's appeal to Americans to fulfill their tradition of liberty, and his reference to slavery, assisted Melville, the reader need only put Chapter 35 of *White-Jacket* beside these excerpts from McNally; his spirit, his facts, and even some of his language (Melville changes "flogged like a dog" to "scourged worse than a hound") were useful elements for Melville's argument and rhetoric. One paragraph of Melville's may show his distillation of the source materials:

> Or will you say that a navy officer is a man, but that an American-born citizen, whose grandsire may have ennobled him by pouring out his blood at Bunker Hill—will you say that, by entering the service of his country as a common seaman, and standing ready to fight her foes, he thereby loses his manhood at the very time he most asserts it? Will you say that, by so doing, he degrades himself to the liability of the scourge, but if he tarries ashore in time of danger, he is safe from that indignity? All our linked states, all four continents of mankind, unite in denouncing such a thought.

In "Flogging not Necessary" (Chapter 36) Melville goes from humanitarian arguments to utilitarian; he was, he said, "ready to come down from the lofty mast-head of an eternal principle, and fight you—Commodores and Captains of the navy—on your own quarter-deck, with your own weapons, at your own paces." With this Melville composed an actual counterblast to the lobbying letters which the Navy had already collected from their "Commodores and Captains" to prove the necessity of flogging.

McNally was of no use to Melville now, but he had two other sources available: articles in Volumes 41 (1824) and 47 (1848) of the *Edinburgh Review* and a pamphlet on flogging. Professor Philbrick has thoroughly discussed the effect of these materials on *White-Jacket;* by quoting generously he demonstrates that for Chapter 35, the Jeffrey article

> was used by Melville as a source of three different categories of information. First, it supplied him with direct quotations from

Collingwood's letters. . . . [He] also found useful material in
Jeffrey's quotations from Newnham Collingwood's editorial remarks. . . . third and most important . . . in Jeffrey's own
statements, for Jeffrey used his review as the occasion for a
vigorous attack on naval abuses, an attack which coincided at many
points with the purposes of *White-Jacket*.[6]

What Melville contributed of his own to this mishmash of information from the *Edinburgh Review* was the closing peroration against dead
precedent and a dream of the liberating future:

> The Past is, in many things, the foe of mankind; the Future is, in
> all things, our friend. In the Past is no hope; the Future is both
> hope and fruition. The Past is the text-book of tyrants; the Future
> the Bible of the Free. Those who are solely governed by the Past
> stand like Lot's wife, crystallized in the act of looking backward,
> and forever incapable of looking before.

This goes on for two more paragraphs about "predestinated" America—
this was written only four years after the phrase "Manifest Destiny" was
coined—and proudly, if chauvinistically, asserts that "we Americans are
the peculiar, chosen people—the Israel of our time; we bear the ark of
the liberties of the world."

Even in the formal elements of balance and antithesis Melville sur-
passed his sources; the epigrammatic snap, the imagery, the aptness and
economy of this single snippet from his four closing paragraphs of
pleading surely exonerate him from any silly charge of theft.

The second significant addition was Melville's reference from Collingwood and Nelson to "the influence wrought by a powerful brain,
and a determined, intrepid spirit over a miscellaneous rabble." He had
already expressed the idea a few chapters earlier, again inspired by
thinking about Nelson and Wellington, when he wrote: "One large
brain and one large heart have virtue sufficient to magnetize a whole fleet
or an army." In a documentary such as *White-Jacket*, and with Captain
Ap Catesby Jones or Commodore Davis as prototypical leaders, Melville
could scarcely embody this heroic concept in an actual captain. To have
done so would have been to write a different book. Even the bare mention of the idea in relation to Mad Jack, whose intrepid heart and brain
had saved the ship, had introduced a dramatic element which had to be

6. Thomas Philbrick, "Melville's 'Best Authorities,'" *Nineteenth-Century Fiction*, XV (September 1960), pp. 171–179.

dropped since it threatened to turn a documentary into a novel. In his next book, *Moby-Dick,* Melville would allow this urgency to have its way, embodying in Captain Ahab—a Nantucket version of Nelson and Collingwood—the great brain and heart, but instead of once again invoking Mad Jack's self-reliance, which saves his ship, Melville will alter course and show the Mad Ahab who, self-reliant without the corrective element of social-reliance, destroys the *Pequod.*

· IO ·

Rambling Around
a Man-of-War

". . . so long as I get somewhere," Alice added as an explana-
tion. "Oh, you're sure to do that," said the Cat, "if only you walk
long enough."

Lewis Carroll, *Alice in Wonderland*

WRITTEN rapidly, *White-Jacket* was clearly not planned in detail but
was written *ad hoc*. It grew almost at random. Quite obviously, Melville
simply began, confident that his subject—life in a man-of-war—and his
time limitation—the voyage from Callao to Norfolk—would easily give
shape to his book from the plentiful materials which his memory and
his library provided.

White-Jacket, then, is disjunctive, spasmodic, but this disturbs only when the reader demands or expects what Melville never intended to write—a novel. It is, to be sure, more spasmodic than the other sailor-accounts, because, unlike their authors, Melville increasingly succumbed to his deep urge to say something meaningful and not merely to spin yarns as did Mercier and Ames. Melville wanted to realize some of the implications of his material, to expand upon them. Mercier's *Scenes* does not expand one hair's breadth, and indeed does not even mention many such fundamental facts of ship-life as crowding and discomfort, flogging and brutality. Comic discomforts such as belly-aches and dous-ings, but never beatings and tyranny—things which were certainly part of the *Constitution* cruise which he wrote about. Cheerful and chatty, *Scenes* reads as though written by Flask of the *Pequod.*

Leech's *Thirty Years from Home* is different from Mercier, better conceived and better written. It is deficient in informative detail about how a man-of-war operates, but it has a less superficial, more dynamic, sense of ship life. Leech's autobiographic purpose gave him an opportunity which Mercier's one-voyage narrative did not have; Leech was telling of his long life on many seas and could therefore select dramatic moments. His, however, is no jolly tar approach. His account of flogging is the most vivid, save Dana's, among Melville's sources, but although he bitterly attacks floggings he does not attack the penal practice itself, nor does he create a Ushant as Melville, using his material, will do. *Thirty Years from Home* might have been written by Starbuck.

Had Melville written on the level he first intended—a pot-boiler amusingly informative—he would have left us only an improved Mercier or Leech. Because he became aroused by his insight into his materials, his book exploded on him—as the whaling voyage more furiously exploded into *Moby-Dick*—and upset the orderly and unambitious documentary. Without this explosion *White-Jacket* would have complied with low level canons of criticism, but it wouldn't have been our present *White-Jacket* which, if no novelistic masterpiece, is a book whose readability and excellence time has only served to strengthen; remembered, while Mercier and Leech are remembered only because of their unwitting aid to *White-Jacket.*

A simple documentary requires little structuring. Melville had many obvious approaches. He could proceed from deck to deck, or from rank to rank, or from duty to duty—or any blend thereof. It was when he included propaganda and metaphysics in *White-Jacket* that disjunctions became noticeable. Melville's tailor image is again useful. The difficulty of patching a jacket was more than that of piecing together patches from

Mercier, Leech, Ames, and Dana; it was also the stitching of pockets and sleeves, of ideas and insights. Melville complained similarly about writing *Moby-Dick,* when he wrote Dana:[1]

> It will be a strange sort of book, tho', I fear; blubber is blubber you know; tho' you may get oil out of it, the poetry runs as hard as sap from a frozen maple tree;—& to cook the thing up, one must needs throw in a little fancy, which from the nature of the thing, must be as ungainly as the gambols of the whales themselves. Yet I mean to give the truth of the thing, spite of this.

This familiar grumble throws some light on the *White-Jacket* problem. Written while the whaling voyage was still probably in the semi-documentary stage, it shows Melville working out a deliberate, preconceived strategy for handling his shipful of whaling objects and men; it shows his awareness of the new documentary form he had created in *White-Jacket,* the perfecting of which was brought about by the very writing of the man-of-war book. The insight into technique which Melville came to more than part-way through *White-Jacket* was for his next book a familiar, personal pattern.

The flogging section of four chapters was one of these disjunctive elements which introduced a new intensity in the writing, out of key with what had preceded and, to a lesser degree, with what is immediately to follow. Having been lifted by Leech to the vividness of his flogging scene, Melville now lowers his emotional level—to that, say, of Mercier—and for more than twenty chapters, 37–60, resumes the relaxed, sauntering manner of the lecturer-guide conducting a tour of a man-of-war, each chapter a vignette or tableau. He moves almost at random. Whatever whimsically attracts him, object or vagrant notion, he pauses to comment on, to describe, or to dramatize. He does not now bother to link chapter with chapter but presents discrete details. The only forward movement of the book is in sheer accumulation of knowledge whereby we come to know and to feel the life on a man-of-war in the 1840's as we can from no other book. It would seem to be, later, the method of the cetological center of *Moby-Dick,* but in that book Melville has a linking plot and a unified, and unifying, set of characters not available or appropriate to him now in *White-Jacket,* a book primarily documentary. It is to this middle section of *White-Jacket*

1. *The Letters of Herman Melville,* edited by Merrell R. Davis and William H. Gilman (New Haven: Yale University Press, 1960), p. 108. Dated 1 May 1850.

that Melville seems most pertinently to refer when, in describing the sewing of his jacket, he mentions its "many odds and ends of patches."

How, for instance, could any writer unify seamlessly the variety of materials which we find here: the recovery from the sea of some casks of old port wine; the chaplain and his conduct of prayers; the frigate in the Bay of Rio; navy ceremonial; the ship's library; killing time in harbor; smuggling; a villainous master-at-arms; a ship's poet; an auction; the purser and his staff; the Bay of Rio; midshipmen as a breed; the effect of weather on sailors; the visit to the ship of Emperor Don Pedro; and so on. Melville takes each subject by itself; the result is a ragbag which we shall rifle rapidly, glancing only at a few eye-catching patches.

•

Chapter 37, "Some superior old 'London Dock' from the Wine-coolers of Neptune," is an instance of the pleasant triviality of much of the middle section and suggests how much shorter (but less effective or interesting) *White-Jacket* would have been without the source books to stir Melville's imagination. What probably moved Melville to this anecdote—sounding so authentic, so reminiscent—was noticing the same general situation independently described in two different authors, and being able to improve, and conceal, his sources by sheer combination, as well as by style and humor.

Mercier tells (p. 70) about some liquor-less sailors longing for some grog miraculously to come floating by to relieve their drouth:

> As we neared the Cape, and began to feel the weather grow gradually colder and colder, the dolorous complaints of our tars could be heard throughout the ship on every deck, cursing bitterly the hard fortune that deprived them of their beloved, stimulating liquid in this uncomfortable weather. How many wishes were expressed that the dreaded barrier between us and the harbour of Valparaiso was but safely rounded—or that they could possibly fall in with some good-natured and obliging craft that would help to replenish our whiskey casks somewhat—or that the man at the mast-head could discover two or three puncheons of good West India, tumbling and rolling as if anxious to be picked up, or a hundred others equally vain and foolish; but 'twas all of no avail; there was Cape Horn as yet to be doubled, and whether in a pacific or cross-grained humour we had yet to determine; not a vestige of a vessel to be seen from aloft for days and days together; and the

only object that cheered our sight in lieu of the wished-for casks of liquor, was the cape pigeons and albatrosses that were hovering around us in great numbers, many of which being enticed by a baited hook, became an easy prey to some of our epicures.

Melville makes this longing sigh of the crew of *Constitution* into a realization for the crew of the *Neversink*, when "A man at the fore-top-sail-yard sung out that there were eight or ten dark objects floating on the sea, some three points off our lee-bow."

They were "a sight that Bacchus and his bacchanals would have gloated over," and when tapped, there issued "a rich purple tide" of port. Captain Claret first ordered the casks put away, but the consequent grumbling of the grog-thirsty crew was silenced the next day when "all hands were electrified by the old familiar sound—so long hushed—of the drum rolling to grog. After that the port was served out twice a day, till all was expended."

This chapter is really but a trifle, a pointillist dot to relieve the dark tone of the flogging chapters just concluded. Seeing Mercier's simple sentences, Melville's dramatizing imagination used them for humorous purposes and to satirize not the brutality of Authority but rather its arbitrary, unpredictable character.

But that is not all. Finding this source in Mercier is an example of the tricky experiences in prospect for the source-hunter. Mercier certainly seems sufficient to explain the chapter, until one comes across the following paragraph in *The Life and Adventures of John Nicol, Mariner* (p. 84):

When off Cape Horn, we perceived an object floating at a small distance from the ship. Not one of us could make out what it was. All our boats being fast, two men went down into the water and swam to it, and made it fast in the slings. When it came on board it was a cask, but so overgrown with weeds and barnacles, the bunghole could not be discovered. I was set to work to cut into it. To our agreeable surprise, it was full of excellent Port wine. All the crew got at little of it, and Captain Portlock gave us brandy in place of the rest.

This slides into Melville's account only slightly altered:

Each puncheon was of a deep-green color, so covered with minute barnacles and shell-fish, and streaming with sea-weed, that it needed long searching to find out their bung-holes; they looked like venerable old *loggerhead-turtles.* How long they had been tossing about, and making voyages for the benefit of the flavor of their contents, no one could tell. In trying to raft them ashore, or on board of some merchant-ship, they must have drifted off to sea. This we inferred from the ropes that lengthwise united them, and which, from one point of view, made them resemble a section of a sea-serpent. They were *struck* into the gun-deck, where the eager crowd being kept off by sentries, the cooper was called with his tools.

"Bung up, and bilge free!" he cried, in an ecstasy, flourishing his driver and hammer.

Upon clearing away the barnacles and moss, a flat sort of shell-fish was found, closely adhering, like a California-shell, right over one of the bungs. Doubtless this shell-fish had there taken up his quarters, and thrown his own body into the breach, in order the better to preserve the precious contents of the cask. The by-standers were breathless, when at last this puncheon was canted over and a tin-pot held to the orifice. What was to come forth? salt-water or wine? But a rich purple tide soon settled the question, and the lieutenant assigned to taste it, with a loud and satisfactory smack of his lips, pronounced it Port!

"Slightly altered?" No, considerably, through details which intensify the physical sense of casks and men, through the prolongation of the discovery, in the dramatization of events. Melville's chapter is not just two merged lantern slides from Mercier and Nicol; it is a motion picture, in which the elements of what were discrete lantern slides suddenly unfreeze, merge, and move about before our eyes.

•

Bart I: . . . (*In a whisper:*) I even suspect him of being a bit of a Platonist.
Bart III: Oh . . . how ghastly! A Platonist . . . what animal's that? . . . (*aside*) A Platonist? . . . Oh yes, it's a kind of platypus!

Eugène Ionesco, *Improvisation*

From the comic sensuality of the grog scene, Melville turns immediately to the ivory tower of ineffectual, even inept, idealism, "The Chaplain and Chapel in a Man-of-war" (Chapter 38). The Chaplain of the *Neversink* is transcendental, appropriate for a book written in 1849. The Chaplain's behavior is in accordance with his reading; it is unrealistic and abstract, unrelated to the needs and problems of the sailors to whom he ministers. Melville pins him to paper as a specimen of *homo absurdus;* his chapter is a sketch of Alcottian ineffectuality worthy of the satiric crayon of a Daumier:[2]

> He was a slender, middle-aged man, of an amiable deportment and irreproachable conversation; but I must say, that his sermons were but ill calculated to benefit the crew. He had drank at the mystic fountain of Plato; his head had been turned by the Germans; and this I will say, that White-Jacket himself saw him with Coleridge's Biographia Literaria in his hand.
>
> Fancy, now, this transcendental divine standing behind a gun-carriage on the main-deck, and addressing five hundred salt-sea sinners upon the psychological phenomena of the soul, and the ontological necessity of every sailor's saving it at all hazards. He enlarged upon the follies of the ancient philosophers; learnedly alluded to the Phaedon of Plato; exposed the follies of Simplicius's Commentary on Aristotle's "De Coelo," by arraying against that clever Pagan author the admired tract of Tertullian— *De Proescriptionibus Hoereticorum*—and concluded by a Sanscrit invocation. He was particularly hard upon the Gnostics and Marcionites of the second century of the Christian era; but he never, in the remotest manner, attacked the every-day vices of the nineteenth century, as eminently illustrated in our man-of-war world. Concerning drunkenness, fighting, flogging, and oppression— things expressly or impliedly prohibited by Christianity—he never said aught. But the most mighty Commodore and Captain sat before him; and in general, if, in a monarchy, the state form the audience of the church, little evangelical piety will be preached. Hence, the harmless, non-committal abstrusities of our Chaplain were not to be wondered at. He was no Massillon, to thunder forth his ecclesiastical rhetoric, even when a Louis le Grand was enthroned among his congregation. Nor did the chaplains who preached on the quarter-deck of Lord Nelson ever allude to the guilty Felix, nor to Delilah, nor practically reason of righteousness, temperance, and judgment to come, when that renowned Admiral sat, sword-belted, before them.

2. A cartoon, date unknown, from *Punch* shows a minister speaking from the pulpit in high passion, while a woman murmurs to her friend, "He's always like this about confetti in the porch."

The temptation has been strong to interpret this portrait as one of the Reverend J. Thomas Bartow, Chaplain of the Frigate *United States* during the Pacific voyage.[3] That may be, but how can we *know?* Melville, as we have seen, would have denied the identification. The Chaplain is, rather, a straw man created for Melville comically to knock down, another phase of his persistent indictment of militarism, here the paradox of the man-of-peace in a man-of-war.

Furthermore, the Chaplain is part of Melville's lifetime interest in the relationship between idealism and reality, a subject treated quickly in *White-Jacket,* but developed, and dramatized, throughout *Moby-Dick* (Ahab is a transcendentalist in reverse), and stated explicitly in the pamphlet on "Chronometricals and Horologicals" in *Pierre,* and suggested in *Billy Budd.*

The "chapel" is a setting as contradictory as the Chaplain himself, being a space among the guns where the sailors sat "wearing out our trowsers and our tempers." Ridiculous and contradictory is the cursing of officers to drive men to prayers; ridiculous, too, the Baptist sailor protesting attendance at a service not of his sect. Democracy and Christianity are themselves contradicted by a man-of-war:

> How can it be expected that the religion of peace should flourish in an oaken castle of war? How can it be expected that the clergyman, whose pulpit is a forty-two-pounder, should convert sinners to a faith that enjoins them to turn the right cheek when the left is smitten?

For much of this Melville seems to be working away from his book sources, from some amalgam of memory and imagination, but as always with him whenever he protracts his satire to support his position by facts, or pseudo-facts, he turns to his staff of writers, and this time he has called on McNally to help him ridicule the role of the Bible aboard ships, and the role of missionary activity among sailors:

3. For the career of Bartow see *United States Navy Chaplains, 1778–1945,* compiled by the Chaplain's Activity of the Bureau of Naval Personnel, Navy Department, under the direction of Clifford Merritt Drury, Washington, U.S. Government Printing Office, 1948. Charles R. Anderson, *Melville in the South Seas* (New York: Columbia University Press, 1939), pp. 369–371, compares Melville's description of the Sunday morning service with an actual sailor account of one of Bartow's services, Melville's irony in striking contrast with the prettiness and sentimentalism of the scribe.

Melville (Chapter 38)	McNally (p. 154)
Although, by the regulations of the Navy, each seaman's mess on board the Neversink was furnished with a Bible, these Bibles were seldom or never to be seen, except on Sunday mornings, when usage demands that they shall be exhibited by the cooks of the messes, when the master-at-arms goes his rounds on the berth-deck. At such times, they usually surmounted a highly polished tin-pot placed on the lid of the chest.	There is a Bible to each mess on board of our ships of war, but they are not used in any way except as an ornament on the top of the mess can, on the mess chest. The cook of a mess will be flogged if the Bible is not in its place as an ornament, but nothing will be said to him for not applying it to the use for which it was intended.

Further, McNally's serious indignation that missionaries concerned themselves with savages in faraway lands to the neglect of Americans in American ships becomes Melville's sarcastic notice of the Neversink Chaplain's circulation of propaganda among the sailors: "One was for the purpose of building a seaman's chapel in China; another to pay the salary of a tract-distributor in Greece; a third to raise a fund for the benefit of an African Colonization Society." Such satire looks back to Typee and Omoo, and forward to The Confidence-Man.

•

Most of the middle section of White-Jacket is set in the harbor of Rio de Janeiro, a circumstance which further explains its somewhat dawdling character. The ship is at rest, the voyage suspended; there is somehow a vacuum to be filled. As he talks, Melville gives the effect of an announcer ad libbing during the intermission of a game, describing half-relevant matters until the game—his journey—resumes. While in harbor, nothing much happens on board ship—one might compare the log of the United States for the equivalent period—and what little did happen, or could properly be imaginatively projected into that period, Melville spins into short, unrelated chapters.

Melville refuses to go ashore for material;[4] he concedes that Brazil

4. The crew of the United States was not granted liberty during its return voyage stop at Rio.

and Rio de Janeiro are touristically interesting, but stresses that "though much might be said of all this, yet must I forbear, if I may, and adhere to my one proper object, *the world in a man-of-war."*

More than ever, then, Melville turns to his sources, weaving paragraphs from suggestions in Mercier, Leech, and Nicol.

If anything connects these disparate chapters it is Melville's attitude towards pomp and circumstance. Omitting few chances to satirize, he ridicules commodores and captains, ritual and meaningless routine. Chapter 39, "The Frigate in Harbor.—The Boats.—Grand State Reception of the Commodore," jeers at the state visitations of the *Neversink's* captain to other ships, and to one English ship particularly. White-Jacket is at this time substituting for one of the gig-men, and helps row the captain about the bay. The visit sounds authentic, but the records make no mention of it nor of Melville's service in the gig. Suspicion increases on finding that one of the details is taken from Leech (on board an English ship). Melville wrote:

> There happened to be a lord on board of this ship—the younger son of an earl, they told me. He was a fine-looking fellow. I chanced to stand by when he put a question to an Irish captain of a gun; upon the seaman's inadvertently saying *sir* to him, his lordship looked daggers at the slight; and the sailor, touching his hat a thousand times, said, "Pardon, your honor; I meant to say *my lord,* sir!"

If we remember that "they told me" is one of Melville's favorite coverings for literary theft and note that the following passage is from the flogging section of Leech, which Melville has already freely looted, then the influence of *Thirty Years from Home* (p. 60) is apparent. An "honest-hearted Irishman" drunkenly addresses the captain as "Billy":

> The captain was excessively proud; even his officers scarcely dared walk the quarter deck on the same side with him. He never allowed himself to be addressed but by his title of "my Lord." Should a sailor, through design or forgetfulness, reply to a command, "Yes, sir," the lordly man would look at him with a glance full of dignity, and sternly reply, "What, sir?" This, of course, would put the offender in mind to correct himself by saying, "Yes, my *Lord."* Judge then of his surprise, indignation, nay, of his lordly horror, when poor old drunken Bob Hammond called him "Billy, my boy!"

Leech's offender is flogged, but Melville, just finished with flogging, alters the episode to arouse a smile rather than a shudder.

Chapter 40, "Some of the Ceremonies in a Man-of-war unnecessary and injurious," moralizes on "the absurd, ridiculous, and mock-heroic" naval practices, completely undemocratic in character, that enlarge the gap between common sailor and officer.

The scene shifts yet again in Chapter 41, "A Man-of-war Library." The chapter was created for at least two reasons: first, Melville was fond of reading and wanted his *Neversink* to have a library, just as had the *United States*—not, however, the same one.[5] Second, he had before him Mercier's section on ship reading, and Mercier's chapter, "The Literary Tars," suggested and supplied him with his chapter. Towards the beginning of "The Literary Tars" Mercier wrote (p. 106):

> When sailing on the boundless Ocean for weeks and weeks together, each day bringing forth the same dull, unvaried round of employment; the same tiresome monotony still pervading the scene; what can be a greater resource to help to dispel the foul fiend *ennui,* than the interesting or amusing volume; it is at a time like this, the unsophisticated tar pores over with pleasurable feelings the pages of history, or imbibes, with heated imagination, the melting pathos of smoe [sic: some] of our beautiful modern poets.

Melville begins his chapter similarly:

> Nowhere does time pass more heavily than with most man-of-war's men on board their craft in harbor.
> One of my principal antidotes against *ennui* in Rio, was reading. There was a public library on board. . . .

The first long paragraph describes the "librarian," who had "once been a clerk in a Post-office ashore; and, having been long accustomed to hand over letters when called for, he was now just the man to hand over books." This librarian kept the books in a large cask, and some of the books "must have been selected by our Chaplain, who so pranced on Coleridge's 'High German horse.' " Transcendentalism again, an attack

5. See Charles R. Anderson, *Melville in the South Seas* (New York: Columbia University Press, 1939), p. 358: "Since none of the ones he mentions are in the list of those transferred from his ship at Callao, the implication is that this was only part, and perhaps a small part, of the ship's library."

to be resumed in *Moby-Dick*. Melville is playing some private joke, surely, but from what source or to what point is uncertain. Having taken Mercier's suggestion, his situation, and having transferred it to the Rio de Janeiro section of *White-Jacket*, Melville then proceeds to construct "A Man-of-war Library." Paragraph one describes the librarian, perhaps an authentic memory; at least he appears in no source yet known. But in the second paragraph the books are mentioned, the very first one being:

> Mason Good's Book of Nature—a very good book, to be sure, but not precisely adapted to tarry tastes—was one of these volumes.

And then he lists difficult books too intellectual and dry for uneducated sailors' tastes. This paragraph in Melville would seem to be his drastic rewriting of Mercier's paragraph (p. 107):

> There was a soft-pated "Johnny Raw," a steady cook on the berth-deck, with scarcely sense enough to know which was *banyan* day, loudly vociferating for number one hundred and sixty, which, as soon as presented, proved to be an essay on conchology; he carried it off at all events, triumphantly, though whether he could read the title page or not, I have my doubts. Next came a light hearted *harum-scarum* fore-topman, up to all manner of mischief, with an eye even at this time seeking for a fit object amongst the crowd to play his intolerable pranks upon; he called for anything at all to pass the time away, number two hundred and four would answer as well as any, 'twas his ship's number, and therefore he chose it: the number in question was brought up, and our fore-topman stalked off with Mason Good's Book of Nature under his arm, to edify himself and the worthies of the larboard gangway.

Melville's third paragraph about a couple of "choice old authors, whom I stumbled upon in various parts of the ship" is clearly his improvisation, or use, of two books from which he, now author in 1849, was then reading: *Morgan's History of Algiers,* and *Knox's Captivity in Ceylon.* That these were at hand in Melville's New York study is suggested by his adequately accurate quotation from the second work.

The fourth paragraph deals with the Elizabethans, especially Shakespeare, which was Melville's overwhelming discovery the year of the composition of *White-Jacket.* Throughout the paragraph Melville was stuffing the *Neversink*'s library with his own immediate literary interests.

The fifth paragraph returns to Mercier. Melville wrote:

I diversified this reading of mine, by borrowing Moore's *"Loves of the Angels"* from Rose-water, who recommended it as *"de charmingest of wolumes;"* and a Negro Song-book, containing *Sittin' on a rail, Gumbo Squash,* and *Jim along Josey,* from Broadbit, a sheet-anchor-man. The sad taste of this old tar, in admiring such vulgar stuff, was much denounced by Rose-water, whose own predilections were of a more elegant nature, as evinced by his exalted opinion of the literary merits of the *"Loves of the Angels."*

This is pure Mercier (p. 108):

One of the galley cooks now popped his curly head amongst the assemblage, and asked in quite a polite style for Moore's "Loves of the Angels." "Never mind," cried Flukes, the main-top wag— "I've got Sittin on a Rail and Gumbo Squash in my *ditty-bag* I can let you have, they will answer you just the same; you will be more at *home* with them at all events." "I'd have you to understand," replied the "coloured gemman"—his lips thickening and his nose dilating with anger, "that I don't read such foolish stupid stuff as you have just mentioned—nothing less than Moore or Byron in the shape of poetry do I think palatable; and when I read prose, always give me a philosophical treatise; I always like something *heavy* to digest."

Melville's sixth and last paragraph in "A Man-of-war Library" is also in part from Mercier, for when he says that

Several other sailors were diligent readers, though their studies did not lie in the way of belles-lettres. Their favorite authors were such as you may find at the book-stalls around Fulton Market; they were slightly physiological in their nature.

he is reworking Mercier's account (p. 109) of the barber's

enquiring at a hazard for number one hundred and twenty; it was passed up to him and proved to be a Treatise on Physiology; "my gracious!" cried the man of soapsuds, "this is too *dull* altogether for me."

Melville of course changes the implication of the "physiology" from the dullness of the treatise to the spicier connotation of the unspecified works. Only two and a half pages long, Melville's library chapter is obviously a rapid pasting job, expendable under the pencil of a severe editor. It does, however, help us to pass the time with its light mockery of unusual librarianship. As he does so often, Melville ends the chapter with a generalization, observing that, imposing public libraries to the contrary, the "books that prove most agreeable, grateful, and companionable, are those we pick up by chance here and there; those which seem put into our hands by Providence; those which pretend to little, but abound in much." What is pleasantly ironic about this statement is that it described Mercier's *Scenes,* which here and elsewhere was so "companionable" to Melville in the construction of *White-Jacket.*

The middle section, then, shows Melville working close to the most literal and uninspired of his uninspired sources; he demonstrates how dullness can be brightened into diversion. He is especially close to the central section of Mercier's *Scenes,* in which Mercier, also in port at Callao, is trying to show that "To beguile the monotony that hangs like an incubus upon him, the sailor has recourse to divers methods; the merry song, the romantic tale, the facetious anecdote, all are brought in force to kill this foul fiend *ennui.*" His "divers methods" become Melville's. The theme, then, of Melville's harbor section is really "Monotony on Board a Man-of-War," and the problem which he so successfully solves, as Mercier does not, is how to make monotony unmonotonous. Thanks in good part, however, to the initial spadework, or rough notes, of Mercier, Melville's imagination was freed to adorn and enliven otherwise mundane materials—to work *out* of them as well as from them.

Melville confronts the monotony theme head-on in Chapter 42, "Killing Time in a Man-of-war in Harbor." Some sailors read, as he has just shown, but some were unable to read:

> Still, they had other pursuits; some were expert at the needle, and employed their time in making elaborate shirts, stitching picturesque eagles, and anchors, and all the stars of the federated states in the collars thereof; so that when they at last completed and put on these shirts, they may be said to have hoisted the American colors.

This was a literary patch sewn into *White-Jacket* from doggerel lines by Mercier (p. 103):

> Near yonder gun sits an industrious blade
> With all the *et ceteras* of a tailor's trade,
> Working a collar for some graceless wight

Who in a bit of *flash* takes great delight;
Upon it flags and stars of every hue
And parti-coloured eagles meet the view,
On which the owner bends his ardent gaze,
Giving the fancy workman every praise.

This is close, and so are the next few paragraphs. Melville mentions the unnecessary "busy-work" imposed on the sailors:

> One other mode of passing time while in port was cleaning and polishing your *bright-work;* for it must be known that, in men-of-war, every sailor has some brass or steel of one kind or other to keep in high order—like house-maids, whose business it is to keep well-polished the knobs on the front-door railing and the parlor-grates.
>
> Excepting the ring-bolts, eye-bolts, and belaying-pins scattered about the decks, this bright-work, as it is called, is principally about the guns, embracing the *"monkey-tails"* of the carronades, the screws, *prickers,* little irons, and other things.
>
> The portion that fell to my own share I kept in superior order, quite equal in polish to Rogers's best cutlery. I received the most extravagant encomiums from the officers; one of whom offered to match me against any brasier or brass-polisher in her British majesty's Navy. Indeed, I devoted myself to the work body and soul, and thought no pains too painful, and no labor too laborious, to achieve the highest attainable polish possible for us poor lost sons of Adam to reach.

Even Melville's flippant self-reference cannot conceal his indebtedness to a passage from Mercier (p. 113):

> . . . our happy tars had nothing at all to do after the nine o'clock inspection; the yards were uniformly squared, and each piece of rigging systematically hauled taut, under the directions of our knowledgeable and efficient boat-swain; the capacious awnings were ready spread fore and aft, imparting a refreshing coolness along the spar-deck; the *belaying-pins, monkey-tails, screws,* and all the other *bright-work,* wore an appearance that might complete with Rogers' most superior cutlery; in fact, every article about the deck was arranged with the neatest precision and accuracy, and "Old Ironsides," both inside and out, could present to the gaze of a stranger, as complete a floating structure of precise elegance and exact regularity, as any ship that ever danced over the bounding billow.

The "happy tars" from Mercier, however, blend in Melville's account with the very unhappy tars from McNally, who serve under a tyrant and are flogged with brutal frequency as they try to keep the ship bright (p. 98):

> the most harassing and unnecessary work was done on board that ship; every handspike, crow-bar, and belaying-pin was scoured bright; the iron straps of snatch blocks, iron travellers round the masts, linch-pins of the guns, ringbolts in the deck, trainbolts in the gun carriages, iron rail round the fore-castle, and the iron straps of the cat blocks were all kept as bright as silver; and many hundreds of floggings did keeping these bright occasion; which was entirely out of order, and as such was laughed at by the rest of the officers on the station.

Melville alternates between Mercier and McNally, his patches taken in the following order: *Scenes* (p. 103), McNally (p. 98), *Scenes* (p. 113), McNally (p. 112), and *Scenes* (p. 113).

McNally complains (p. 112) about the lack of space for the diversion of foremast hands:

> Such petty and unnecessary annoyances were very likely to make men discontented, who knew them to be uncalled for and tyranni- cal. No person was allowed to remain on the orlop deck, and none on the lower gun deck, except the cooks; the larboard side of the main deck was the parade of the officers, and the starboard side was occupied with the commodore's tailors, shoemakers, and cabi- netmakers. . . .

Melville touches this up with a flick of his accustomed contempt for the petty tyranny of officers:

> But, after all, there was not much room, while in port, for promenading, at least on the gun-deck, for the whole larboard side is kept clear for the benefit of the officers, who appreciate the advantages of having a clear stroll fore and aft; and they well know that the sailors had much better be crowded together on the other side than that the set of their own coat-tails should be im- paired by brushing against their tarry trowsers.

Immediately, then, Melville mentions checkers as a diversion, as sug- gested by this passage from *Scenes* (p. 113), immediately following that quoted above:

Groups of light-hearted sailors might be observed scattered about the decks in glorious confusion, some killing time with the assistance of chequer or back-gammon boards; others (though in opposition to the strictest orders of the service) throwing the fatal and cursed dice with all a determined gambler's anxiety. . . .

This set Melville to decorating. Unlike some tyrannical officers, Captain Claret allowed "checkers"; Melville ironically lauds his liberality, a concession his great heart made under certain drastic pressures:

But Captain Claret's leniency in permitting checkers on board his ship might have arisen from the following little circumstance, confidentially communicated to me. Soon after the ship had sailed from home, checkers were prohibited; whereupon the sailors were exasperated against the Captain, and one night, when he was walking round the forecastle, bim! came an iron belaying-pin past his ears; and while he was dodging that, bim! came another, from the other side; so that, it being a very dark night, and nobody to be seen, and it being impossible to find out the trespassers, he thought it best to get back into his cabin as soon as possible. Some time after—just as if the belaying-pins had nothing to do with it—it was indirectly rumored that the checker-boards might be brought out again, which—as a philosophical shipmate observed—showed that Captain Claret was a man of a ready understanding, and could understand a hint as well as any other man, even when conveyed by several pounds of iron.

When anything is "confidentially communicated," as he says this information was, to one of Melville's narrators, it is certain that a bookish source is the communicator.

Sources for the latter half of the chapter have not appeared. Melville seems, perhaps deceptively, to be working from his own memories, as he develops the trope, through illustrative episode and forthright statement, of the ship as a prison. An ex-convict named "Shakings" (the name is in Mercier [pp. 64–65]), contrasts his former term in Sing Sing with his incarceration aboard the *Neversink*, "this State's Prison man-of-war world of ours."

Idle and thirsty, the sailors in port often pass their time in smuggling liquor, despite severe penalties of flogging. To this hazardous sport Melville devotes all of Chapter 43, "Smuggling in a Man-of-war." This time he leaned heavily on Mercier's information from "The Unexpected Seizure" (pp. 157–161), telling of the discovery of a number of skins of rum attached to a nearby buoy, to which from time to time the men would quietly swim, bringing rum back to the ship. Mercier's story is told at length; the moans and groans of the sailors when their hidden liquor is discovered, seized, and poured into the ocean—this furnishes his comedy. Melville drastically curtails his source; his low-keyed chapter is one of the least interesting in the book. Detailed examination of the stitching of these particular patches is therefore unimportant.

·

Melville's chapter on smuggling sprawls, as if he were not deeply involved in his subject nor in the writing of it. It is patched carelessly, casually, as if to fill up idle hours on board ship in the harbor of Rio.

Chapter 44, which follows, is different in tone and tension, evidenced in its tighter construction and in the vividness of the portrait of Bland as "A Knave in Office in a Man-of-war." From the anecdotal tone of his "boys will be boys" attitude towards smuggling—a social evil of no great consequence—Melville shifts to a mesmeric fascination with pure human evil, a mystery of iniquity in a man-of-war world.

Melville's chapter is of a length scarcely called for by a character whose subsequent role in *White-Jacket* is insignificant. It is portraiture for the portrait's sake, Goya-esque in its verbal way. It is one phase, almost the first, in Melville's long-sustained interest in Satanism, an interest displayed just two months before in *Redburn,* in the character of Jackson, to be shown again shortly in the overly-carpentered Fedallah of *Moby-Dick,* to emerge five years later in the metamorphoses of the Confidence Man, and thirty years later to culminate in Claggart— Bland's twin—in *Billy Budd.*

Bland has a prototype, possibly in actuality,[6] but more certainly, demonstrably, in a favorite Melville source. William McNally's embittered, harsh description of Sterritt in *Evils and Abuses* (pp. 89–90) is the first draft of Melville's figure:

> There was an individual on board of that ship whose name was Sterritt; but he was better known in the navy, by the cognomen of "Jemmy Leggs." He had been on board the frigate Constitution, as a master at arms, and had there incurred such hatred, for his tyranny and villainy, that his life was unsafe. On the arrival of that ship in Boston, he was sent on shore, in order to give him a chance

6. There was a Master-of-Arms on board the *United States* who, like Bland, was temporarily demoted, but we know nothing else about this Thomas A. Warbass (Muster Roll 586).

to escape the vengeance of the crew. He fled to New York, where
he was pursued by the sailors, and he took refuge by shipping
again in the navy, on board of the receiving ship; and when the
Fairfield was commissioned he was taken on board, in his former
capacity of master at arms, where free liberty was given him to
indulge his disposition. This man was destitute of every moral or
honorable principle—destitute alike of every good feeling that
reigns in the human breast; and the punishment which he had at
different times received from seamen, for his cruelty towards them,
only increased his malignity and hatred. He had been several times
so badly bruised and injured by them, that his life was despaired
of—and on one occasion, they had committed an act upon his
person which left him of the neuter gender, or of "no sex, at all,"
as Byron expresses it. But he recovered; and the seamen, who are
ever ready to ascribe to supernatural agency the most common
occurrences, believed him to be in league with his great prototype,
the devil. When the Fairfield was in Marseilles, the crew at-
tempted to hang him. It was in the evening, and he was sitting at
the galley, drinking a pot of coffee, which he had gotten by the
fears of one of the cooks; for none would have given him any
thing, from love. A rope was passed down the fore scuttle, with
the hangman's knot in it, and thrown over his head; the rest of the
conspirators hauled upon deck, for it was rove through a block on
the fore yard; but, unfortunately, he caught under one of the
hammocks while making his unexpected exit, and got his hands
between his neck and the rope, which gave him a chance to shout
murder, and he was rescued by the marines. A number of the crew
were put in irons, on suspicion, but nothing transpired to prove
who were concerned in the affair. His own brother was on board,
but he hated him as much as any man. Had he not caught under
the hammock, he would have died the death befitting such a man.
This monster was allowed to carry a "colt," and use it upon any
man that he thought proper; thus giving him the same power that
the law vests in a captain. He would flog a man on the berth deck,
and then report him to the officer of the deck, who would flog him
again.

"Jemmy Leggs" was the name the sailors gave to Claggart,[7] a name
which Melville had seen in Mercier as well as in McNally. The Jemmy

7. Cf. *Billy Budd:*
—"Didn't I say so, Baby Budd?"
"Say what?" demanded Billy.
"Why, *Jemmy Leggs is down* on you."
"And what," rejoined Billy in amazement, "has *Jemmy Leggs* to do with that

Leggs of McNally's book is a rough, unmitigated rascal; Melville's Bland has charm and suavity consonant with his very name. "He was a neat and gentlemanly villain, and broke his biscuit with a dainty hand. . . . In short—in a merely psychological point of view, at least— he was a charming blackleg." Bland's literary descendant, Claggart, is of course a far more complex character, a genuinely great dramatic creation, with a superiority to be seen in his very name which in contrast to the obviousness of "Bland" has a complexity and indefinite suggestiveness which is menacing, combining as it does such words as "clang," "clangor," "laggard," "blackguard," and maybe even "clever."

Melville utilizes two specific details from McNally. Although Bland did not, like Sterritt, explicitly suffer castration, Melville hints at the possibility: "More than once a master-at-arms ashore has been seized by night by an exasperated crew, and served as Origen served himself, or as his enemies served Abelard." Second, Sterritt's narrow escape from being hanged by the crew becomes a similar attack on Bland:

> While in office, even, his life had often been secretly attempted by the seamen whom he had brought to the gangway. Of dark nights they had dropped shot down the hatchways, destined "to damage his pepper-box," as they phrased it; they had made ropes with a hangman's noose at the end, and tried to *lasso* him in dark corners.

In drawing the features of Bland from McNally's Sterritt, Melville's mind is fixed inescapably on the problem of evil. Bland was "an organic and irreclaimable scoundrel, who did wicked deeds as the cattle browse the herbage." This stated, admitted, what then becomes of the questions of Good and Evil? What becomes of the Transcendentalist dismissal of "pain as but a tickle" ("Tell that," said Melville in a letter to Hawthorne,[8] "to a man with the raging toothache!")? If the world is the creation of God, who is good, how explain the motiveless malignancy of

---

cracked afterguardsman?"

"Ho, it was an afterguardsman then. A cat's paw. . . ."

George Monteiro, "Melville and Keats," *Emerson Society Quarterly,* No. 31 (1963), p. 55, suggests that Melville may have taken the name from a passage in Keats' letter to Bailey, 23 January 1818: "There were some miserable reports of Rice's health—I went and lo! Master Jemmy had been to the play the night before and was out at the time—he always comes on his Legs like a Cat—," but such a source seems distant compared with Melville's immediate knowledge of McNally, Mercier, and of nautical life.

8. *Letters,* p. 131.

an Iago, of a Bland, of a Claggart? The rest of Melville's chapter deals ambiguously with this dark theme.

Bland as a model or anticipation of Claggart has been frequently dealt with in the large literature now accumulated around *Billy Budd*. Sterritt as the model for Bland has already been mentioned by Thomas Philbrick in "Another Source for *White-Jacket*" and by Harrison Hayford and Merton Sealts in their authoritative edition of *Billy Budd*. There is still an opportunity, even a necessity, for the student of morality and of psychology to restudy the question of Melville's villains—stretching in a line before us like the phantom kings before Macbeth: Jackson, Bland, Fedallah, Babo, the Confidence Man, and Claggart. In so doing the student will find this chapter of *White-Jacket* tantalizing and elusive. He will agree, however, with Melville's conclusion about Bland: "It was asserted that, had Tophet itself been raked with a fine-tooth comb, such another ineffable villain could not by any possibility have been caught." These words are adapted from McNally, used not in reference to Sterritt but to other villainous officers of whom he wrote (p. 127): "Had hell been raked with a fine tooth comb, two such villains could not have been found."

McNally gave much information to Melville for the writing of *White-Jacket,* but surely his finest help was his description of Sterritt, which became one of Melville's most interesting patches.

•

Supervisor. Don't poke fun at my finery. It is all that sustains me at the moment. Except the thought of those who should be wearing it. They would certainly be here with me, if they were alive. As it is, let me present—my grandfather, his cane. My great-uncle: his watch and chain. My father: his hat. My Uncle Albert: his gloves. The rest is myself.

Jean Giraudoux, *The Enchanted*

Item: a dozen pairs of shorts
shirts, stockings, sandals, and a sailor's cap

Item: six sailor blouses, with appropriate ties
anchors embroidered on sleeves . . .

Conrad Aiken, "The Costumes"

Chapter 47, "An Auction in a Man-of-war," brings the jacket once again prominently into the story. The chapter is aboundingly comical, showing how amid an auction held on shipboard of various sailor effects, White-Jacket's own jacket not only does not sell but is jeered at by the crew. The auction was, as Huntress long ago showed, Melville's adaptation of a chapter from *Scenes*.[9] We may mention how much Melville's skill in dialogue contributes to the natural comedy of situation, how keen his ear is in catching the sailor voice. In *White-Jacket* the vernacular was stealing into literature a generation before Eggleston or Mark Twain.

The scene was introduced partly for comic relief, but it plays a symbolic role as it reminds us, now in the middle of the book, of the life and death of the jacket, of its decline, its soiling, its inutility, its genuine menace and danger to its owner. Floridly Melville concludes the chapter:

> While this scene was going forward, and my white jacket was thus being abused, how my heart swelled within me! Thrice was I on the point of rushing out of my hiding-place, and bearing it off from derision; but I lingered, still flattering myself that all would be well, and the jacket find a purchaser at last. But no, alas! there was no getting rid of it, except by rolling a forty-two-pound shot in it, and committing it to the deep. But though, in my desperation, I had once contemplated something of that sort, yet I had now become unaccountably averse to it, from certain involuntary superstitious considerations. If I sink my jacket, thought I, it will be sure to spread itself into a bed at the bottom of the sea, upon which I shall sooner or later recline, a dead man. So, unable to conjure it into the possession of another, and withheld from burying it out of sight forever, my jacket stuck to me like the fatal shirt on Nessus.

How transcendentally White-Jacket mockingly held this "superior old jacket," is shown two chapters later, in Chapter 50, "The Bay of all Beauties." This is perhaps the most inessential chapter in the entire book; it is not about life in a man-of-war, it is simply a rhetorical cascade to describe the great bay of Rio. Melville calls upon the tricks he had used in the overloaded chapters of *Mardi,* the manner revealed by the opening sentence: "I have said that I must pass over Rio without a description; but just now such a flood of scented reminiscences steals over me, that I must needs yield and recant, as I inhale that musky air." Literary taradiddle.

9. Keith Huntress, "Melville's Use of a Source for *White-Jacket," American Literature,* XVII (March 1945), pp. 66–74.

The eighth paragraph is the richest, the ripest, and the rottenest, beginning "Amphitheatrical Rio! in your broad expanse might be held the Resurrection and Judgment-day of the whole world's men-of-war . . ."—a single sentence stretching across and down the page for almost 300 words in a series of prepositional phrases ("of" parallels to the one just quoted). It is stilted and strained word-building; the intended rapture and ecstasy dribbles away through the stylistic cracks in the structure.

The chapter has no action until the very end and then it is thrust, joltingly, in. The men are ordered to furl the sails:

> At the sound I sprang into the rigging, and was soon at my perch. How I hung over that main-royal-yard in a rapture! High in air, poised over that magnificent bay, a new world to my ravished eyes, I felt like the foremost of a flight of angels, new-lighted upon earth, from some star in the Milky Way.

The paragraph intrudes. It is possible, of course, that the spacious excitement is ironic and that Melville is satirizing again the Rousseauistic dreamer, in the mast-head, the creature of purity, who regards himself angelically, but who, like another Lucifer, will forty-one chapters later realistically and untranscendentally plunge into the Cartesian vortices, the sea.

•

Surprisingly few of White-Jacket's actions were derived from Melville's own activities on board the *United States*. Melville's memories furnished tone and impression more than act and fact. The major events in White-Jacket's personal story did not happen to Melville but were events endured by others, adapted by Melville to his *White-Jacket* persona: the arraignment at the masthead (from Sleeper), the auction of the jacket (from Mercier), the fall from the yard-arm (from Ames and others), are a few examples. It happens at some times, however, that an event involving another actor, not White-Jacket, may well have been Melville's own experience.

One such episode is the burden of Chapter 59, "A Man-of-war Button divides two Brothers," a fictive situation traced by Wilson Heflin back to a probable episode in Melville's own service on board the *United States*. White-Jacket is not the chief actor but is, however, the one to whom the dilemma of the actor is confided. The chief actor is a young man named "Frank." He comes to White-Jacket to blurt out his anxiety over the approach of the supply ship for the *Neversink,* which is, according to a newspaper he has accidentally found, due soon to arrive in the harbor of Rio with his brother on board as an officer-of-the-deck. Frank is afraid that the unavoidable meeting that sheer proximity will bring about between the two brothers will be shameful and embarrassing to both of them, for he, Frank, has been for three years a roaming vagabond, while his brother has become a successful officer in the United States Navy. Frank's fears turn out to be groundless, for although the meeting between the two brothers does happen, such is the bustle and confusion attendant on the supplying operations, that the officer brother does not notice his enlisted brother from the *Neversink.*

Heflin has showed that a confrontation similar to Frank's and his brother's might possibly have taken place, under similar circumstances, between Herman Melville and his cousin Stanwix Gansevoort. During the week of 14 February 1844 the supply ship *Erie,* with Stanwix Gansevoort as an officer-of-the-deck, anchored beside the *United States* in the harbor of Callao (not Rio), and for several days the *Erie* transferred supplies to the frigate. Whether the cousins actually met, and whether recognition took place, are questions as yet unanswered. It is tempting to accept Melville's chapter and White-Jacket's unfrank story of Frank—altered from cousins to brothers, shifted from an Atlantic port to a Pacific one—as essentially true, oblique biography to be truly read back to its basic conflict only by members of the Gansevoort and Melville families, or, long after, by the perceptive eye of Wilson Heflin.

•

While the *Neversink* rests at anchor in the harbor of Rio, little or nothing would normally take place on board ship worthy of significance —at least nothing *really* happened on board the *United States* according to its logbook—but Melville, needing to enliven an otherwise sagging section of his book, makes much happen by creating a situation which sets up, makes mandatory, the magnificent account of Surgeon Cadwallader Cuticle, a name which rolls from the tongue as freely as pedantry from the lips of the great doctor himself. Surgeon of the Fleet, a de-humanized (or de-hearted) creature a little less than physically mortal, he has been made immortal, by Melville's satiric genius, with devastating and delightful efficiency.

The preparation for this lethal account is a special transition of less than two pages, Chapter 60, "A Man-of-war's man Shot at," which tells of the attempt by a sailor, denied shore leave, to swim ashore only to be shot in the leg by the sentry, who hits him in the "right thigh just above the knee." The sailor himself is ironically unimportant, since he subsequently dies, having served as a vehicle to demonstrate the virtuosity and viciousness of Cadwallader Cuticle. Nevertheless the account of his wound is important because it introduces the subject of the difficulties and dangers on the treatment of gunshot wounds, a topic on which Melville, as innocent in knowledge of medical mysteries as any normal man-in-the-street, made himself temporarily proficient—as he did on other subjects elsewhere—by rapid consultation and deft skimming and pilfering from published sources. Which sources? Professor Willard Thorp in his fine Preface to the Northwestern-Newberry edition of *White-Jacket* says that Melville relied primarily on five articles ("Amputation," "Anatomy," "Gun-Shot Wounds," "William Hunter," and "Tourniquet") from *The Penny Cyclopaedia of the Society for the Diffusion of Useful Knowledge* (London, 1833–1843), 27 volumes. It seems to me that absolute certainty on this point is impossible to establish, but that it is more probable that Melville had read these articles and then turned to the basic medical authorities from which the encyclopedists themselves had taken their materials. In fact, after close study of these articles and after equally close reading of the several medical books listed below, I find it hard to believe that *The Penny Cyclopaedia* contributed much to Melville; although all the information which Thorp cites from the *Cyclopaedia* is, to be sure, there, there is also much more in Melville which is not there and which is to be found only in the basic medical authorities, Guthrie and Hennen especially. To conclude this matter I assert the primacy of four books, here listed in diminishing order of importance, which Melville brilliantly exploited to create a masterpiece of medical satire, malicious characterization, and comic action, carried on contrapuntally against the horror of insensitivity, brutality, and, subsequently, death. Melville's sources, and the primary sources for *The Penny Cyclopaedia,* were as follows:

A Treatise on Gun-Shot Wounds, on Injuries of Nerves, and on Wounds of the Extremities Requiring the Different Operations of Amputation, in which The Various Methods of performing these Operations are shown, together with their After-treatment; and Containing an account of The Author's successful Case of Amputation at the Hip-joint. By G. J. Guthrie (London: Burgess and Hill, 1820), Second Edition.

Principles of Military Surgery, Comprising Observations on the Arrangement, Police, and Practice of Hospitals, and on the History, Treatment, and Anomalies Variola and Syphilis. Illustrated with Cases and Dissections. By John Hennen, M.N.F.R.S.E., Inspector of Military Hospitals (London and Edinburgh: John Wilson, Princes Street, Soho; and Adam Black, 1829), Third Edition.

William Fergusson, F.R.S.E., *A System of Practical Surgery* (Philadelphia: Lea & Blanchard, 1848), Third American Edition (from the last English edition).

John and Charles Bell, *The Anatomy and Physiology of the Human Body* (New York: Collins & Co., 1827), two volumes, Fifth American Edition (reprinted from the sixth London edition of 1826), by John D. Godman, M.D.

•

In describing the sailor's wound (the man is significantly nameless because of his ironic insignificance), Melville makes much of the deceptive nature of gunshot wounds—that some seem small and therefore inoffensive but are dangerous, as was the wound in question:

> The ball struck with great force, with a downward obliquity, entering the right thigh just above the knee, and, penetrating some inches, glanced upward along the bone, burying itself somewhere, so that it could not be felt by outward manipulation. There was no dusky discoloration to mark its internal track, as in the case when a partly-spent ball—obliquely hitting—after entering the skin, courses on, just beneath the surface, without penetrating further. Nor was there any mark on the opposite part of the thigh to denote its place, as when a ball forces itself straight through a limb, and lodges, perhaps, close to the skin on the other side. Nothing was visible but a small, ragged puncture, bluish about the edges, as if the rough point of a tenpenny nail had been forced into the flesh, and withdrawn. It seemed almost impossible, that through so small an aperture, a musket-bullet could have penetrated.
>
> The extreme misery and general prostration of the man, caused by the great effusion of blood—though, strange to say, at first he said he felt no pain from the wound itself—induced the Surgeon, very reluctantly, to forego an immediate search for the ball, to extract it, as that would have involved the dilating of the wound by the knife; an operation which, at that juncture, would have been almost certainly attended with fatal results. A day or two, therefore, was permitted to pass, while simple dressings were applied.

Hennen's chapter on "The Treatment of Wounds" (especially p. 48) may have served Melville in that description of the sailor's injured limb:

> The effects of a gun-shot wound differ so materially in different men, and the appearances are so various, according to the nature of the part wounded, and the greater or lesser force with which it has been struck, that no invariable train of symptoms can be laid down as its *necessary* concomitants. If a musket or pistol ball has struck a fleshy part, without injuring any material blood-vessel, we see a hole about the size of, or smaller, than the bullet itself, with a more or less discoloured lip forced inwards; and, if it has passed through the parts, we find an everted edge, and a more ragged and larger orifice at the point of its exit; the haemorrhage is in this case very slight and the pain inconsiderable, insomuch that in many instances the wounded man is not aware of his having received any injury. If, however, the ball has torn a large vessel, or nerve, the haemorrhage will generally be profuse, or the pain of the wound severe, and the power of the part lost. Some men will have a limb carried off or shattered to pieces by a cannon ball, without exhibiting the slightest symptoms of mental or corporeal agitation; nay, even without being conscious of the occurrence; and when they are, they will coolly argue on the probable result of the injury: while a deadly paleness, instant vomiting, profuse perspiration, and universal tremor, will seize another on the receipt of a slight flesh wound. This tremor, which has been so much talked of, and which, to an inexperienced eye, is really terrifying, is soon relieved by a mouthful of wine or spirits: or by an opiate; but above all, by the tenderness and sympathizing manner of the surgeon, and his assurances of his patient's safety. Where some important vital organ is injured, considerable pain and much anxiety is a general consequence; these will be more particularly considered in treating of the wounds of particular parts.

The sailor's wound interests the other doctors from the ships of the Pacific Squadron:

> The Surgeons of the other American ships of war in harbor occasionally visited the Neversink, to examine the patient, and incidentally to listen to the expositions of our own Surgeon, their senior in rank. But Cadwallader Cuticle, who, as yet, has been but incidentally alluded to, now deserves a chapter by himself.

The chapter which Cuticle "deserves" he now gets, followed by two other chapters of action, the first being the consultation of the surgeons and the second being the very operation, or amputation, itself. Melville's three (or four if Chapter 60, preparing all this, is included) chapters on Cuticle are insufficiently known, never having been closely studied, because *White-Jacket* itself has been insufficiently read. Since the Cuticle episode exposes once again Melville's practice of composition—let us call it the pilfering procedure—we may perhaps be permitted to conduct a dissection which should not kill Melville's comedy as Cuticle killed the sailor.

Cadwallader Cuticle, the Horned Woman, and an Amputation

My surgeons are a savage band.
Surely their patient is ill-fated.

Stanley Kunitz, "My Surgeons"

He always tells a story well, and a plenty are related in this
volume.

George Ripley, review of *White-Jacket*
in New York *Daily Tribune*

GEORGE Ripley was, of course, correct. A born story-teller, Melville could always spin a good yarn. It was this ability, practiced on his family upon his return from the South Seas, that had led him to literature as a profession. Ripley was right, too, in saying that there were plenty of good stories in *White-Jacket*. Some of them, to be sure, had originally been the invention of other men, but Melville in adopting them had improved them.

What is evident from Chapter 60 onward is a different quality in the writing in *White-Jacket*. Throughout the central section Melville had been primarily documentary or journalistic. Along with some yarning he had in a leisurely manner expatiated on "life in a man-of-war," going from deck to deck with his camera, from person to person with his tape-recorder. He had portrayed a transcendental chaplain as well as, in Bland, an unmitigated and descendental villain. It had all been entertaining and instructive, but doodling—chapters thrown off rapidly with a skill which the mundane sources he raided only served to accentuate—but it had been (except for the flogging chapters) the tiger patting the ball playfully around his cage, his true powers leashed. Almost as if to stave off self-disgust, Melville's writing strengthened and became at last genuinely literary in the larger sense of the word. Now not just sailors' yarns but stories with a serious point, stories which stick in the minds and sensibilities of all readers. Consequently, the last third of *White-Jacket*, no less full of yarns, contains the great scenes generally selected by critics for praise, by readers for pleasure.

A striking example of this new strength is the satire of Cadwallader Cuticle, Surgeon of the Fleet. Pompous and heartless, Cadwallader Cuticle is as ridiculous as his possible echoic prototype Cadwallader Morgan, the surgeon in Smollett's *Roderick Random*. The name "Cuticle" is Melville's particularly appropriate substitution for "Morgan." Cuticle is no more like substance than his name, which is merely hard skin, a lifeless husk to be shed or clipped away. His sensual insignificance is neatly encapsuled in one paragraph:

> He was a small, withered man, nearly, perhaps quite, sixty years of age. His chest was shallow, his shoulders bent, his pantaloons hung round skeleton legs, and his face was singularly attenuated. In truth, the corporeal vitality of this man seemed, in a good degree, to have died out of him. He walked abroad, a curious patchwork of life and death, with a wig, one glass eye, and a set of false teeth, while his voice was husky and thick; but his mind seemed undebilitated as in youth; it shone out of his remaining eye with basilisk brilliancy.

It would be irrelevant and perhaps disrespectful to consider for more than a passing moment the possibility that Cuticle was based upon William Johnston, Chief Surgeon of the Pacific Squadron. Realistically, Melville could scarcely have known him, possibly not even met him, nor was, of course, such acquaintance necessary for the pesudo-fictional creation. Johnston was not needed for *White-Jacket,* although of course a surgeon was required to fill out the complement of the *Neversink* crew, for completeness of documentation. Cuticle was created from the general atmosphere of Smollett's medical satire in *Peregrine Pickle* and *Roderick Random,* from other sources still unknown, from the disgust of a Swift and the mockery of a Molière, and from the imagination of Melville, who had now found the central target of his books: the officers of the ship, men not necessarily evil in themselves but rendered evil by the fulfillment of their functions in such a heartless institution as a naval vessel—men rendered heartless and inhuman by power, by rank, and by accompanying pride. Melville operates on Cuticle as skillfully as Cuticle on his patient, but where Cuticle's patient died because of Cuticle's surgical skill, Cadwallader Cuticle lives, paradoxically, because of Melville's lethal lines. Melville's literary operation was motivated from humane concern, whereas Cuticle had no humanity, no heart. Melville sarcastically qualified this:

> Yet you could not say that Cuticle was essentially a cruel-hearted man. His apparent heartlessness must have been of a purely scientific origin. It is not to be imagined even that Cuticle would have harmed a fly, unless he could procure a microscope powerful enough to assist him in experimenting on the minute vitals of the creature.

Cuticle, then, is a non-man, all brain and no heart; he is a technological man, all operation and no substance. He does not even have the physical parts of a man. The title of Poe's story, written ten years before, "The Man that Was Used Up" (significant, that "that"), might well have served Melville. Cuticle is made up of replaceable parts like a machine, not of an organic heart and bowels. He is heartless scientism.[1] His

---

1. Charles G. Finney in *The Circus of Dr. Lao* [1935] (New York: Bantam Books, 1964), pp. 53–54 has a description of the heartless, mechanical, artificial Lawyer, made so by his profession (and many operations on him), so that when "One hundred years after he died they opened his coffin. All they found were strings and wires."

remarkable skill in operating is that of a non-man, as Melville (Chapter 63) sardonically describes the doctor divesting himself of "himself" before performing the amputation:

> He snatched off his wig, placing it on the gun-deck capstan; then took out his set of false teeth, and placed it by the side of the wig; and, lastly, putting his forefinger to the inner angle of his blind eye, spirted out the glass optic with professional dexterity, and deposited that, also, next to the wig and false teeth.
>
> Thus divested of nearly all inorganic appurtenances, what was left of the Surgeon slightly shook itself, to see whether any thing more could be spared to advantage.

•

Such a non-man, monster in human terms, was Cadwallader Cuticle, the admiration of his profession, or of his craft. Before analyzing Melville's account of the amputation which Cuticle performs on a nameless sailor (nameless, no more important to Cuticle than the dissected dog on the medical-school table), we should notice Melville's early stress on Cuticle's monstrosity, partly through the reaction of the cabin-boy (i.e., the ordinary person's point of view) to his master's room: "[He] often told us of the horror he sometimes felt when he would find himself alone in his master's retreat." At times he was seized with the idea that Cuticle was "a preternatural being," especially on one occasion when a flare of "thick, bluish vapor" emanating from an ignited box of Lucifer matches gave an odor of brimstone to the cabin. Melville's action pun—Cuticle as Lucifer—consumes a long paragraph and enforces the surgeon's inhumanity even further than the description, immediately preceding, of the mask of the horned woman hanging on the wall, an object much regarded by the learned surgeon. The original story of this horned woman and her mask has never been related to *White-Jacket,* but it is a bit of medical history, of pathology, which Melville interestingly, powerfully, utilized in his indictment and damnation of Luciferian Cuticle. As such, but also in itself, it is worthy of recall; Melville's full description of the mask is as moving as it is informative:

> In particular, the department of Morbid Anatomy was his peculiar love; and in his state-room below he had a most unsightly collection of Parisian casts, in plaster and wax, representing all imaginable malformations of the human members, both organic and

induced by disease. Chief among these was a cast, often to be met with in the Anatomical Museums of Europe, and no doubt an unexaggerated copy of a genuine original; it was the head of an elderly woman, with an aspect singularly gentle and meek, but at the same time wonderfully expressive of a gnawing sorrow, never to be relieved. You would almost have thought it the face of some abbess, for some unspeakable crime voluntarily sequestered from human society, and leading a life of agonized penitence without hope; so marvelously sad and tearfully pitiable was this head. But when you first beheld it, no such emotions ever crossed your mind. All your eyes and all your horrified soul were fast fascinated and frozen by the sight of a hideous, crumpled horn, like that of a ram, downward growing out from the forehead, and partly shadowing the face; but as you gazed, the freezing fascination of its horribleness gradually waned, and then your whole heart burst with sorrow, as you contemplated those aged features, ashy pale and wan. The horn seemed the mark of a curse for some mysterious sin, conceived and committed before the spirit had entered the flesh. Yet that sin seemed something imposed, and not voluntarily sought; some sin growing out of the heartless necessities of the predestination of things; some sin under which the sinner sank in sinless woe.

But no pang of pain, not the slightest touch of concern, ever crossed the bosom of Cuticle when he looked on this cast. It was immovably fixed to a bracket, against the partition of his stateroom, so that it was the first object that greeted his eyes when he opened them from his nightly sleep. Nor was it to hide the face, that upon retiring, he always hung his Navy cap upon the upward curling extremity of the horn, for that obscured it but little.

Once again Melville has made his reading serve his art. Exactly *where* he had read about the mask of the horned woman has not yet been discovered, but there was such a mask and such a woman. Most probably Melville saw it in some popular periodical of the 1840's similar to the *Penny Magazine*, copiously illustrated with woodcuts or engravings of catch-all topics—a mid-nineteenth-century equivalent of *Life* or *Look*. Or in an American or English equivalent of the popular French journal of the 1830's and 1840's, *Magasin pittoresque* (pp. 394–396; picture on p. 396), for 1841, where the original disclosure of the horned woman was made to the world. Published there was a long article about the monstrous horn growth of Baron de Maine, but accompanying this account was a brief paragraph, with picture, of "The Sunday Widow," otherwise known as "The Horned Mother."

Her story is sad. For years she had endured her tragic disfigurement;

at age 84, weary of the horn, she submitted to an operation for its removal. The operation was the striking success (*eut un succès complet*) of a specialist named Dr. Souberbielle. Eight months after this amputation the Sunday Widow died. The irony of this did not elude Melville in establishing the fate of the sailor.

A few days before the amputation, the Sunday Widow allowed her portrait, horn and all, to be made in wax by Monsieur Guy the Elder, an expert maker of anatomical casts for exhibit in museums of medical pathology. It was from this mask that the *Magasin pittoresque* secured a faithful drawing.

Melville probably wrote as the result of seeing the illustration and not the mask itself, although we may never truly know. When he visited Paris early in 1850 his *White-Jacket* was in press. It is idle but amusing to speculate that on this Parisian visit Melville made a special point to see the original of that which he had just so movingly described. Masks were available then; maybe they still are, although the only large collection in Paris now open is at the Hospital Saint Louis, with no one mask like that of the Sunday Widow and, anyhow, of too late a date for Melville to have seen. He might have seen it in the Musée Dupuytren in the Ecole de Médecine, but this cannot be verified since the museum is closed. The casts were crated at the beginning of World War II; the list of contents of each box was nailed inside so that there is no available directory to show whether the mask of the horned woman is in one of the hundreds of crates still awaiting reexhibition.

•

"A Consultation of Man-of-war Surgeons" (Chapter 62) is one in which "consultation" is simply conquest by Cuticle over his subordinates, the surgeons from the fleet, his puppets, each given a farcically appropriate name, being "in order of appearance" in this little drama, Surgeons Bandage, Sawyer, Wedge, and Patella. The comedy of their verbal evasions or of their squirming sycophancy (and yet, each in his way does oppose Cuticle) must, like any play, be seen to be enjoyed for its fine fun, and analytic description destroys the delicate, and also broad, play of humor as Cuticle forces against the true will of the group his own eager desire to operate.

To operate or not to operate, that is the question. Cuticle is indecently anxious to perform an extremely dangerous and difficult amputation. Even Guthrie admitted it (p. 296): "This operation has seldom been performed. Surgeons have agreed in calling it a dreadful and a horrible operation." Nevertheless, he felt that this was prejudice, and his pages are an attempt to overcome this prejudice. It is significant that Melville makes his character Cuticle refer to Guthrie openly, which is perhaps a proof that Melville himself had utilized that essential work. In Chapter 63 Cuticle says, "There is a fine example, somewhat similar, related in Guthrie; but, of course, you must have met with it, in so well-known a work as his Treatise upon Gun-shot Wounds."

But Guthrie (p. 313) was really arguing for amputation from wounds which occurred "from cannon or grape shot, or the explosion of shells." And he then added, "Few surgeons would think of performing it for a wound by a musket-ball, although cases do happen that require it. . . ." Cuticle in forcing this special amputation, resulting from a gunshot wound only, was going against the greatest of authorities, Guthrie himself. And yet it is evident that Cuticle himself, in defying social opinion and the advice of fellow-experts (as Ahab later defied the advice of other whalemen), was acting like Guthrie, who in an impressively detailed and extremely long study of the history of amputations at the thigh, adduced the evidence of authorities from the time of Celsus down to his own day, honestly presenting the pros and cons, but concluding against majority opinion that early or immediate amputation is preferable. Melville read and digested the sense and spirit of this argument to summarize it dramatically, if tropically, in the person and the words of Cadwallader Cuticle, wherein Cuticle, like Guthrie, arrives at the conclusion he wants rather than the one demanded by the evidence. Cuticle professes to the surgeons before they give their opinions (Chapter 62):

> "But, gentlemen, I find myself placed in a very delicate predicament. I assure you I feel no professional anxiety to perform the operation. I desire your advice, and if you will now again visit the patient with me, we can then return here, and decide what is best to be done. Once more, let me say, that I feel no personal anxiety whatever to use the knife."

However, Cuticle contradicts these words as he resists the opinions of his fellow practitioners who one by one advise against amputation, each one angering Cuticle, who has difficulty suppressing his vexation and rage. His most persistent opposition comes from Surgeon Wedge, who is full of what Cuticle calls "hard words," those words being the technical terminology of the anatomical exercise to be performed. The following paragraph of Wedge's opinions, with language so technical that it does not appear in *The Penny Cyclopaedia* (and so is probably from Guthrie, Hennen, and Bell), shows Melville's use of his library:

> "Surgeon Wedge, of the Malay," said Cuticle, in a pet, "be pleased to give *your* opinion; and let it be definitive, I entreat:" this was said with a severe glance toward Bandage.
> "If I thought," began Wedge, a very spare, tall man, elevating himself still higher on his toes, "that the ball had shattered and divided the whole *femur,* including the *Greater* and *Lesser Trochanter,* the *Linear aspera,* the *Digital fossa,* and the *Intertrochanteric,* I should certainly be in favor of amputation; but that, sir, permit me to observe, is not my opinion."

This is language, terminology, which owes much, probably most, to Guthrie (p. 302 especially) with the addition of terms from other books. Guthrie is representative:

> Having laid the patient on the sound side, upon a table of a common height, and putting the diseased thigh at right angles with the trunk, I began my incision immediately behind the top of the great trochanter, carrying it obliquely backwards and downwards, to the inside of the thigh, and from thence obliquely upwards, to within two inches of the crural artery. I then began the second incision at the same place with the former, carrying it in an opposite direction over the upper extremity of the trochanter, and from thence obliquely forwards and downwards, to within the same distance of the vessel as in the former.

Surgeon Bandage, Surgeon Sawyer, and Surgeon Wedge had successfully, if circuitously, opposed Cuticle. Surgeon Patella, youngest of the group and therefore most uncertain of his status and most fearful of the great Surgeon Cuticle, hems and haws to such an extent that Cuticle, desperate for support for his extreme position, takes Patella's words for approval; Surgeon Sawyer has just recommended that the patient be treated with "tonics and gentle antiphlogistics, locally applied," an opinion to enrage the Chief Surgeon, who turns to young Patella:

> "Surgeon Patella, of the Algerine," said Cuticle, in an ill-suppressed passion, abruptly turning round on the person addressed, "will *you* have the kindness to say whether *you* do not think that amputation is the only resource?"
> Now Patella was the youngest of the company, a modest man, filled with a profound reverence for the science of Cuticle, and

desirous of gaining his good opinion, yet not wishing to commit himself altogether by a decided reply, though, like Surgeon Sawyer, in his own mind he might have been clearly against the operation.

"What you have remarked, Mr. Surgeon of the Fleet," said Patella, respectfully hemming, "concerning the dangerous condition of the limb, seems obvious enough; amputation would certainly be a cure to the wound; but then, as, notwithstanding his present debility, the patient seems to have a strong constitution, he might rally as it is, and by your scientific treatment, Mr. Surgeon of the Fleet"—bowing—"be entirely made whole, without risking an amputation. Still, it is a very critical case, and amputation may be indispensable; and if it *is* to be performed, there ought to be no delay whatever. That is my view of the case, Mr. Surgeon of the Fleet."

"Surgeon Patella, then, gentlemen," said Cuticle, turning round triumphantly, "is clearly of opinion that amputation should be immediately performed. For my own part—individually, I mean, and without respect to the patient—I am sorry to have it so decided. But this settles the question, gentlemen—in my own mind, however, it was settled before. At ten o'clock to-morrow morning the operation will be performed. I shall be happy to see you all on the occasion, and also your juniors" (alluding to the absent *Assistant Surgeons*). "Good-morning, gentlemen; at ten o'clock, remember."

And Cuticle retreated to the Ward-room.

•

Cadwallader Cuticle "retreats" to the ward-room but advances to the operation. He prevails against the common sense of the surgeons. Delighted to display his technical virtuosity and his immense learning, he describes the operation while he performs it, and discusses the history of amputation, mentioning glibly names famous in such a medical survey, all of which are cited at some length in Guthrie's pages. "The Operation" (Chapter 63) is in its way a summation, a distillation, of all that Guthrie has said, and Cuticle himself is an incarnation, much compressed and heightened and caricatured, of Guthrie, just as Snodhead, Von Sleet, and others in *Moby-Dick* are parodies of and allusions to Captain Scoresby and his book, *An Account of the Arctic Regions*. Scoresby's pedantry is no more burdensome than Guthrie's, and it is perhaps regrettable for their reputations that these two men, eminent and honorable scholars in their respective fields, each having produced indispensable books on his subject, must serve as the butt of Melville's satire.

One of Melville's most brilliant adaptations was of a passage by Hennen, on the peculiarity and unpredictability of the course of bullets within the body. Melville wrote:

"Now, young gentlemen, not the least interesting consequence of this operation will be the finding of the ball, which, in case of non-amputation, might have long eluded the most careful search. That ball, young gentlemen, must have taken a most circuitous route. Nor, in cases where the direction is oblique, is this at all unusual. Indeed, the learned Hennen gives us a most remarkable—I had almost said an incredible—case of a soldier's neck, where the bullet, entering at the part called Adam's Apple—"

"Yes," said Surgeon Wedge, elevating himself, "the *pomum Adami.*"

"Entering the point called *Adam's Apple,*" continued Cuticle, severely emphasizing the last two words, "ran completely round the neck, and, emerging at the same hole it had entered, shot the next man in the ranks. It was afterward extracted, says Hennen, from the second man, and pieces of the other's skin were found adhering to it. But examples of foreign substances being received into the body with a ball, young gentlemen, are frequently observed."

And this is what Hennen had supplied Cuticle:

The ball is, in many instances, found very close to its point of entrance, having nearly completed the circuit of the body. In a case which occurred to a friend of mine in the Mediterranean, the ball, which struck about the Pomum Adami, was found lying in the very orifice at which it had entered, having gone completely round the neck, and being prevented from passing out by the elasticity and toughness of the skin which confined it to this circular course.

For once, Wedge defeats Cuticle, who begrudgingly concedes it by saying,

"For once, Surgeon Wedge, you use the only term that can be employed; and let me avail myself of this opportunity to say to you, young gentlemen, that a man of true science"—expanding his shallow chest a little—"uses but few hard words, and those only when none other will answer his purpose; whereas the smatterer in science"—slightly glancing toward Wedge—"thinks, that by mouthing hard words, he proves that he understands hard things."

"The Operation" (Chapter 63) is so long and varied, so crammed with things and events, that to summarize were to quote it entire, and to attempt to expose Melville's utilization of his library in full detail would be to cut rudely into Melville's wit, for the condensation and interweaving is dense, a Gordian knot. The economy of that wit is evident when Melville's chapter is contrasted with the lengthy medical discourses which furnished him in his "hard words," his brilliant satire. Melville's embodiments, incarnations, and dramatizations of tiresome (to non-medical men, of course) tomes and prosy passages of description and argument are amazing examples of creative transformation.

"The Operation" is crowded with events and with gruesome materials (knives, saws, bandages and sponges, blood-pails), and the events are at once grimly sardonic as Cuticle, "withered, shrunken, one-eyed, toothless, hairless Cuticle; with a trunk half dead—a *memento mori* to behold," starts operating on (and essentially killing) this "sailor, who, four days previous, had stood erect—a pillar of life, with an arm like a royal-mast, and a thigh like a windlass."

Cadwallader Cuticle lectures and demonstrates as he operates, a Niagara of words conceitedly flowing from his thin lips; he points to a human skeleton suspended by the operating table, to show exactly what he is going to do to the patient, lying there listening to the words of his own condemnation:

> "Surgeon Wedge," said Cuticle, looking round severely, "we will dispense with your commentaries, if you please, at present. Now, young gentlemen, you can not but perceive, that the point of operation being so near the trunk and the vitals, it becomes an unusually beautiful one, demanding a steady hand and a true eye; and, after all, the patient may die under my hands."
>
> "Quick, Steward! water, water; he's fainting again!" cried the two mess-mates.
>
> "Don't be alarmed for your comrade, men," said Cuticle, turning round. "I tell you it is not an uncommon thing for the patient to betray some emotion upon these occasions—most usually manifested by swooning; it is quite natural it should be so. . . ."

Cuticle's "Anatomy Lesson" is a far cry from the masterpiece by Rembrandt, which stresses the concern, the humanity, and the delicate considerate skill of the doctors; Melville draws in the style of Hieronymous Bosch, or perhaps more pertinently, in the manner of William Hogarth, who might well have supplied a distinguished body of illustrations to Melville's man-of-war book.

To conclude our study of Cadwallader Cuticle and his behavior, and of Melville's development of the man and of his actions, we might turn to Melville's "authoritative" words about the role of the tourniquet in amputation; this was a subject on which Hennen discoursed at length—as did Guthrie—but on which Melville, source-guided, spoke comically as he further demonstrated the skill of Cuticle the technician:

> "But you noticed that I did not use the tourniquet; I never do. The forefinger of my steward is far better than a tourniquet, being so much more manageable, and leaving the smaller veins uncompressed. But I have been told, young gentlemen, that a certain Seignior Seignioroni, a surgeon of Seville, has recently invented an admirable substitute for the clumsy, old-fashioned tourniquet. As I understand it, it is something like a pair of *calipers,* working with a small Archimedes screw—a very clever invention, according to all accounts. For the padded points at the end of the arches"—arching his forefinger and thumb—"can be so worked as to approximate in such a way, as to—but you don't attend to me, young gentlemen," he added, all at once starting.

Admittedly this is extremely close to the following passage from *The Penny Cyclopaedia*'s article on "Tourniquets."

> The tourniquet is now not so generally used as formerly. Many surgeons prefer to have the artery compressed during an amputation by an assistant; because the tourniquet is not free from the objection of compressing the veins as well as the artery, and is liable to accidents which cannot be instantly repaired. An instrument has also been recently invented by Signor Signoroni, a surgeon at Milan, which seems likely to supersede the tourniquet altogether. It is composed of two arches of steel, connected by a hinge at one end, and each bearing at the other end a pad. By an Archimedes screw ingeniously placed at the hinge, the pads can be approximated and separated like the ends of the blades of a pair of callipers, and can be immoveably fixed in any position. In use one pad is put over the artery, and the other on the opposite part of the limb, and the screw is worked till, in their tendency to approximate, the pads have sufficiently compressed the artery, upon which alone the pressure is thus made to fall.

Misspelling Signoroni and having Cuticle place him in Seville instead of Milan are Melville's means of stressing Cuticle's inability to use "hard words," words which were Wedge's *forte* and which Melville himself, by library work, has himself been able to wedge into his narrative.

Further material on the role of tourniquets is in a long passage from Guthrie (p. 374), which indicates that more than one source may have contributed to Cuticle's discourse on the tourniquet:

> When amputation by the circular incision is preferred, the tourniquet may be used to stop the circulation of the blood; and especially where the surgeon is not much accustomed to operative surgery, the assistants bad, and the loss of a larger quantity of blood than usual might prove fatal. It should however be slackened as soon as the principal vessels are secured; for the natural retraction of the muscles is prevented by the strap of the instrument, which often causes some difficulty in high operations, in sawing the bone, by preventing the retraction of the soft parts. In consequence of these, and other inconveniences attending the use of the tourniquet in operations high in the thigh, I recommend compression to be made on the artery against the os pubis, in preference; but this requires a self-confidence young operators do not in general possess. . . . I may add, that when I have performed the operation without a tourniquet, my patient has lost little blood, and that when I have used a tourniquet, I have frequently had considerable haemorrhage. . . .

The operation is a success for Cuticle but not for the patient, who dies; Cuticle's reaction is characteristic of his essential callousness:

> "Please, sir," said the Steward, entering, "the patient is dead."
> "The body also, gentlemen, at ten precisely," said Cuticle, once more turning round upon his guests. "I predicted that the operation might prove fatal; he was very much run down. Good morning"; and Cuticle departed.

Melville properly allows these words to radiate their own frightening, damning implications, and ends his chapter with a simplicity which is in touching contrast to the series of actions which he has so strongly satirized:

> The following evening the mess-mates of the top-man rowed his remains ashore, and buried them in the ever-vernal Protestant cemetery, hard by the Beach of the Flamingoes, in plain sight from the bay.

· 1 2 ·

The Arraignment
of White-Jacket

C HAPTER 66, "Fun in a Man-of-war," is primarily just that, an inconsequential chapter describing the ways whereby sailors amuse themselves, in games like "those of a single-stick, sparring, hammer-and-anvil, and head-bumping." Head-bumping consists in two Negroes (whites will not answer) butting at each other like two rams. This pastime was an especial favorite with the captain. In the dogwatches, Rose-Water and May-Day were repeatedly summoned into the lee waist to tilt at each other, for the captain's amusement. Perhaps the only "point" made in this chapter is the whimsical and unpredictable character of officialdom, which at one moment will tolerate and even encourage a sport, and the next minute flog men for engaging in it. Much of this was adapted from Mercier's *Scenes,* "The Nigger Pugilists" (pp. 193–200), a yarn about two Negroes who fight over a Valparaiso trollop. Like Ague-cheek and "Sebastian" they are reluctant to fight but are urged on by the watching sailors. The main form their fight takes is head-bumping. Little really happens in *Scenes* until the watch warns of the officers' coming, and all fade from sight. Melville drastically shortened and altered Mercier's yarn, with a brevity fitting the inconsequentiality of the whole business. He gives it some dramatic point only by exposing the behavior of the officers, at one moment good fellows and the next sadistic floggers. "Of all insults, the temporary condescension of a master to a slave is the most outrageous and galling." Rose-Water and May-Day are not the only slaves, and as Hamlet might have said, "The *Neversink*'s a prison, my Captain."

•

There is another justification for this slight chapter—to give breathing space between the brilliance of the Cuticle satire and the intense drama of Chapter 67, "White-Jacket arraigned at the Mast," one of the high points of the entire book.

The arraignment is unusual in that it is one of the few scenes in which White-Jacket himself is exposed to a crisis. The episode was for some time interpreted as a fact of Melville's own biography, one of the "ugly experiences during the cruise that were among the most lurid of his life. . . . And that day as the scourge hung over him for an offence he had not committed, he seems to have been as murderously roused as at any other moment in his life."[1] This was written in 1921; it was not until 1939 that Charles R. Anderson persuasively argued that "The evidence seems to indicate overwhelmingly that Melville invented this dramatic moment in his life."[2]

Anderson's suggestion, carefully made, can now be confirmed. As elsewhere in *White-Jacket*—and in other books as well—Melville was again consulting his "best authorities," the sailor-writers. The man who later said with comic exaggeration that he had "swum through libraries"

1. Raymond Weaver, *Herman Melville, Mariner and Mystic* (New York: George H. Doran, 1921), pp. 243, 245.

2. Charles R. Anderson, *Melville in the South Seas* (New York: Columbia University Press, 1939), p. 411.

to authenticate his whaling lore, swam just as much through libraries to authenticate his naval lore. This time Melville is working from a source so mundane that Mercier for a moment looms literary: the author is "Hawser Martingale" [John Sherburne Sleeper], and his book is *Tales of the Ocean*.

The day following the flogging of the Negroes, White-Jacket obeys an order to help tack the ship. He congratulates himself on the speed of his response, feeling that he "deserved a public vote of thanks, and a silver tankard from Congress." He is, however, ordered before an angry Captain Claret, who accuses him, from one of his officer's reports, of failing to appear at his assigned post. When White-Jacket demurs by pointing out that he knew nothing of such an assignment (an error of the lieutenant's), Claret angrily charges him with contradicting an officer and therefore doubly to be flogged. The gratings are prepared— will the narrator so ardent in his indictment of flogging now himself be flogged?[3] There follows an eloquent passage of rebellious and murderous intention:

> I had now been on board the frigate upward of a year, and remained unscourged; the ship was homeward-bound, and in a few weeks, at most, I would be a freeman. And now, after making a hermit of myself in some things, in order to avoid the possibility of the scourge, here it was hanging over me for a thing utterly unforeseen, for a crime of which I was as utterly innocent. But all that was as naught. I saw that my case was hopeless; my solemn disclaimer was thrown in my teeth, and the boatswain's mate stood curling his fingers through the *cat*.
> There are times when wild thoughts enter a man's heart, when he seems almost irresponsible for his act and his deed. The Captain stood on the weather-side of the deck. Sideways, on an unobstructed line with him, was the opening of the lee-gangway, where the side-ladders are suspended in port. Nothing but a slight bit of sinnate-stuff served to rail in this opening, which was cut right down to the level of the Captain's feet, showing the far sea beyond. I stood a little to windward of him, and, though he was a large, powerful man, it was certain that a sudden rush against him, along the slanting deck, would infallibly pitch him headforemost into the ocean, though he who so rushed must needs go over with him. My blood seemed clotting in my veins; I felt icy cold at the

---

3. *The British Seaman* tells (p. 33) of a sailor who is reproved, and almost flogged, although he had really done nothing. He resolves to keep out of trouble, with double caution.

tips of my fingers, and a dimness was before my eyes. But through that dimness the boatswain's mate, scourge in hand, loomed like a giant, and Captain Claret, and the blue sea seen through the opening at the gangway, showed with an awful vividness. I can not analyze my heart, though it then stood still within me. But the thing that swayed me to my purpose was not altogether the thought that Captain Claret was about to degrade me, and that I had taken an oath with my soul that he should not. No, I felt my man's manhood so bottomless within me, that no word, no blow, no scourge of Captain Claret could cut me deep enough for that. I but swung to an instinct in me—the instinct diffused through all animated nature, the same that prompts even a worm to turn under the heel. Locking souls with him, I meant to drag Captain Claret from this earthly tribunal of his to that of Jehovah, and let Him decide between us. No other way could I escape the scourge.

Nature has not implanted any power in man that was not meant to be exercised at times, though too often our powers have been abused. The privilege, inborn and inalienable, that every man has, of dying himself, and inflicting death upon another, was not given to us without a purpose. These are the last resources of an insulted and unendurable existence.

Great oaks come from little acorns, and Melville's scenes grew from a chapter, "Impressment of Seamen," in Sleeper's *Tales of the Ocean*. Sleeper tells of a Yankee sailor who having resisted a British impressment party was to be taught "a lesson which might be of use to him hereafter."

Accordingly the offender was lashed to a gun, by the inhuman satellites of tyranny, and his back was bared to the lash. Before a blow was struck, he repeated his declaration that he was an American citizen, and the sworn foe of tyrants. He demanded his release —and assured the captain in the most solemn and impressive manner, that if he persisted in punishing him like the vilest malefactor, for vindicating his rights as an American citizen, the act would never be forgiven—but that his revenge would be certain and terrible. The captain laughed aloud at what he regarded an impotent menace—and gave the signal to the boatswain's mate. The white skin of the young American was soon cruelly mangled, the blows fell thickly and heavily on the quivering flesh. He bore the infliction of this barbarous punishment without a murmur or a groan and when the signal was given for the executioner to cease, although the skin was hanging in strips on his back, which was thickly covered with clotted blood, he showed no disposition to

"The Revenge of the Flogged Sailor," from *Tales of the Ocean*, by "Hawser Martingale" (John S. Sleeper) (Boston: 1842).

faint or to falter. His face was somewhat paler than it was wont to be—but his lips were compressed, as if he were summoning determination to his aid, and his dark eyes shot forth a brilliant gleam, showing that his spirit was unsubdued, and that he was bent on revenge, even if his life should be the forfeit.

His bonds were loosened, and he rose from his humiliating posture. He glared fiercely around. The captain was standing within a few paces of him with a demoniac grin upon his features, as if he enjoyed to the bottom of his soul the disgrace and the tortures inflicted on the poor Yankee. The hapless sufferer saw that smile of exultation—and that moment decided the fate of the oppressor. With the activity, the ferocity, and almost the strength of a tiger the mutilated American sprang upon the tyrant, and grasped him where he stood, surrounded by his officers, who for the moment seemed paralyzed with astonishment—and before they could recover their senses and hasten to the assistance of their commander, the flogged American had borne him to the gangway, and then clutching him by the throat with one hand, and firmly embracing him with the other, despite his struggles, he leaped with him into the turbid waters of the Demerara! They parted to receive the tyrant and his victim—then closed over them, and neither was ever afterwards seen. Both had passed to their last account—

"_____Unanointed, unannealed,
With all their imperfections on their heads."

The external differences between the scene in Sleeper and that in Melville are of course considerable. In some ways Melville's episode seems muted compared with its source, for Sleeper has a completed action, a real and not an imagined flogging, an executed indignity and injustice, and a genuine murder and suicide. These external matters were not for Melville's book. The power of his passage is in its inwardness, its psychological rather than its external action. First of all he was writing a documentary sort of work using materials of a cruise which was a matter of record. Then, too, by following Sleeper's scene exactly, Melville would have ended his own book, for with the execution of vengeance would have occurred the death of the narrator. But more to the point is that Melville was concerned with his general attack on flogging, one of the three central aims of his book, and that the whimsical punishment threatened White-Jacket was sufficiently emphasized by being drawn to the very brink of the fact. Besides, the reprieve gave Melville a chance once again to bring in the handsome hero, Jack

Chase, who with Colbrook, a Corporal of the Marines, stepped forward and testified for White-Jacket's character, effecting his release.

Most important, however, is Melville's vision of the experience in psychological and ethical terms. In an absurd world, how may a man maintain his manliness, his being, his selfhood except by strongly assertive acts, by positive choices and not by submissions? "The privilege, inborn and inalienable, that every man has, of dying himself, and inflicting death upon another, was not given to us without a purpose. These are the last resources of an insulted and endurable existence." It is a passionate affirmation, rewritten and expanded in the closing paragraphs of "Knights and Squires" (*Moby-Dick,* Chapter 26). There Melville laments the submissiveness of Starbuck, "the fall of valor" of a man who, physically brave, had not an equivalent moral bravery. White-Jacket unlike Starbuck is determined not to present the "undraped spectacle of a valor-ruined man."

The wheel swings full circle, perhaps. What was first seen as an autobiographical episode, an "actuality," was proved to be a fiction, which now proves to have been an appropriation and an adaptation— but which may be further interpreted as an imaginative "actuality" of Melville's own life. Sleeper's episode for Melville is almost *déja vu. It* did not happen to Melville on board the *United States.* It happened to Melville in his study, in his mind, as he read, altered, and transfigured Sleeper's lurid scene into a scene of moral grandeur. White-Jacket has asserted himself in such a way, has reached such a state that he will soon be ready—naked, defiant, himself—to rip off the white jacket itself and become a man among men. The later, and even greater, episode of the Fall is here prepared for, and what occurs in that climactic scene vitally relates to the arraignment and defiance drawn from the crudities of "Hawser Martingale."

War in a Man-of-War

T HREE themes have emerged from the detailed documentation and description of the first two-thirds of *White-Jacket* to give focus as well as force to an otherwise rambling discourse. These themes are life on board a man-of-war, the ship as microcosm, and the maturation of White-Jacket, the least developed of the three. These three themes now receive powerful dramatizations during the last third of the book. The third theme is the substance of the closing episode, White-Jacket's fall from the yard-arm; the second theme is the substance of the comic-tragic Mutiny of the Beards; and the first theme is now set forth in the vivid battle scenes of Chapter 74, "The Main-top at Night," and Chapter 75, "Sink, Burn, and Destroy."

Up to now Melville has shown us the ship in its physical and social aspects; he now shows us the ship in its functional, and final, phase.

Life in a man-of-war involves death in a man-of-war. An instrument of destruction, the man-of-war is not adequately described until destruction itself is portrayed. This is the ultimate use of the ship, to sink, burn, and destroy. With constructional tact Melville waited until Chapters 74 and 75 before confronting this essential, sad, and savage subject. For this the previous pages of information and description have in a sense been preparing.

•

"The Main-top at Night" and the chapter following, "Sink, Burn, and Destroy," are a diptych; the first panel depicts the historic sea-fight between the *United States* and the *Macedonian* early in the War of 1812; the second tells of the Battle of Navarino, when the fleets of Britain, France, and Russia completely destroyed the Turkish fleet. Both were glorious triumphs—or bitter defeats, depending on the point of view— in the pages of history, but Melville shows them as senseless slaughter and brutality, essential folly beneath a specious glory. The triumphs of captains are the defeats of mankind.[1]

The setting in which the stories are told is the main-top on a moonlit night. Melville's is a marine painting:

> From our lofty perch, of a moonlight night, the frigate itself was a glorious sight. She was going large before the wind, her stun'-sails set on both sides, so that the canvass on the main-mast and fore-mast presented the appearance of two majestic, tapering pyramids, more than a hundred feet broad at the base, and termi- nating in the clouds with the light copestone of the royals. That immense area of snow-white canvass sliding along the sea was indeed a magnificent spectacle. The three shrouded masts looked like the apparitions of three gigantic Turkish Emirs striding over the ocean.

1. John D. Langhorne, sailor, scribbled in his copy of *White-Jacket:* "is it not strange that Mr. Melville, having such ideas about fighting should voluntarily enlist on board a man of war?" It was not a good question; Melville enlisted so as to get home from the Sandwich Islands. He probably had little idea of the constricted conditions in which he would have to live during the voyage, and he certainly anticipated no actual fighting. It was the experience of the ship and his subsequent thinking and reading which led him to attack the man-of-war func- tion. Furthermore, his complaints were no different, except in their rhetorical power and deeper insight into events, from some of his sailor sources, Leech especially.

Few passages show better how far Melville has gone in mastering difficult material. As every painter and writer knows, "beautiful" scenes are the most difficult; they are scenes which God has already achieved, and for the artist to "do" something with them, to make something more than a technicolor slide or a sentimental paragraph, demands a sure technique to eliminate treacly prettiness. Moonlight nights reduce lesser writers to rhymes of moon-June, and ships in full-sail are a cliché; it takes a Coleridge or a Ryder to surmount the merely picturesque elements. Melville now describes a scene which could have been calendar art, but isn't. By his showing us sharply the ship itself in terms of a pyramid, the fluid, shimmering ship is seen wittily in terms of the most solid and stable of objects, a space-bound and time-enduring pyramid; Melville avoids sentimentalism and may be permitted the phrase "magnificent spectacle" because he has made it one. More startling than the static pyramid trope is the kinetic one of the striding Turkish Emirs, an image probably taken from some Oriental source (as maybe was the pyramid figure), as yet untraced.

The idyllic setting in the theme is, further, in ironic contrast to the violent stories the sailors tell, stories of death on the deck below. In Melville life aloft is always contrasted with life on the main-deck, an almost metaphysical opposition of idealism and materialism, of dream and fact, of art and action.

In the first chapter Jack Chase acts as master of ceremonies; in the second he is narrator and hero. He first regales his shipmates with snatches of poetry from his favorite Camoëns' *Lusiad*[2] and from balladry, after which the gathering is diverted "by sundry *yarns* and *twisters* of the top-men." The setting and the basic spirit constitute Melville's adaptation of the social atmosphere prevalent throughout Mercier's *Scenes* (even the word *twisters* is there, italicized with *yarns*), which served not so much as "source"[3] but as reminder of how he might set up *his* two yarns or twisters about warfare.

The fight of the *Macedonian* versus the *United States* was the one episode which Melville could not have omitted telling. No account of the *Neversink-United States* could be complete if the highest moment in the history of the ship were left out. When the *United States* defeated

2. For Melville's interest in this work see Lawrance Thompson, *Melville's Quarrel With God* (Princeton: Princeton University Press, 1952), pp. 346–349, especially.

3. It should be noted, however, that the "Soirée on the Forecastle," pp. 200–210, is a gathering very similar, especially in its opening two pages, to Melville's opening paragraphs. Note also the earlier yarn-spinning session on pp. 48ff.

United States vs. Macedonian. Painting by Antonio Jacobsen, courtesy of the Historical Society of Pennsylvania.

United States vs. Macedonian. Scrimshaw sperm whale tooth, from the collection of the author.

the *Macedonian* on 12 October 1812, she reached her triumphant moment, a proud day in the history of the United States Navy. To have omitted this would have been like omitting Agincourt in a play about Henry V.

The story is told to the main-top club by "an old negro, who went by the name of Tawney, a sheet-anchor-man, whom we often invited into our top of tranquil nights, to hear him discourse. He was a staid and sober seaman, very intelligent, with a fine, frank bearing, one of the best men in the ship, and held in high estimation by every one."

Tawney, the "staid and sober seaman" who tells his own story, may have been a fact, a memory of Melville's, for there had been Negroes on board the *United States,* but Tawney is more significantly a fiction; at least the story he tells is taken almost entirely from Leech's *Thirty Years from Home* (pp. 126ff.), and although Melville uses only a small part of Leech's twenty-five-page account, the narrative continuity is essentially from Leech, with a few lurid details from Nicol and the British Seaman interwoven. As a documentary account of the battle between the *Macedonian* and the *United States* Leech's version is historically authentic, and it is also well written; but for a sharp impressionistic account of the chaos and savagery of battle at sea, with the naval details utilized to indict the very action they seem to celebrate, Melville's is superior.

Melville does not follow Leech's pages *seriatim* but removes useful bits from various pages to paste together in his new pattern, to suit his different purpose, which is fundamentally propagandistic. Melville, for example, describes in sequence: (1) Captain Cardan's adamant insistence that Tawney and other Americans impressed on the *Macedonian* must fight in the battle, against their own country; (2) Captain Cardan's surrender to Captain Decatur; and, (3) the guns of the two ships. Although all these items are in Leech, (1) is from page 128, (2) from page 103, and (3) from page 149. Following these matters, Melville drops Leech for the moment to attack the Articles of War, and to question some of the moral attitudes of Captains.[4]

After his moralistic attack, Melville returns to the story of the battle, taking items from pages 144, 145, 132, and 133 of Leech, stitching with them several scraps from *John Nicol, Mariner,* as well as some from the British Seaman's account of the Battle of Navarino.

One scrap seems to have come from both Leech and Nicol, although the latter's claim to influence is perhaps the greater. Melville wrote:

> One afternoon, I was walking with him along the gun-deck, when he paused abreast of the main-mast. "This part of the ship," said he, "we called the *slaughter-house* on board the Macedonian. Here the men fell, five and six at a time. An enemy always directs its shot here, in order to hurl over the mast, if possible. The beams and carlines overhead in the Macedonian *slaughter-house* were spattered with blood and brains. About the hatchways it looked like a butcher's stall; bits of human flesh sticking in the ring-bolts. A pig that ran about the deck escaped unharmed, but his hide was so clotted with blood, from rooting among the pools of gore, that when the ship struck the sailors hove the animal overboard, swearing that it would be rank cannibalism to eat him."

4. Little if any of this is found in Leech, and although much of it is Melville's alone, one suspects that some may be from a source as yet unknown.

Tracing the sources for this one paragraph one discovers the intricacy of Melville's patchwork. At first glance Leech (p. 132) would seem to be—and up to now has been held to be—the sole and sufficient source for Melville's lines, as he furnished Melville with the metaphor of the slaughterhouse:

> Certainly there was nothing very inspiriting in the aspect of things where I was stationed. So terrible had been the work of destruction round us, it was termed the slaughter-house. Not only had we had several boys and men killed or wounded, but several of the guns were disabled.

Then, however, one finds the term "slaughter-house" defined by John Nicol in his useful-to-Melville account of a naval battle off Cape St. Vincent (p. 170):

> The seamen call the lower deck, near the main-mast, the slaughter-house, as it is amid-ships, and the enemy aim their fire principally at the body of the ship.

Having found two possible sources, one might rest, explaining that the added details of the carnage were taken in part from Leech and from the imagination of Melville, until one reads in Melville's much-thumbed copy of the British Seaman's *Life on Board a Man-of-War* (p. 172):

> When I came under the half-deck, a scene of carnage now presented itself to my view that had been hid during the darkness of the night. All the upper part of the deck was splashed with blood and brains; lumps of human flesh sticking to it; and in the eyebolts of the deck several of the same disgusting remnants of mortality met my view. We had killed a bullock the day before, the four quarters of which were hung up here; but they were so covered with human carnage that we were obliged to consign to the water neck and crop. The Captain had a goat and kid aboard, (the latter a pretty little animal). They both ran about the decks all the time of the action, and neither of them were hurt. Two beautiful ring-doves, also, which hung in a cage above the after grating, escaped uninjured, although pieces of human flesh were found sticking to the wires of the cage. We had a sheep, however, killed by a shot, and it was thrown overboard.

Such a passage served for factual suggestions in Melville, but certainly it served more significantly to arouse Melville's disgust with the animality of war. What needs to be remembered is that a specific source stirs Melville to action, but the surrounding context of the passage he "borrows" also contributes to Melville's writing in ways which are subtly but strongly felt but difficult, almost impossible to prove except by citation of an impossible, unwieldy fullness. There is no need to quote Leech in full (twenty-five pages!) since the significant passages have already been quoted and discussed by Anderson (pp. 390–394). What is important here is Melville's intention in so placing his battle chapters. Early in *White-Jacket* (Chapter 17), he had described war games and contrasted them with a scene from real war, and in so doing had utilized some of the present material from Leech and details from the British Seaman—saving, however, the bulk of his source-supplies for use now, late in the book. Ten chapters before the present battle scenes, in "Man-of-war Trophies" (Chapter 64), he had introduced his anti-war theme, his indictment of savage civilized man. Now, nearing the end of his book, Melville reuses his sources to describe two real battles with climactic, summary force. Melville concludes his chapter "The Main-top at Night" with a reference to the great Lord Nelson, but so weary is White-Jacket of carnage—even though it comes to him only through Tawney's twister—that he rejects the thought of military glory after death, desiring rather the rhythmic union with nature. Interestingly, this hint of *"Kom süsser Tod"*:

Peace to Lord Nelson where he sleeps in his mouldering mast! but rather would I be urned in the trunk of some green tree, and even in death have the vital sap circulating round me, giving of my dead body to the living foliage that shaded my peaceful tomb.

seems to have been suggested by the concluding lines in Nicol's book (p. 187):

I have been a wanderer, and the child of chance, all my days; and now only look for the time when I shall enter my last ship, and be anchored with a green turf upon my breast; and I care not how soon the command is given.

White-Jacket's weariness is only momentary, however, as he turns to the second of the two battles, this one in the baroque style of Jack Chase, built by Melville with a care and a complexity akin to a literary cross-word puzzle.

•

Melville's composition of the second battle scene, "Sink, Burn, and Destroy" (Chapter 75), is complex but its sources are traceable. The very title of the chapter was thrust at Melville by Leech's lines (p. 189):

> This wanton destruction of property was in accordance with our instructions, "to *sink, burn,* and *destroy*" whatever we took from the enemy. Such is the war-spirit! SINK, BURN, and DESTROY! how it sounds! Yet such are the instructions given by Christian (?) nations to their agents in time of war. What Christian will not pray for the destruction of such a spirit?

In this passage, and elsewhere in Leech, Melville also saw his larger theme, the ironic clash of Christian ideals and Christian practices.

Of "Sink, Burn, and Destroy," White-Jacket says, "Among [the] innumerable *'yarns and twisters'* reeled off in our main-top during our pleasant run to the North, none could match those of Jack Chase, our captain." First Melville rapidly hints at some of the previous romantic exploits of gallant Jack Chase,[5] as smuggler and as Don Juan, and then adds:

> But more than all, Jack could tell of the battle of Navarino, for he had been a captain of one of the main-deck guns on board Admiral Codrington's flag-ship, the Asia. Were mine the style of stout old Chapman's Homer, even then I would scarce venture to give noble Jack's own version of this fight, wherein, on the 20th of October, A.D. 1827, thirty-two sail of Englishmen, Frenchmen, and Russians, attacked and vanquished in the Levant an Ottoman fleet of three ships-of-the-line, twenty-five frigates, and a swarm of fire ships and hornet craft.

Well might Melville hesitate, for factual and for literary reasons. In the first place, the Muster Roll of the *Asia* bears neither the name of John J. Chase, nor of Jack Chase, and unless (as could have happened) he had adopted an alias, Jack Chase did not serve on Codrington's ship; nor was he at the Battle of Navarino, since his name is not on the Muster Rolls of the other ships in the British contingent.[6] One must be skeptical of Chase's participation in that historic battle, when the

5. Since much of what is attributed to Jack Chase is derived from sources, one is inclined to suspect a similar origin for Melville's account of Chase's past.
6. Public Records Office, London. Admiralty 37/7302.

Turkish fleet was for once and for all rendered impotent. "It was a glorious victory," but it was literally unseen by our hero.

Jack Chase tells a yarn, or a twister, which is his memory of the Battle of Navarino, himself made into a heroic participant. A twister is what Huck Finn later called a "stretcher," and the word is suitably employed by Melville, for he has twisted, or wrested, the story from the British Seaman, whose book had already been of service in writing *White-Jacket*. "Noble Jack's own version of this fight" is a "twister" from the British Seaman, with a few scraps taken from John Nicol and Samuel Leech.

Melville (Chapter 75)

"We bayed to be at them," said Jack; "and when we *did* open fire, we were like dolphin among the flying-fish. 'Every man take his bird' was the cry, when we trained our guns. And those guns all smoked like rows of Dutch pipe-bowls, my hearties! My gun's crew carried small flags in their bosoms, to nail to the mast in case the ship's colors were shot away. Stripped to the waistbands, we fought like skinned tigers, and bowled down the Turkish frigates like nine-pins. Among their shrouds —swarming thick with small-arm men, like flights of pigeons lighted on pine-trees—our marines sent their leaden pease and gooseberries, like a shower of hail-stones in Labrador. It was a stormy time, my hearties! The blasted Turks pitched into the old Asia's hull a whole quarry of marble shot, each ball one hundred and fifty pounds. They knocked three port-holes

Leech, Nicol, and British Seaman

Nicol (pp. 169–170):

Soon as they were in sight, a signal was made from the Admiral's ship for every vessel, as she came up, to make the best of her way, firing upon the French ships as she passed, and "every man to take his bird," as we jokingly called it.

Leech (p. 133): Our men fought like tigers. Some of them pulled off their jackets, others their jackets and vests; while some, still more determined, had taken off their shirts, and, with nothing but a handkerchief tied round the waistband of their trowsers, fought like heroes.

British Seaman (p. 144): Shortly before this, I had heard a dreadful crash as if the whole ship's side had been stove in, and now I learned that it was occasioned by two marble-shot into one. But we gave them better than they sent. 'Up and at them, my bull-dog!' said I, patting my gun on the breech; 'tear open hatchways in their Moslem sides!' White-Jacket, my lad, you ought to have been there. The bay was covered with masts and yards, as I have seen a raft of snags in the Arkansas River. Showers of burned rice and olives from the exploding foe fell upon us like manna in the wilderness. *'Allah! Allah! Mohammed! Mohammed!'* split the air; some cried it out from the Turkish port-holes; others shrieked it forth from the drowning waters, their top-knots floating on their shaven skulls, like black-snakes on half-tide rocks. By those top-knots they believed that their Prophet would drag them up to Paradise, but they sank fifty fathoms, my hearties, to the bottom of the bay. 'Ain't the bloody 'Hometons going to strike yet?' cried my first loader, a Guernsey man, thrusting his neck out of the port-hole, and looking at the Turkish line-of-battle ship near by. That instant his head blew by me like a bursting Paixhan shot, and the flag of Neb Knowles himself was hauled down forever. We dragged his hull to one side, and avenged him with the cooper's anvil, which, endways, we rammed home; a mess-mate shoved in the dead man's bloody Scotch cap for the wad, and sent it flying into the line-of-battle ship. By the god of

of 120 pound weight each, striking the main-deck . . . [which] had knocked two ports into one, and wounded five men.

British Seaman (p. 147): The face of the water was covered with pieces of wreck; masts and yards drifted about on the surface. . . . (p. 148) pieces of burning wood and showers of burned rice and olives from the Turkish ships rained down upon us in plentiful profusion. . . .

British Seaman (p. 148): all were Mahometans, as we saw by the lock of hair left on the crown of their heads, by which Mahomet, according to their own belief, lifts them to Paradise.

Nicol (p. 167): One lad put his head out of the port-hole, saying, "D—n them, are they not going to strike yet?"

Nicol (p. 50): I looked to their gun, and saw the two horns of my *study** [* Anvil] across its mouth; the next moment it was through the Jason's side.

war! boys, we hardly left enough of that craft to boil a pot of water with. It was a hard day's work—a sad day's work, my hearties. That night, when all was over, I slept sound enough, with a box of cannister shot for my pillow! But you ought to have seen the boat-load of Turkish flags one of our captains carried home; he swore to dress his father's orchard in colors with them, just as our spars are dressed for a gala day."

"Though you tormented the Turks at Navarino, noble Jack, yet you came off yourself with only the loss of a splinter, it seems," said a top-man, glancing at our captain's maimed hand.

"Yes; but I and one of the Lieutenants had a narrower escape than that. A shot struck the side of my port-hole, and sent the splinters right and left. One took off my hat rim clean to my brow; another *razeed* the Lieutenant's left boot, by slicing off the heel; a third shot killed my powder-monkey without touching him."

"How, Jack?"

"It *whizzed* the poor babe dead. He was seated on a *cheese*

Leech (p. 188) . . . our captain told us, if they fired, to not "leave enough of her to boil a tin pot with."

British Seaman (p. 165): I found a number of them stretched on the deck, sleeping as soundly as if they had been in a feather bed, with a pillow of down under their head, instead of a box of cannister.

Nicol (p. 55): When Captain Reeves came ashore, he completely loaded the long-boat with flags he had taken from the enemy. When one of the officers inquired what he would do with them, he said, laughing, "I will hang one upon every tree in my father's garden."

British Seaman (p. 144): I saw Captain Bathurst coming down the poop ladder, when the tail of his cocked hat was carried away by a splinter from the bulwarks. . . .

Nicol (p. 168): One of my mess-mates had the heel of his shoe shot off; the skin was not broke, yet his leg swelled and became black.

Nicol (p. 171): One lad who was stationed by a salt-box, on

of wads at the time, and after the dust of the powdered bulwarks had blown away, I noticed he yet sat still, his eyes wide open. *'My little hero!'* cried I, and I clapped him on the back; but he fell on his face at my feet. I touched his heart, and found he was dead. There was not a little finger mark on him.

which he sat to give out cartridges, and keep the lid close, —it is a trying birth,—when asked for a cartridge, he gave none, yet he sat upright; his eyes were open. One of the men gave him a push; he fell all his length on the deck. There was not a blemish on his body, yet he was quite dead, and was thrown overboard.

Comparing Melville's two pages with the parallel column of patches taken from his "best authorities" is a startling and disturbing study. The snap judgment may be: Melville's version has nothing original in it; ergo, it is plagiarized. This is to forget that in such a view much writing of history is then plagiarism because fact 1 from author A is put with fact 2 from author B, etc., to assemble an argument, to build up a narrative, to order a description. Melville was first of all in *White-Jacket* a historian, and he was concerned that his be a true account of life on board a man-of-war. One's judgment of Melville's practice will depend partly on one's concept of "truth." To write a true battle scene Melville took significant bits from three different battles described by three different authors; he then dramatically gave that narrative to a real character to recount because, in a sense, Chase, who had never fought at Navarino, serves well as a kind of fusion in himself of the three chief sources. Melville's, or Chase's, description is an accurate or truthful account of *a* naval battle, but it is not exclusively one of just *the* Battle of Navarino.

Melville is moving towards the fiction of *Moby-Dick;* his dramatic instinct conquers droning historicism. Jack Chase's battle account is thoroughly in keeping with his character—vivid, flamboyant—or rather, his character is itself created by such narratives throughout *White-Jacket.* Which comes first, the character or the actions? Who can tell the dancer from the dance? This account plays John Chase not so much as John J. Chase of the *United States* but "glorious Jack Chase," a persona of Melville's and not a figure for the *Dictionary of National Biography.*

Characteristic of Melville is Melville's ironic duplicity which allows his hero, whom he obviously and genuinely admired, to celebrate war so forthrightly and so glowingly to describe slaughter and bloodshed, in order tellingly to drive home the point that war is an absolute evil by which the best are corrupted, that "thus it would seem that war almost makes blasphemers of the best of men, and brings them all down to the Feejee standard of humanity. . . . the fighting man is but a fiend." With this Melville is ready in one of his noblest and most idealistic of indictments to conclude his chapter with a challenge to his readers which reads like lines from an ardent existentialist manifesto, and in which we glimpse the passion and the power that is to make *Moby-Dick:*

> But all events are mixed in a fusion indistinguishable. What we call Fate is even, heartless, and impartial; not a fiend to kindle bigot flames, nor a philanthropist to espouse the cause of Greece. We may fret, fume, and fight; but the thing called Fate everlastingly sustains an armed neutrality.
>
> Yet though all this be so, nevertheless, in our own hearts, we mold the whole world's hereafters; and in our own hearts we fashion our own gods. Each mortal casts his vote for whom he will to rule the worlds; I have a voice that helps to shape eternity; and my volitions stir the orbits of the furthest suns. In two senses, we are precisely what we worship. Ourselves are Fate.

·14·

The Sequel of War
in a Man-of-War

THE two naval fights just narrated as "twisters" in the main-top of
the *Neversink* serve an essential thematic, not just a dramatic, purpose. More than flamboyant fireworks, they are, horribly, "life in a man-
of-war," a life which may mean death. The battle chapters expose the
central purpose for which the man-of-war was created, to "sink, burn,
and destroy," an intention and a performance which reduces, Melville
says, Christian civilization to a Feejee level. Significantly, this passionate
indictment is absent from Ames, Mercier, and Nicol, writers who left
unexamined the unprincipled, inconsistent world which they passively
served. The two intense spasms of these chapters are followed by a

relaxed but relentless continuation of Melville's attack, the ensuing scenes being rolling echoes of the cannons' terrible thunder. Echoes and consequences of those battles are Chapter 76, "The Chains," and Chapter 77, "The Hospital in a Man-of-war," two chapters of semi-documentary material to balance against and to complete the tense dramatic ones.

Weary of tales of war, White-Jacket seeks a place of peace somewhere on the main-deck. "After the battle-din of the last two chapters, let us . . . in the sequestered fore-chains of the Neversink, tranquillize ourselves, if we may." For the first time, but not the last, the fore-top has failed him.

He remembers the "chains," a small, somewhat hidden platform, but on going there he discovers one of the gun-captains, a pious Baptist and "a sincere, humble believer." The irony of the situation—"But how, with those hands of his begrimed with powder, could he break that *other* and most peaceful and penitent bread of the Supper?"—strikes White-Jacket, saddened from only imaginative participation in battle, as he finds this un-Claudian character who has found some sort of prayer to serve his turn. A year before the fighting Quaker whalemen in *Moby-Dick,* and two years before the "Chronometricals and Horologicals" of *Pierre,* Melville dramatizes the clash of idealism and expediency:

> Ah! the best righteousness of our man-of-war world seems but an unrealized ideal, after all; and those maxims which, in the hope of bringing about a Millennium, we busily teach to the heathen, we Christians ourselves disregard. In view of the whole present social frame-work of our world, so ill adapted to the practical adoption of the meekness of Christianity, there seems almost some ground for the thought, that although our blessed Savior was full of the wisdom of heaven, yet his gospel seems lacking in the practical wisdom of earth—in a due appreciation of the necessities of nations at times demanding bloody massacres and wars; in a proper estimation of the value of rank, title, and money. But all this only the more crowns the divine consistency of Jesus; since Burnet and the best theologians demonstrate, that his nature was not merely human—was not that of a mere man of the world.

The chapter of "The Chains" was inserted not to inform but to indict, to reiterate a moral theme that is now dominant as the book moves to its close. Drawing away from but not abandoning this theme, "The Hospital in a Man-of-war" introduces factual materials—but in keeping with

the battle chapters—facts about the inadequate care of the wounded.[1] It
is a Kafka-esque world of depth and death, "a subterranean vault, into
which scarce a ray of heaven's glad light ever penetrated, even at noon."
Surgeon Cadwallader Cuticle, in command of this lightless world, we
have already seen. His assistants are appropriate for him and his realm.
There is Pills, "a small, pale, hollow-eyed young man, with that peculiar
Lazarus-like expression so often noticed in hospital attendants." Pelican,
the assistant surgeon, is equally apt for this world of death-in-life. The
two aides are like eccentrics from Dickens, and Melville satirically scores
them. His chief condemnation, however, is for Cuticle, who not only
neglects the hospital but will not use his discretionary power at other
times—for instance, to stop or to limit the floggings. Men do not matter
in this military machine which amputates not merely the limbs of individuals, but an entire world.

If the picture of the sick-bay is bleak and sterile there was nevertheless, in times of peace, a desirable function which the sick-bay served—it
could be a refuge in a storm, a time when the sailors goldbricked to get
into sick-bay. This was especially so when the ship approached Cape
Horn, when the steward's list would lengthen:

> But, notwithstanding all this, notwithstanding the darkness and
> closeness of the Sick-bay, in which an alleged invalid must be
> content to shut himself up till the Surgeon pronounces him cured,
> many instances occur, especially in protracted bad weather, where
> pretended invalids will submit to this dismal hospital durance, in
> order to escape hard work and wet jackets.
>
> There is a story told somewhere of the Devil taking down the
> confessions of a woman on a strip of parchment, and being
> obliged to stretch it longer and longer with his teeth, in order to
> find room for all the lady had to say. Much thus was it with our
> Surgeon's Steward, who had to lengthen out his manuscript Sick-
> list, in order to accommodate all the names which were presented
> to him while we were off the pitch of Cape Horn. What sailors call
> the *"Cape Horn fever,"* alarmingly prevailed; though it disap-
> peared altogether when we got into fine weather, which, as with
> many other invalids, was solely to be imputed to the wonder-
> working effects of an entire change of climate.
>
> It seems very strange, but it is really true, that off Cape Horn
> some *"sogers"* of sailors will stand cupping, and bleeding, and

1. Ames wrote (p. 224) that "the medical department of our Navy is much
and scandalously neglected."

blistering, before they will budge. On the other hand, there are cases where a man actually sick and in need of medicine will refuse to go on the Sick-list, because in that case his allowance of *grog* must be stopped.

This Cape Horn Fever came from Ames (p. 193) when, off the Patagonian coast, cold weather "produced a complaint jocosely called by our men 'the Cape Fever,' " and the men "sogered" and tried to get on the doctor's list.

To close his hospital chapter, Melville blasts at privilege and preference extended to the officers in the food:

> On board of every American man-of-war, bound for sea, there is a goodly supply of wines and various delicacies put on board— according to law—for the benefit of the sick, whether officers or sailors. And one of the chicken-coops is always reserved for the Government chickens, destined for a similar purpose. But, on board of the Neversink, the only delicacies given to invalid sailors was a little sago or arrow-root, and they did not get *that* unless severely ill; but, so far as I could learn, no wine, in any quantity, was ever prescribed for them, though the Government bottles often went into the Ward-room, for the benefit of indisposed officers.
>
> And though the Government chicken-coop was replenished at every port, yet not four pair of drum-sticks were ever boiled into broth for sick sailors. Where the chickens went, some one must have known; but, as I can not vouch for it myself, I will not here back the hardy assertion of the men, which was that the pious Pelican—true to his name—was extremely fond of poultry. I am the still less disposed to believe this scandal, from the continued leanness of the Pelican, which could hardly have been the case did he nourish himself by so nutritious a dish as the drum-sticks of fowls, a diet prescribed to pugilists in training. But who can avoid being suspicious of a very suspicious person? Pelican! I rather suspect you still.

Not even the closing comedy about Pelican's leanness can conceal Melville's indebtedness to William McNally's *Evils and Abuses* (pp. 168–169):

> The difference between seamen's and officers' quarters in hospitals would not be a matter of much consequence, but the same unequal distribution extends to the good things of the hospital department,

on board of the ships. There is abundance of wines, porter, and other things of the sort, furnished for the use of the sick, on board of ships in commission; but in the course of eleven years, I declare, with the greatest regard to truth, that I never saw or knew a half dozen of wine to be given to the crews during that period; but I have known a commissioned officer allowed a bottle of porter every day, and a bottle of wine every two days, when he was sick with a disease that he had brought on himself. The only article that sailors usually receive, if very sick, is a little sago or arrow root, and then it is very seldom that any wine is put into it, to make it palatable. I never can forget what I heard a dying man say, on board the Lexington, at Buenos Ayres. When the doctor was very anxious to do something for him, he replied, "It's too late, now, doctor; if you had tried to do something before, you might have done me good; but now it's too late. I want my will made out, and my wages left to my mother: she lives in Richmond, Va." These were nearly the last words he spoke; in an hour he was a corpse. Deny this who can. There are generally chickens put on board for the use of the sick, but it rarely happens that any of them ever find their way to the mouth of a seaman. If a chicken dies, during the day or night, it is sure to be one belonging the doctor— at least, it is put into his coop, by the cabin or ward-room steward, and a live one taken out and put into their own—as these worthies take particular delight in *weathering* the doctor, and keeping their own stock good. A coroner's inquest will be held under the fore-castle, who will report that the doctor's chicken came to its death by some cause unknown, and the body is committed to the sharks. Pandora's box holds nothing that does not fall to the lot of the doctor's fowls, on board of a ship of war.

Melville's stitching of his jacket is as active as ever.

•

The jacket, so long forgotten, returns for the next to the last time in Chapter 78, "Dismal Times in the Mess." Priming, an old gunner's mate in White-Jacket's mess, grumbles about the sickness of Shenly, a mess member, the fatal fall of Baldy, and the death of the amputee, implying that all three accidents occurred because there were thirteen in the mess, that the inclusion of White-Jacket had not only crowded the mess but had hexed it—" 'Blast you, and your jacket, say I.' " To this White-Jacket replies:

"My dear mess-mate," I cried, "don't blast me any more, for Heaven's sake.[2] Blast my jacket you may, and I'll join you in *that;* but don't blast *me;* for if you do, I shouldn't wonder if I myself was the next man to keel up."

The distinction between the external, the jacket, and the essential, the *me,* is emphatically made, a meaning to be employed in the closing scene of the book when, indeed, White-Jacket does become the "next man to keel up."

Jack Chase steps in, reproving Priming for his intolerance, and the gunner's mate rolls off, "growling as he went." White-Jacket curses his jacket, and concludes the chapter with "Jacket! jacket! thou hast much to answer for, jacket!"

Following the chapter on the "cursed jacket," Melville added a four-chapter group dealing with death and its immediate consequences on board ship—that is, a ship crew's reactions to the sickness, death, and funeral of one of their shipmates. Since death *en masse* had been vividly and appropriately treated in the two battle scenes a few chapters before, the death of an individual through illness or accident was a frequent enough event to call for its description in such a documentary as *White-Jacket.* The death of a shipmate is part of the life of a ship.

The four chapters pick up again from the closing lines (and so from McNally, as shown) of "The Hospital in a Man-of-war" (Chapter 77), so that the jacket chapter is but a brief break in a sequence originating in the two battle episodes. The sequence of chapters is logical if loose, and even the jacket chapter, seemingly digressive, connects with the others since the jacket is held by the superstitious sailors to be the *cause* of ill fortune.

The death scene of Shenly is not to be found in the sources so far located for *White-Jacket.* There are, to be unsure, suggestions, wisps of ideas-for-development in McNally and Mercier, but that these hints have any genuine connection, give significant stimulation to Melville's imagination, can not be proved. The death scene is a powerful one, the close atmosphere "in this subterranean sick-bay, buried in the very bowels of the ship, and at sea cut off from all ventilation," is physically and psychologically oppressive; and Melville suggests that such surroundings may have contributed to Shenly's death. Once dead, Shenly's body is laid out; a separate chapter (80), gruesome as the grave-digger's scene in *Hamlet* (and maybe suggested by that), describes the stitching

2. Printed in original as "sale."

of Shenly's shroud by two grizzled sail-makers, Dickensianly named Thrummings and Ringrope. Their concern for their stitching technique makes them callous to the human tragedy present in the corpse at their side. The succeeding Chapter 81, "How they Bury a Man-of-war's-man at Sea," is one short page in which irreverence and reverence are realistically blended: "But there is something in death that ennobles even a pauper's corpse." The clash of ship routine and cursing men with the holy and solemn occasion sounds authentic:

> *"I am the resurrection and the life!"* solemnly began the Chaplain, in full canonicals, the prayer-book in his hand.
> "Damn you! off those booms!" roared a boatswain's mate to a crowd of top-men, who had elevated themselves to gain a better view of the scene.
> *"We commit this body to the deep!"* At the word, Shenly's messmates tilted the board, and the dead sailor sank in the sea.

Although Melville had seen such burials on board the *United States,* it is quite probable that this episode was partially suggested by a passage from Ames (pp. 189–190):

> "Keep down, there, d——n your eyes, keep down off those lee hammock nettings; boatswain's mate, drive those fellows off those nettings." The chaplain began, "I am the resurrection and the life."—"Silence, G-d d——n you," thundered the first lieutenant.
> . . .

The concluding chapter of this quartet deals summarily with "What remains of a Man-of-war's-man after his Burial at Sea," when his "will" is "proved" by the purser.

Melville was near the end of his information and of his narrative. As an intermission between the Mutiny of the Beards and the Fall from the Yard-Arm, he inserted as contrast two expository passages, the first, Chapter 89, dealing with "The Social State in a Man-of-war," hinting at horrors (sexual perversion primarily) not to be told on board naval ships, and Chapter 90, "The Manning of Navies." The second is the most bestitched chapter in the entire book, as if Melville had sewn into one small garment all the attractive (to him) but unused patches from his sources—notes which any journalist or scholar wishes to use in the motion of his book, but which he can't quite fit in. Leech, McNally, and Nicol all gave their blood to save this chapter. So intricate is this stitching operation that tracing it in full would be as prodigal of space as it would be involved.

One special passage, however, must be especially noticed here because of its relationship to the scene, the Fall, which will follow, the monsters here preparing the way for the later one which brushes the passive form of White-Jacket in the sea's depths:

> And as the sea, according to old Fuller, is the stable of brute monsters, gliding hither and thither in unspeakable swarms, even so is it the home of many moral monsters, who fitly divide its empire with the snake, the shark, and the worm.

Thus, towards the end, in one of his most felicitous quotations, Melville states one of the most profound meanings of his book, and foreshadows its climactic scene.

·15·

The Mutiny
of the Beards

The nautical sketches are unsurpassed.
Review in The Albion, 30 March 1850

THE ab ovo way in which sections of White-Jacket grew during Melville's progress through his manuscript is clearly shown in several sections, especially in that sequence of chapters we shall term "The Mutiny of the Beards."

Following his eloquent sequence on war and its horrible human consequences, Melville returns to his documentary purpose to tell about life in a man-of-war. Naturally, he turns for help to his favorite storehouse, noticing in Mercier's *Scenes* (pp. 97–98) the doggerel verses

about schools on board a frigate, and noticing, too, on the same page
(p. 98), the humorous description of shaving on board ship. Both scenes
are part of a long "poetic" section, 396 mismetered lines in which Mercier
threw together a summary of the ship's social structure, most useful
before, and now, to Melville's expository purpose. From Mercier's facts
he begins to write and from them he quickly takes off—the beginning is
interesting as literary appropriation; the departure is splendid as creative
transmutation and transcendence.

Melville's Chapter 83, "A Man-of-war College," describes two
schools on the *Neversink:*

> There were two academies in the frigate. One comprised the
> apprentice boys, who, upon certain days of the week, were indoc-
> trinated in the mysteries of the primer by an invalid corporal of
> marines, a slender, wizzen-cheeked man, who had received a
> liberal infant-school education.

This Melville saw in *Scenes* (p. 98):

> Between the other guns there's much more noise,
> It is the school for our apprentice boys,
> Who round the tables sit, with roguish smile,
> Their minds intent on other things the while,—
> Whilst their efficient tutor's standing near,
> To be engaged in study all appear;
> You see them with their pencil, slate, and book,
> With downcast eyes and solemn, studious look,
> But the first moment he withdraws his glance
> They then commence to caper and to prance,
> And in the *skylark,* pencil, book and slate
> Are all forgot, with fun they're so elate.

From this Melville departs only in phrasing, neither expanding nor
dramatizing his source. For the other school (which had come first in
Scenes) Melville has this to work from (pp. 97–98):

> But to the *starboard* side,—just cast your looks
> Upon that screen that's pendent from the hooks,
> And oftentimes proceeds from there such din
> As makes you wonder what there was within;
> This is the *middies'* school—how much they learn
> I leave for abler judges to discern:

But let it not be thought that I have meant
That their professor is not competent;
No such thing—we all are well aware
That his abilities are bright and fair,
And tho' but *young*, his tact and skill to teach
Hundreds, *more vain*, their life-time would not reach.

This is not much, but Melville's imagination is ignited by the possibilities and he dramatized the lines to the full. First he sketches out in realistic detail the setting (ship), the actors (students), and the star (professor), infusing these details with the caustic irony unleashed in the Cadwallader Cuticle episode. Similarly, Melville's target is intellectual vanity, here pedantry in education—as Cuticle had been the medical pedant—and as, later, the two disputing priests of Tranquo's whale temple (*Moby-Dick,* Chapter 102) satirize theological chop-logic.

Melville's expansion of unpromising materials is no accident but part of his general attack on the entire military institution, which makes monstrous those men who, while not called upon actually to fight, nevertheless serve war and are thus dehumanized. The group is summarized:

> *"The Professor"* was the title bestowed upon the erudite gentleman who conducted this seminary, and by that title alone was he known throughout the ship. He was domiciled in the Ward-room, and circulated there on a social par with the Purser, Surgeon, and other *non-combatants* and Quakers. By being advanced to the dignity of a peerage in the Ward-room, Science and Learning were ennobled in the person of this Professor, even as divinity was honored in the Chaplain enjoying the rank of a spiritual peer.

The Professor of course is relatively harmless; he cannot mutilate bodies as does Cuticle although he can and does muddle minds. At once learned, pedantic, and fatuous, he expounds naval tactics, gunnery technology. His battle situation sketched on the blackboard, so very correct, is lifeless compared with the slapdash but practical actualities of his saucy students who will, then in speech and later in action, proceed from empirical rather than theoretical knowledge. The ineffectuality of it all is suggested by the closing lines:

> "I now add that, agreeably to the method pursued by the illustrious Newton in treating the subject of curvilinear motion, I consider the *trajectory* or curve described by a moving body in space as

consisting of a series of right lines, described in successive intervals of time, and constituting the diagonals of parallelograms formed in a vertical plane between the vertical deflections caused by gravity and the production of the line of motion which has been described in each preceding interval of time. This must be obvious; for, if you say that the passage *in vacuo* of this cannon-ball, now held in my hand, would describe otherwise than a series of right lines, &c., then you are brought to the *Reductio ad Absurdum,* that the diagonals of parallelograms are——"

"All hands reef top-sails!" was now thundered forth by the boatswain's mates. The shot fell from the professor's palm; his spectacles dropped on his nose, and the school tumultuously broke up, the pupils scrambling up the ladders with the sailors, who had been overhearing the lecture.

More powerfully, more complexly, Melville will use this kind of situation again, in Chapter 47 of *Moby-Dick,* when the metaphysical reveries of Ishmael, as futile and impractical as the Professor's theorizing, are interrupted by the cry "Thar She blows!" and "the ball of Free Will" drops from his hand as the crew rush pell-mell to lower the boats. Whales, actions, life, always in Melville abash and satirize theories, dreams, idealisms. What makes the *Moby-Dick* scene greater, among other things, is its mockery of metaphysics for, after all, Ishmael is then being a philosophical pedant.

From virtually nothing in *Scenes,* but probably helped further by some other book (which some day will turn up), or from his memory of Lockwood, professor on board the *United States*—or from a combination of the two—Melville creates a vignette of wry amusement.

•

If you cannot be free, be as free as you can.
Ralph Waldo Emerson, *Journals,* 1838

The school and the professor are diverting creations of flesh from dust, but even more remarkable is the "Mutiny of the Beards" (Chapters 84–87) section, which begins with such mundane matter as "Man-of-war Barbers," but ends with one of Melville's finest and most moving character creations: John Ushant.

Immediately following his verses on schools, Mercier had described the activity of the ship's barbers (p. 98):

The Barber's shop will next attract your view,
Where you perceive a pleasant, motley crew,
Who round this *sanctorum* with great patience stand
Waiting, to come under the shaver's hand;
The operators they great tact display
In sending so quick "each new reap'd" face away;
And make their razors move with easy grace
Over each son of Neptune's sun-burnt face;
No flattering compliments are bandied o'er,
No "pray sit down sir" as it is ashore;
But in true sailor style you'll hear them say,
"Give us a scrape old fellow, quick's your play:"
"Whose turn is next?" the operators cry,
" 'Tis mine! 'tis mine!" a dozen tars reply:
"Yours?" cries an old main-top man; "well done Jack,
I see of lying, you ain't lost the knack;
Why damme, man, you're not a moment here
And now you're trying to make things appear
As if your turn was next, you count too fast;"
"So 'tis!" a wag replies, *"next to the last."*
"Patterson?" another cries, "I want a shave—
Not such as you to me last Wednesday gave,
For 'pon my soul, your razor was so dull
I thought my face was off at every pull;
And if you serve me that way any more,
I shan't forget you when the cruise is o'er:"
The barber cries, "just try it once again,
I'm sure *this* razor will not give you pain;
For when I've shaved you, I'll a wager make,
My very *establishment* I'll put at stake
You'll say it is the best and keenest blade
That e'er was on your face by barber laid."

From the mere detail and spirit of this passage and from a special prose section in *Scenes,* "The Barber's Shop" (pp. 134–139), Melville composes his setting for the ensuing Mutiny of the Beards. The setting is established, it should be noted, in straightforward exposition, and for once Melville alters his source not by expansion or dramatization but rather by compression and simplification. In *Scenes* (pp. 135–137 especially) there is much "jawing" among the tars about precedence, about the barber's ineptitude with the razor, and so on—rough comedy which Melville does not bother to rework, choosing rather to sum up the conditions in three paragraphs (as against five pages of *Scenes*) so that he may get on with his little drama of the Mutiny of the Beards. Having thus set the stage for his pocket drama, Melville (in Chapter 84) introduces the hero:

> Above all, the Captain of the Forecastle, old Ushant—a fine specimen of a sea sexagenarian—wore a wide, spreading beard, grizzled and gray, that flowed over his breast, and often became tangled and knotted with tar. This Ushant, in all weathers, was ever alert at his duty; intrepidly mounting the fore-yard in a gale, his long beard streaming like Neptune's. Off Cape Horn it looked like a miller's, being all over powdered with frost: sometimes it glittered with minute icicles in the pale, cold, moonlit Patagonian nights. But though he was so active in time of tempest, yet when his duty did not call for exertion, he was a remarkably staid, reserved, silent, and majestic old man, holding himself aloof from noisy revelry, and never participating in the boisterous sports of the crew. He resolutely set his beard against their boyish frolickings, and often held forth like an oracle concerning the vanity thereof. Indeed, at times he was wont to talk philosophy to his ancient companions—the old sheet-anchor-men around him—as well as to the hare-brained tenants of the fore-top, and the giddy lads in the mizzen.
>
> Nor was his philosophy to be despised; it abounded in wisdom. For this Ushant was an old man, of strong natural sense, who had seen nearly the whole terraqueous globe, and could reason of civilized and savage, of Gentile and Jew, of Christian and Moslem. The long night-watches of the sailor are eminently adapted to draw out the reflective faculties of any serious-minded man, however humble or uneducated. Judge, then, what half a century of battling out watches on the ocean must have done for this fine old tar. He was a sort of sea-Socrates, in his old age "pouring out his last philosophy and life," as sweet Spenser has it; and I never could look at him, and survey his right reverend beard, without bestowing upon him that title which, in one of his satires, Persius gives to the immortal quaffer of the hemlock—*Magister Barbatus* —the bearded master.

A grand figure himself, Ushant (the "sea-Socrates") is the prototype of Perth, the blacksmith in *Moby-Dick,* and he culminates in old Dansker in *Billy Budd*. Ushant acts more positively than they (and less Socratically), who cunningly protect themselves against the world's punishments by non-commitment, their wisdom coming Delphically forth in cryptic utterances, in whispered hints.

Chapter 84 sets the stage and introduces the hero. Chapter 85, "The great Massacre of the Beards," now humorously describes the dramatic action, the plot, a disastrous situation set off in parody, a nautical *Rape of the Lock*. Captain Claret orders all the sailors to shave. ("He was afterward discovered to have been tipsy at the time.") The crew is beside itself with rage, having nursed their beards throughout the long voyage and now anticipating parading them soon at home. Their vanity has been touched, their manhood menaced. "The excitement was intense throughout the whole evening" and there were even murmurs of mutiny—"I thought it impossible that they would seriously think of such a folly; but there is no knowing what man-of-war's-men will sometimes do, under provocation—witness Parker and the Nore."[1] That night during the first watch the sailors drive two boatswain's mates from their guard stations, cutting communications between gun and spar-deck. Violence seems unavoidable, inevitable, until the cool and heroic Mad Jack intervenes to save the *Neversink* for a second time against the folly of its Captain. On the first occasion Mad Jack had saved the ship in an action borrowed by Melville from Mercier's *Scenes;* this time he saves it through an action found in McNally's *Evils and Abuses* (pp. 114–115):

> . . . at the same time the Java's men were on liberty and sailing round the harbor, which tended to foster the spirit of discontent that was ready to burst into open mutiny. When the hands were turned to, one day, shortly after our arrival, the master's mate and boatswain, as usual, went on the berth deck to drive the men up; but four or five hundred of them refused to go, and triced up all the ladders fore and aft, except the after one, to prevent any one doing so, and swore vengeance against all who dared to let them down. Word was carried to the first lieutenant that the crew were in a state of mutiny. I was by his side when the report was made. His countenance underwent a slight change, but his compressed lips told that his resolution was taken. He went down the after ladder and ordered the men on deck, who had by this time collected in a body between the guns and abaft the sick bay; one of them said, "Mr. M——, we want liberty; we have been on the station nearly two years and never had any, while the crews of all other vessels have. Why can't we have the same? what have we done?" The first lieut. replied in his usual tone, "This is a pretty

---

1. The theme of mutiny is almost a constant in Melville's writings, first showing in *Typee* and repeated in each book through *Moby-Dick*.

way to get liberty you rascals; you ought to be ashamed to disgrace
yourselves in this way; the commodore will give you liberty in
proper time; let down the ladders and go on deck: don't let me see
any more of such nonsense as this." They did as he ordered them;
but had it not been for the coolness that he displayed, and the light
manner in which he treated their contempt for the authority of the
boatswain and master's mate, a scene would have taken place that
afternoon that would have disgraced our navy and caused the
shedding of innocent blood.

The *Neversink* crew cravenly, or prudently, capitulates to the Captain's petty command, submitting their faces to the barbers with many
grumbles and groans, but submitting. The comedy of their shearing and
shaving is lively, extended. Even valiant Jack Chase yields; he steps
forward to allow his fine flowing beard to be removed—"striking the
flag that Nature herself has nailed to the mast!"—and, being Jack Chase,
he delivers a florid speech, a kind of address from the scaffold. The
mock-epic tone is maintained energetically throughout and is, as Ague-
cheek would say, "admirable fooling."

The Mutiny of the Beards is probably pure fiction. The *United States*
Log has no record of such an order. Perhaps Melville constructed the
drama from the report he might have heard of an order issued to the
Pacific Squadron on the voyage out, as told in a Journal kept by Dr.
Maxwell, Surgeon on board the *United States* at the time: The day is 28
June 1842:

On the same day, Henry La Reintree was appointed Commodore's
Secretary, in place of William I. Allen, resigned because an order
was issued that every man shave off his moustache on a level with
his ears; the only whiskers we were allowed to wear was parallel
with the ear. He was so mortified that he resigned rather than
comply.[2]

The submission, and abasement, of the men leads into the climactic
event of the Mutiny of the Beards: the defiance and the triumph of John
Ushant.

Several men resist longer than the majority of their comrades, and
their extended resistance is honored by Melville as he describes them in
noble comparatives; they resemble Layard's Assyrian Kings, or they are

2. John Haskell Kemble, ed., *Visit to Monterey in 1842* by Dr. R. T. Maxwell
(Los Angeles: Glen Dawson, 1955), p. 16.

like Roman Senators being despoiled by the Goths. These heroes are arraigned before the mast; threatened with flogging, they at last submit. Only John Ushant holds out. Reluctantly, for even Captain Claret had his humanities, the order is given to flog the dauntless old man:

> One, two, three, four, five, six, seven, eight, nine, ten, eleven, twelve lashes were laid on the back of that heroic old man. He only bowed over his head, and stood as the Dying Gladiator lies.

Ushant is placed in the brig for the remainder of the voyage. On arrival at the home port he rents a boat and is rowed, sitting alone, to the shore "amid the unsuppressible cheers of all hands. It was a glorious conquest over the Conqueror himself, as well worthy to be celebrated as the Battle of the Nile." Adept at describing defiant men, Melville does well in his creation of old John Ushant. Even the outrageous pun in the name has a kind of admirable appropriateness.

We have noted that the setting for the Mutiny of the Beards had been elaborated from Mercier's *Scenes* and that the incipient mutiny had been taken from McNally's *Evils and Abuses*. Where did the hero, John Ushant, come from? Probably not from the actual voyage of the *United States,* although its Log Book conceals better than it reveals; as of this date he has not been traced to any literary source, although this is still a reasonable, if unpredictable, possibility.

Perhaps recklessly, I wish to nominate, as the prototype of John Ushant, Joseph Palmer,[3] the Fitchburg farmer-butcher who said "You shan't" to a world which shouted at him, "You must!" In 1830 Joseph Palmer sported a fine bushy beard at a time when beards were not only unfashionable but also un-Christian, the adornment only of infidel Jews. Palmer tartly reminded his critics that our Saviour once wore a beard.

The affronted community of Fitchburg acted. Three men waylaid

3. Joseph Palmer was born 13 May 1789 at No Town (*i.e.,* Leominster), Massachusetts, and died at Fruitlands, Harvard, Massachusetts, 30 October 1873. The details are still obscure, but Palmer was in some way connected with the short-lived 1843 Fruitlands Community, established at Harvard, Massachusetts, by Bronson Alcott and Charles Lane, delightfully described by Louisa May Alcott in *Transcendental Wild Oats.* Palmer bought Fruitlands from Lane when the Community broke up, and he ran it as a farm until his death. Equally unsatisfactory in detail is the story of Palmer's beard-rebellion, although in recent years popular articles have made the story generally familiar. We must await the researches of Mrs. Crocker of Fitchburg for an accurate biography of Palmer. Both she and Mr. William Tyler Harrison, Curator of the Fruitlands Museum, have kindly answered my questions.

Palmer on the street to remove the offending beard. Fighting back stoutly, Palmer was able to open his pen-knife, slashing his opponents so that they retreated, leaving the beard intact. Predictably, in the light of community feeling, Palmer was arrested for disturbing the peace. Refusing to pay a fine of ten dollars, he was sent to the Worcester Jail, where he remained for a year, writing, it has been said, letters to the Worcester *Spy*. At one time, amateur "barbers" visited his cell, but, lying on his bunk, Palmer kicked out so resolutely that again the would-be violators withdrew. He was at last released, a victor, to be, in effect, rowed back to Fitchburg to the cheers of many fellow-Americans.

His case was then a national scandal, and since then it has been a national admiration. If the Unpardonable Sin was the violation of the sanctity of a human soul, as both Hawthorne and Melville believed, then this treatment of Palmer had been such a sin. His rebellion had a comic and heroic grandeur worthy of Melville's memorable scene. He was doughty as was Ushant.

·16·

The Unmanning
of Navies

USHANT'S flogging prepares the way for the documentary but
denunciatory Chapters 88–90 which follow: "Flogging through
the Fleet," "The Social State in a Man-of-war," and "The Manning of
Navies." Anger inflames Melville's pages in the relentless indictment of
the accidental evil within the military institution and of the essential
evil at the heart of man. Heavily documented though these chapters are,
deeply indebted as they are to "sources," they hold the reader, though
at a lower intensity, almost as closely as the Ushant scenes preceding and
the fall from the yard-arm which follows. The intricacy of Melville's
manipulations of his sources in this section makes any account of the

process also intricate—but also interesting because Melville's masterful use and transcendence of facts shows in his rigorous reshaping of those facts to a passionate purpose.

Man's inhumanity to man is now unreservedly Melville's resounding theme—the Unpardonable Sin. Ushant's flogging forces—or allows— Melville again to revive the topic already so vividly treated much earlier, now connected with other naval brutalities. And once again Melville turns primarily to Leech, having prudently saved a striking episode from his source which might now significantly serve him. This is Leech's description of flogging through the fleet, most brutal (save, possibly, for keel-hauling—merely mentioned by Melville) of punishments, more so than straightforward hanging. Although Melville saw 163 floggings in the thirteen months' time, he was spared the horrible sight of flogging through the fleet. Leech's *Thirty Years from Home* provides him with the essential details of his account; the pedantry of parallel passages cannot diminish the power with which both men expose a shocking act:

Melville (Chapter 88)

Leech (pp. 61–62)

　　But though this barbarity is now abolished from the English and American navies, there still remains another practice which, if any thing, is even worse than *keel-hauling.* This remnant of the Middle Ages is known in the Navy as *"flogging through the fleet."* It is never inflicted except by authority of a court-martial upon some trespasser deemed guilty of a flagrant offence. Never, that I know of, has it been inflicted by an American man-of-war on the home station. The reason, probably, is, that the officers well know that such a spectacle would raise a mob in any American sea-port. . . .
　　All hands being called "to witness punishment" in the ship to which the culprit

　　It may be asked how a man could endure whippings which would destroy an ox or a horse. This is a very natural question, and but for the consciousness I feel of being supported in my statements by the universal testimony of old men-of-war's-men, I should hesitate to publish them. The *worst* species of this odious torture, however, remains to be described— flogging through the fleet.

　　This punishment is never inflicted without due trial and sentence by a court-martial, for belongs, the sentence of the court-martial condemning him is read, when, with the usual solemnities, a portion of the punishment is inflicted. In order that it shall not lose in severity by the slightest exhaustion in the arm of the executioner, a fresh boatswain's mate is called out at every dozen.

As the leading idea is to strike terror into the beholders, the greatest number of lashes is inflicted on board the culprit's own ship, in order to render him the more shocking spectacle to the crews of the other vessels.

The first infliction being concluded, the culprit's shirt is thrown over him; he is put into a boat—the Rogue's March being played meanwhile—and rowed to the next ship of the squadron. All hands of that ship are then called to man the rigging, and another portion of the punishment is inflicted by the boatswain's mates of that ship. The bloody shirt is again thrown over the seaman; and thus he is carried through the fleet or squadron till the whole sentence is inflicted.

In other cases, the launch—the largest of the boats—is rigged with a platform (like a headsman's scaffold), upon which halberds, something like those used in the English army, are erected. They consist of two stout poles, planted upright. Upon the platform stand a Lieutenant, a Surgeon, a Master-at-arms, and the executioners

some aggravated offence. After the offender is thus sentenced, and the day arrives appointed by his judges for its execution, the unhappy wretch is conducted into the ship's launch—a large boat—which has been previously rigged up with poles and grating, to which he is seized up; he is attended by the ship's surgeon, whose duty it is to decide when the power of nature's endurance has been taxed to its utmost. A boat from every ship in the fleet is also present, each carrying one or two officers and two marines fully armed. These boats are connected by tow lines to the launch.

These preparations made, the crew of the victim's ship are ordered to man the rigging, while the boatswain commences the tragedy. When he has administered one, two or three dozen lashes, according to the number of ships in the fleet, the prisoner's shirt is thrown over his gory back; the boatswain returns on board, the hands are piped down, the drummer beats a mournful melody, called the rogue's march, and the melancholy procession moves on. Arriving at the side of another ship, the brutal scene is repeated, until every crew in the fleet has witnessed it, and from one to three hundred lashes have lacerated the back of the broken-spirited tar to a bleeding pulp.

with their "cats." They are rowed through the fleet, stopping at each ship, till the whole sentence is inflicted, as before.

In some cases, the attending surgeon has professionally interfered before the last lash has been given, alleging that immediate death must ensue if the remainder should be administered without a respite. But instead of humanely remitting the remaining lashes, in a case like this, the man is generally consigned to his cot for ten or twelve days; and when the surgeon officially reports him capable of undergoing the rest of the sentence, it is forthwith inflicted. Shylock must have his pound of flesh.

Leech (p. 88)

. . . a court-martial sat upon him, and returned the shamefully disproportionate sentence of three hundred lashes through the fleet, and one year's imprisonment! Any of my shipmates who are living, will certify to the truth of this statement, brutal and improbable as it may appear.

Nor was that sentence a dead letter; the unhappy man endured it to the letter. Fifty were laid on alongside of the Macedonian, in conformity with a common practice of inflicting the most strokes at the first ship, in order that the gory back of the criminal may strike the more terror into the crews of the other ships. This poor tortured man bore two hundred and twenty, and was pronounced by the attending surgeon unfit to receive the rest. Galled, bruised, and agonized as he was, he besought him to suffer the infliction of the remaining eighty, that he might not be called to pass through the degrading scene again; but this prayer was denied! He was brought on board, and when his wounds were healed, the captain, Shylock-like, determined to have the whole pound of flesh, ordered him to receive the remainder!

Leech (p. 50)
. . . it resembles roasted
meat burnt nearly black before
a scorching fire; yet still the
lashes fall; the captain continues
merciless.

To say, that after being
flogged through the fleet, the
prisoner's back is sometimes
puffed up like a pillow; or to
say that in other cases it looks
as if burned black before a
roasting fire; or to say that you
may track him through the
squadron by the blood on the
bulwarks of every ship, would
only be saying what many seamen have seen.

Several weeks, sometimes
whole months, elapse before
the sailor is sufficiently recovered to resume his duties.
During the greater part of that
interval he lies in the sick-bay,
groaning out his days and
nights; and unless he has the
hide and constitution of a
rhinoceros, he never is the
man he was before, but, broken
and shattered to the marrow of
his bones, sinks into death before his time. Instances have
occurred where he has expired
the day after the punishment.
No wonder that the Englishman, Dr. Granville—himself
once a surgeon in the Navy—
declares, in his work on Russia,
that the barbarian "knout" itself is not a greater torture to
undergo than the Navy cat-
o'-nine-tails.

Leech (p. 62)
He is then placed under the
surgeon's care, to be fitted for
duty—*a ruined man*—broken in
spirit! all sense of self-respect
gone, forever gone! If he survive, it is only to be like his
own brave bark, when winds
and waves conspire to dash her
on the pitiless strand, a
wretched, hopeless wreck; a
living, walking shadow of his
former self. Shameful blot!
most foul and disgraceful stain
on the humanity of England!
How long before this worse
than barbarism will disappear
before the mild influences of
civilization and Christianity?

Chapter 89, which follows this frightening account of flogging, is on "The Social State in a Man-of-war." It attacks another naval abuse, the employment of marines on board ship, and the sadistic power often used by these marines against the sailors:

> Through all the endless ramifications of rank and station, in most men-of-war there runs a sinister vein of bitterness. . . . It were sickening to detail all the paltry irritablities, jealousies, and cabals, the spiteful detractions and animosities, that lurk far down, and cling to the very kelson of the ship. It is unmanning to think of.

Some of these evils, Melville sadly and angrily concludes, "are unavoidably generated through the operation of the Naval code; others are absolutely organic to a Navy establishment, and, like other organic evils, are incurable, except when they dissolve with the body they live in."

·

The third chapter, 90, in Melville's catalogue of man-of-war evils is the densest and most carefully stitched of all, "The Manning of Navies." Here Melville followed his sources closely, linking their facts with his charges, to indict crimping, impressment, the use of foreigners in the navy, and the nightmare of life in a man-of-war in general:

> "The gallows and the sea refuse nothing," is a very old sea saying; and, among all the wondrous prints of Hogarth, there is none remaining more true at the present day than that dramatic boat-scene, where after consorting with harlots and gambling on tomb-stones, the Idle Apprentice, with the villainous low forehead, is at last represented as being pushed off to sea, with a ship and a gallows in the distance. But Hogarth should have converted the ship's masts themselves into Tyburn-trees, and thus, with the ocean for a background, closed the career of his hero. It would then have had all the dramatic force of the opera of Don Juan, who, after running his impious courses, is swept from our sight in a tornado of devils.
> For the sea is the true Tophet and bottomless pit of many workers of iniquity; and, as the German mystics feign Gehennas within Gehennas, even so are men-of-war familiarly known among sailors as "Floating Hells." And as the sea, according to old Fuller, is the stable of brute monsters, gliding hither and thither in

unspeakable swarms, even so is it the home of many moral monsters, who fitly divide its empire with the snake, the shark, and the worm.

The opening sentence is directly from McNally (p. 57): "It is an old saying, 'that the gallows and the sea refuse nothing,' but in this I do not entirely concur. A ship is perhaps the best place in which an idle youth could be placed." The second sentence reminded Melville of Hogarth's Idle Apprentice, and McNally's further sentences, not quoted here, deal with foreigners in the American Navy, an abuse which Melville then treats in *his* chapter. The image of the sea with its "stable of brute monsters, gliding hither and thither" is made an emblem of moral experience, and foreshadows the great depth-monster scene two chapters later. It suggests perhaps the dramatized hells of the cutting-in of the whale and of the try-works in *Moby-Dick*. Melville has certainly found his artistic formula, his secret of power, which strains for full release— to be retarded for a few months, until the composition of *Moby-Dick*, but nonetheless exposed by these bits.

The close stitching and patching is evident as one studies the sources of the next two paragraphs, short though they are:

> Nor are sailors, and man-of-war's-men especially, at all blind to a true sense of these things. *"Purser rigged and parish damned,"* is the sailor saying in the American Navy, when the tyro first mounts the linen frock and blue jacket, aptly manufactured for him in a State Prison ashore.
> No wonder, that lured by some *crimp* into a service so galling, and, perhaps, persecuted by a vindictive lieutenant, some repentant sailors have actually jumped into the sea to escape from their fate, or set themselves adrift on the wide ocean on the gratings, without compass or rudder.

The information about the bluejackets is one tiny bit from a forty-line discussion in McNally (pp. 28–29) of the "clothing furnished by the government." The sentence Melville has adapted is "This clothing is, I believe, generally made up in some of the state prisons, and in the most wretched manner, so much so that every man-of-war's man has to sew them over before they are worn, or immediately afterwards."

Melville's discussion of *crimping* takes off from a line ten pages earlier (p. 18) in McNally: *"Crimping* is a word well understood by all persons acquainted with the navy" etc.; Melville, however, quickly sews to this a patch from Nicol, an anecdote about the desperation of some crimped men. Melville's single sentence, "persecuted by a vindictive lieutenant . . ." is really a radical reduction of sentences from John Nicol's narrative, a book to which Melville refers later in his chapter:

> . . . one circumstance . . . I cannot avoid mentioning, as a dreadful example of what man will dare, and the perils he will encounter, to free himself from a situation he dislikes. A man-of-war had been washing her gratings, when the India fleet hove in sight. They are washed by being lowered overboard, and allowed to float astern. Four or five men had slipped down upon them, cut them adrift, and were thus voluntarily committed to the vast Atlantic, without a bit of biscuit, or a drop of water, or any means of guiding the gratings they were floating upon, in the hope of being picked up by some vessel. They held out their arms to us, and supplicated, in the wildest manner, to be taken on board. The captain would not. The Nottingham was a fast sailing ship, and the first in the fleet. He said, "I will not; some of the stern ships will pick them up." While he spoke, these unfortunate and desponding fellow-creatures lessened to our view, while their cries rung in our ears. I hope some of the stern ships picked them up. Few things I have seen are more strongly impressed upon my memory, than the despairing looks and frantic gestures of these victims in quest of liberty. Next morning the frigate they had left came alongside of us, and inquired if we had seen them. The captain gave an indirect answer to their inquiries, as well he might [pp. 153–154].

Nicol's is a full passage, an episode; Melville's excerpt is but a passing detail. This is one of the rare instances of Melville's tossing away the dramatic elements of his source, but the reasons are perhaps obvious: first of all he did not need the story at this point—it was not *to* the point—and second, it would have taken considerable effort at any place to enlarge this story. We may idly wonder whether Ahab's inhuman refusal of aid to the captain of the *Rachel* is not somehow a variant of Nicol's anecdote.

Melville's detailed indictment of naval evils and abuses comes, logically, from McNally's *Evils and Abuses*. McNally wrote (p. 127) that "he is not ignorant of the law which declares that no slave or person liable to be sold as a slave, shall be borne on the books of any vessel of the U.S. navy, and he knows that there were slaves on board the Java, that their masters received their pay, and that slaves are employed in the navy yard as laborers, to the exclusion of white persons and free persons of color." Melville simplified this to read, "It may have been, in part, owing to this scarcity of man-of-war's-men, that not many years ago, black slaves were frequently to be found regularly enlisted with the crew of an American frigate, their masters receiving their pay." Melville's larger point, however, was that the man-of-war was itself a prison, and life therein slavery; and it is this metaphorical extension of fact which is not in the sources.

Melville scores another turn:

> . . . the free introduction of foreigners into any Navy can not be sufficiently deplored. During the period I lived in the Neversink, I was repeatedly struck by the lack of patriotism in many of my shipmates.[1]

On the sea the sailor's loyalties are landless:

> The only patriotism is born and nurtured in a stationary home, and upon an immovable hearth-stone; but the man-of-war's-man, though in his voyagings he weds the two Poles and brings both Indies together, yet, let him wander where he will, he carries his one only home along with him: that home is his hammock. *"Born under a gun, and educated on the bowsprit,"* according to a phrase of his own, the man-of-war's-man rolls round the world like a billow, ready to mix with any sea, or be sucked down to death in the Maelstrom of any war.

This is getting close to the spirit of Chapter 14 in *Moby-Dick* about the independent, far-ranging Nantucket whaleman. Rhythm and image hint of the greater paragraph to come, but this curious rhetorical flareup, vivid amid the details of impressment and recruitment of sailors, is another sign of the greater Melville, now finding himself. This, then, is a celebration rather than indictment, a celebration of the sailor as an uncommitted spirit, much as Melville later honored the Nantucket whaleman in *his* uncharted ocean home, hovered in sleep above herds of rushing whales.

The sailor-tailor who in the first chapter complained about his fumbling fingers, his awkward stitching, now sews his sources deftly, intricately, in the brighter second half of this chapter. The lighter tone, or the diminished outrage, is perhaps explainable by the close factual presentation of material drawn immediately, and little altered, from the

---

1. See McNally, pp. 44ff.

Edinburgh Review.[2] Much like the chain rods in fissionable materials, this collection of sheer facts dissipates Melville's anger, his attack, allowing him to discuss the happy sailor, to quote Dibdin songs (some encountered in *Scenes*). He even creates Landless, a sailor who has learned the secret of survival—don't cause trouble:

> This Landless was a favorite with the officers, among whom he went by the name of *"Happy Jack."* And it is just such Happy Jacks as Landless that most sea-officers profess to admire; a fellow without shame, without a soul, so dead to the least dignity of manhood that he could hardly be called a man. Whereas, a seaman who exhibits traits of moral sensitiveness, whose demeanor shows some dignity within; this is the man they, in many cases, instinctively dislike. The reason is, they feel such a man to be a continual reproach to them, as being mentally superior to their power. He has no business in a man-of-war; they do not want such men. To them there is an insolence in his manly freedom, contempt in his very carriage. He is unendurable, as an erect, lofty-minded African would be to some slave-driving planter.
>
> Let it not be supposed, however, that the remarks in this and the preceding chapter apply to *all* men-of-war. There are some vessels blessed with patriarchal, intellectual Captains, gentlemanly and brotherly officers, and docile and Christianized crews. The peculiar usages of such vessels insensibly soften the tyrannical rigor of the Articles of War; in them scourging is unknown. To sail in such ships is hardly to realize that you live under the martial law, or that the evils above mentioned can any where exist.

Landless is a patch from Leech (pp. 72–74):

> The crew were all delighted at his return, as he was quite popular among them for his lively disposition and his talents as a comic singer, which last gift is always highly prized in a man of war. So joyous were we all at his escape from punishment, that we insisted on his giving a concert, which went off well. Seated on a gun surrounded by scores of the men, he sung a variety of favorite songs, amid the plaudits and *encores* of his rough auditors.
>
> By such means as these, sailors contrive to keep up their spirits amidst constant causes of depression and misery. One is a good singer, another can spin tough forecastle yarns, while a third can crack a joke with sufficient point to call out roars of laughter. But

2. This is fully discussed in Thomas Philbrick, "Melville's 'Best Authorities,'" *Nineteenth-Century Fiction*, XV (September 1960), pp. 171–179.

for these interludes, life in a man of war, with severe officers, would be absolutely intolerable; mutiny or desertion would mark the voyages of every such ship. Hence, officers in general highly value your jolly, merry-making, don't-care sort of seamen. They know the effect of their influence in keeping away discontented thought from the minds of a ship's company. One of these official favorites paid our frigate a visit while we lay at Lisbon. We had just finished breakfast, when a number of our men were seen running in high glee towards the main hatchway. Wondering what was going forward, I watched their proceedings with a curious eye. The cause of their joy soon appeared in the person of a short, round-faced, merry-looking tar, who descended the hatchway amid cries of "Hurrah! here's happy Jack!" As soon as the jovial little man had set his foot on the berth deck, he began a specimen of his vocal powers. The voice of song was as triumphant on board the Macedonian, as it was in days of yore in the halls of Ossian. Every voice was hushed, all work was brought to a stand still, while the crew gathered round their favorite, in groups, to listen to his unequalled performances. Happy Jack succeeded, while his visit lasted, in communicating his own joyous feelings to our people, and they parted from him at night with deep regret.

Landless is also made up of another patch—from the British Seaman, who tells of his first experiences with the whim of Authority, and who is then advised by one of his messmates (p. 36):

"First and foremost," said he, "always touch your castor when an officer speaks to ye's; and I'll tell you what, matey, never give them any *law;* for, d'ye see, as how they dosn't like *sea lawyers* at all, devil a bit on 'em; but just, you know, take Jem Riley's advice, and shove through them as easy as you can; and if you do get your share of slops on a sarving-out day, don't be afraid of it, boy; it's only two or three 'O Lords!' and two or three 'O Gods!' and what then? it's all over at night: you gets a drop of grog from your messmates, and turns in pretty hearty; and next morning you're up the first pipe, and as brisk as a middy after passing."

Jem Riley's advice becomes that of Landless in Melville's very close imitation:

His advice to a young lad, who shipped with us at Valparaiso, embodies the pith and marrow of that philosophy which enables some man-of-war's-men to wax jolly in the service.

"Shippy!" said Landless, taking the pale lad by his neckerchief,

as if he had him by the halter; "Shippy, I've seen sarvice with Uncle Sam—I've sailed in many *Andrew Millers.* Now take my advice, and steer clear of all trouble. D'ye see, touch your tile whenever a swob (officer) speaks to you. And never mind how much they rope's-end you, keep your red-rag belayed; for you must know as how they don't fancy sea-lawyers; and when the sarving out of slops comes round, stand up to it stiffly; it's only an oh Lord! or two, and a few oh my Gods!—that's all. And what then? Why, you sleeps it off in a few nights, and turns out at last all ready for your grog."

When, further, we find that the four lines of one of Landless's favorite songs are taken from a song sung at the Aquatic Theatricals on board Mercier's "Old Ironsides" (pp. 123–124), and that once again we have the fusion of three sources just for one short section of *White-Jacket,* we have eloquent testimony to the force which Melville must have meant us to give to the tailoring trope with which he opened the book—with which, in the humorous way congenial to Melville, he tipped us off to the compositional method of now *White-Jacket,* and proleptically, of *Moby-Dick.*

·

With Chapter 91, Melville is almost ready to end his book: "Smoking-club in a Man-of-war, with Scenes on the Gun-deck drawing near Home." The lightened spirits of the previous chapter now inflate to gaiety. It is the interlude between the savage indignation against the social evils and abuses and the intensity of the private, personal passage of White-Jacket's fall from the yard-arm. The banter of the sailors as they gather to smoke—smoking is always an occasion for sheer sensuous enjoyment in Melville, for mindless gaiety—is highly pictorial, as he tells us: "Take a Flemish kitchen full of good fellows from Teniers; add a fire-side group from Wilkie; throw in a naval sketch from Cruik-shank; and then stick a short pipe into every mother's son's mouth, and you have the smoking scene at the galley of the Neversink." Verbal similarities, identical tone, show that most of Melville's chapter—or at least its narrative core—was straight from "The Galley Politicians" in Mercier's *Scenes* (pp. 130ff.), where the sailors gather: "Now on board a frigate, the precincts of the galley on the gun-deck (the only part of the ship wherein they are allowed to smoke,) is the regular news-room. . . ."

Chapter 91 closes with Melville's restatement of his central metaphor:

> But we have seen that a man-of-war is but this old-fashioned
> world of ours afloat, full of all manner of characters—full of
> strange contradictions; and though boasting some fine fellows here
> and there, yet, upon the whole, charged to the combings of her
> hatchways with the spirit of Belial and all unrighteousness.

Melville is ready to conclude his book, but such is the force and
complexity of his conclusion, such its fascinating revelations, that his
concluding episode demands of the pale-faced usher the closest attention, the most involved exposition. Here is revealed Melville's un-
equivocal display of the mastery which will soon create *Moby-Dick*.

·17·

The Fall
from the Yard-Arm

—What did you see?
                                        —I saw myself and God.
I saw the ruin in which godhead lives:
Shapeless and vast: the strewn wreck of the world:
Sadness unplumbed: misery without bound.
Wailing I heard, but also I heard joy.
Wreckage I saw, but also I saw flowers. . . .
And thus, I saw myself.

                                        —And this alone?

—And this alone awaits you when you dare
To that sheer verge where horror hangs, and tremble
Against the falling rock; and, looking down,

Search the dark kingdom. It is to self you come,—
And that is God. It is the seed of seeds:
Seed for disastrous and immortal worlds.

It is the answer that no question asked.
    Conrad Aiken, *Preludes for Memnon or Preludes to Attitude*

The fall (bababadalgharaghtakamminarronkonnbronntonnerronntu-
onnthunntrovarrhounawnskawntoohoohoordenenthurnuk!)
    James Joyce, *Finnegans Wake* (3.15–17)

It's something fails us. First we feel. Then we fall.
    James Joyce, *Finnegans Wake* (627.11)

•

CERTAINLY the most celebrated single section of *White-Jacket* is the scene in which the narrator, White-Jacket, falls from the yard-arm into the sea, saving himself from drowning only by desperately divesting himself of his self-made, encumbering jacket. This episode is the climax of the book, almost the close, for the chapter which follows is merely the moralistic rounding off of Melville's story.

First a sailor examined the passage. He was Thomas O. Selfridge, who wrote a splenetic attack on Melville's book,[1] assailing its accuracy in general as well as in detail. About the fall Selfridge was emphatic:

> The last adventure of the White Jacket is tenfold more pre-posterous than the one to which we have just alluded—He informs us, that one night, being on the Main topgallant yard in the act of reeving the studding-sail haliards [sic], the entanglement of his jacket caused him to be thrown into the sea a distance of more than one hundred feet; to which he adds an account of his sensations, rescue, &c—
> We will take leave to make a few comments on this most singu-lar accident—
> In the first place, the haliards [sic] in question, are always rove in a man of war, unless the yard is prepared to be sent down; secondly, how is it possible that a jacket, looped together, with

1. See Charles R. Anderson, "A Reply to Herman Melville's *White-Jacket* by Rear-Admiral Thomas O. Selfridge, Sr.," *American Literature*, VII (May 1935), pp. 123–144.

short skirts, could either by a light breese [sic], or by the motion
of the ship, be thrown over one's head?; thirdly, an object falling
from the position indicated, could hardly escape coming in contact
with the topsail yard, the channels, or the spare yard projecting
from the latter; & lastly, is it credible that a man, so exhausted &
prostrated, could have the power to resume his duties in ten
minutes—To any one who has the least knowledge of the sea, this
adventure must carry on its very fact its own refutation. . . .[2]

This is harsh, captious, and, as we shall see, irrelevant. Such close in-
spection, of course, exposed the inauthentic elements—*i.e.,* those not
actual Melville experiences—in *White-Jacket,* that plagued Melville all
his life. When he was an old man a young enthusiast named Peter Tofts
visited him, later reporting that Melville "had to be handled with care."
He found Melville reticent about his past; particularly "[he] was almost
offended when I inquired so curiously about his falling from the
maintopgallant yard of the frigate." Anderson's book in 1939 showed
why the reticence.

During the past half-century scholars and critics have subjected
Melville's dramatic passage to close scrutiny. Raymond Weaver discussed the adventure as Melville's own personal experience on board the
frigate *United States,* treating it as Melville's brush with death in the
late summer of 1844. In this literal-biographical view he was followed
by John Freeman, and Lewis Mumford. Unwittingly, however, these
men were writing largely from fiction, for ten years later Charles R.
Anderson demolished by documentary evidence the assumption that the
Fall was autobiography. This done, he then showed that Melville had
taken the episode from Nathaniel Ames's forgotten volume, *A Mariner's Sketches,* published in Providence in 1831.

Following Anderson, who discovered Melville's source but did not
analyze his adaptation of it, critics have commented appreciatively on
Melville's prose mastery in the Fall. The most detailed analysis of the
passage is that by Matthiessen in which he nicely demonstrates some of
Melville's special felicities, but, curiously, without really touching on the
relationship between Melville and his source, Ames.[3] Thus while many
have spoken appreciatively of the technical skill and the symbolical
power of the Fall, they have paid general rather than precise tribute and
have not analyzed the passage closely enough to uncover its true com-

2. *Ibid.,* pp. 130–131.
3. F. O. Matthiessen, *American Renaissance* (New York: Oxford University
Press, 1941), pp. 394–395.

plexity and its subtle operations. The oversight is natural. Critics have generally reserved their most careful dissections for passages from *Moby-Dick* and not for *White-Jacket,* a documentary which Melville for various reasons belittled. Nevertheless, in this minor work Melville concluded with a major passage, one which revealed a new and striking power prophetic of that displayed shortly with such fullness in *Moby-Dick.*

Before we move into Melville's creative adaptations let us read both Ames and Melville:

Melville (Chapter 92)   Ames (pp. 227–230)

Having reeved the line through all the inferior blocks, I went out with it to the end of the weather-top-gallant-yard-arm, and was in the act of leaning over and passing it through the suspended jewel-block there, when the ship gave a plunge in the sudden swells of the calm sea, and pitching me still further over the yard, threw the heavy skirts of my jacket right over my head, completely muffling me. Somehow I thought it was the sail that had flapped, and, under that impression, threw up my hands to drag it from my head, relying upon the sail itself to support me meanwhile. Just then the ship gave another sudden jerk, and, head foremost, I pitched from the yard. I knew where I was, from the rush of the air by my ears, but all else was a nightmare. A bloody film was before my eyes, through which, ghostlike, passed and repassed my father, mother, and sisters. An unutterable nausea oppressed me; I was consious of gasping;

I was going aloft and had got as far as the futtock shrouds, when a ratlin broke under my feet, and I fell backwards. My first sensation was surprise; I could not imagine where I was, but soon ascertained from the rushing of the air by my ears that I was falling and that headforemost.

Dr. Johnson says that the near approach of death wonderfully concentrates a man's ideas. I am sure it did mine for I never thought so *fast* before or since, as I did during the few seconds that I was tumbling. In an instant the recollection came into my head that one of the quarter deck guns (Mo. 20) was directly under me, and I should in all probability, be dashed to pieces upon it. I would have given the world to vent my feelings in cries, I tried to gather my limbs together, to contract my muscles, to shrink my body into as small there seemed no breath in my body. It was over one hundred feet that I fell—down, down, with lungs collapsed as in death. Ten thousand pounds of shot seemed tied to my head, as the irresistible law of gravitation dragged me, head foremost and straight as a die, toward the infallible centre of this terraqueous globe. All I had seen, and read, and heard, and all I had thought and felt in my life, seemed intensified in one fixed idea in my soul. But dense as this idea was, it was made up of atoms. Having fallen from the projecting yard-arm end, I was conscious of a collected satisfaction in feeling, that I should not be dashed on the deck, but would sink into the speechless profound of the sea.

With the bloody, blind film before my eyes, there was a still stranger hum in my head, as if a hornet were there; and I thought to myself, Great God! this is death! Yet these thoughts were unmixed with alarm. Like frost-work that flashes and shifts its scared hues in the sun, all my braided, blended emotions were in themselves icy cold and calm.

So protracted did my fall seem, that I can even now recall the feeling of wondering how much longer it would be, ere all was over and I struck. Time seemed to stand still, and all the worlds seemed poised on their poles, as I fell, soul-becalmed, through the eddying

a compass as possible, and with unspeakable terror awaited the 'death shock.'

All this while there was a blood red light before my eyes, through which a thousand horrible forms were constantly gliding. Then I thought of home, and the forms of all that I hold dear on earth, and many others, 'strangers of distinction,' beside, floated before me. Then the recollection of the infernal gun and the consequent smash across the breech of it, put all these phantoms to flight, and I felt that peculiar sickness and distress at the stomach which it is said one experiences when on the point of undergoing a sudden and violent and painful death, and I thought to myself, 'surely it must be almost time for the shock.'

A shock I certainly did receive, and that no very gentle one across the back of the head, neck and left shoulder, and in an instant all was dark and still. "It is all over," thought I, "this is the state between death and resurrection." I really thought I had passed the first

whirl and swirl of the Maelstrom air.

At first, as I have said, I
must have been precipitated
head foremost; but I was conscious, at length, of a swift,
flinging motion of my limbs,
which involuntarily threw themselves out, so that at last I must
have fallen in a heap. This is
more likely, from the circumstance, that when I struck the
sea, I felt as if some one had
smote me slantingly across the
shoulder and along part of my
right side.

As I gushed into the sea, a
thunder-boom sounded in my
ear; my soul seemed flying
from my mouth. The feeling of
death flooded over me with the
billows. The blow from the sea
must have turned me, so that I
sank almost feet foremost
through a soft, seething, foamy
lull. Some current seemed
hurrying me away; in a trance
I yielded, and sank deeper down
with a glide. Purple and pathless was the deep calm now
around me, flecked by summer
lightnings in an azure afar. The
horrible nausea was gone; the
bloody, blind film turned a
pale green; I wondered whether
I was yet dead, or still dying.
But of a sudden some fashionless form brushed my side—
some inert, coiled fish of the
sea; the thrill of being alive
again tingled in my nerves, and
the strong shunning of death
shocked me through.

For one instant an agonizing

and awaited with increased terror for the second, when to my
utter dismay, I felt myself
falling a second time, but the
sensation was different; the
blow that I had received turned
me, and I was descending feet
foremost.

But no words can express my
delight, my ecstasy, at finding
myself *overboard,* instead of on
the gun. I kept going down,
down, till it appeared to me
that the seven fathoms and a
half, (the depth of water at our
anchorage,) had more than
doubled since we let go our
anchor.

revulsion came over me as I found myself utterly sinking. Next moment the force of my fall was expended; and there I hung, vibrating in the mid-deep. What wild sounds then rang in my ear! One was a soft moaning, as of low waves on the beach; the other wild and heartlessly jubilant, as of the sea in the height of a tempest. Oh soul! thou then heardest life and death: as he who stands upon the Corinthian shore hears both the Ionian and Aegean waves. The life-and-death poise soon passed; and then I found myself slowly ascending, and caught a dim glimmering of light.

Quicker and quicker I mounted; till at last I bounded up like a buoy, and my whole head was bathed in the blessed air.

I had fallen in a line with the main-mast; I now found myself nearly abreast of the mizzen-mast, the frigate slowly gliding by like a black world in the water. Her vast hull loomed out of the night, showing hundreds of seamen in the hammock-nettings, some tossing over ropes. . . . I essayed to swim toward the ship; but instantly I was conscious of a feeling like being pinioned in a featherbed, and, moving my hands, felt my jacket puffed out above my tight girdle with water. I strove to tear it off; but it was looped together here

After a while I became stationary and soon began slowly to ascend. When I looked up, I saw high, very high above me, a dim, greenish light, which became brighter

and brighter till at last I bounded on the surface like a cork.

I immediately swam to the accommodation ladder and went on board. My shoulder and neck were much bruised by striking against a spare main-topsail yard, that was stowed over the starboard quarter, and my head felt 'sort o' queer,' from sundry thumps and knocks and thumps it had received in the fall, which however were mere 'cakes and gingerbread.'

It may seem incredible, impossible, that I should be able to recollect my feelings after and there, and the strings were not then to be sundered by hand. I whipped out my knife, that was tucked at my belt, and ripped my jacket straight up and down, as if I were ripping open myself. With a violent struggle I then burst out of it, and was free. Heavily soaked, it slowly sank before my eyes.

so long a time had elapsed, but my sensations are as fresh in my memory as they were at the moment when I was satisfactorily demonstrating, in my own unlucky person, the principles of gravitation.

I have generally been peculiarly fortunate in my tumbles, most usually alighting upon my head. . . .

As Matthiessen stated, one aspect of Melville's mastery in the Fall passage was in his almost overpowering evocation of the sensations of the experience. It would be crude to say that Melville came to this on cue, but it is interesting to notice the words with which Ames swung into *his* narration:

I have often read different descriptions of one's sensations when drowning, hanging, starving, being buried alive, &c. I never had nor do I wish to have the comfort of being resuscitated from drowning though I have no doubt it can be done; but coming into this world once is quite enough for me, for if I was once fairly out of it, I should not thank any one for dragging me back into it by the ears, as Hercules did Cerberus of old, an experiment that is said to have made the dog extremely sick.

As for hanging, or as sailors call it, 'taking a walk up Ladder lane, and down Hemp street,' I have no inclination to terminate my sublunary griefs that way, whatever might be the decision of jury in this case, and I am too much of a *bon vivant* to relish any approximation towards starving to death.

One writer has favored us with his sensations while buried under the fallen roof of a theatre. . . .

Having had, while in the Pacific, the pleasure of performing an aerial excursion, which commenced at the main cat-hairpins of the frigate United States and terminated near the bottom of Callao Bay, I will take the liberty to give a history of my own voyage, and my reflections during it, for the benefit of future tumblers.

Ames was writing, he implies, at a time when "sensations" in literature were being stressed—partly in the wake, or the febrile continuation, of the Gothic tradition—but he was a few years too early to have read the advice which, in Edgar Poe's comic sketch, "How to Write a Blackwood Article," Mr. B[lackwood] had given to the gushing featherbrain calling herself Miss Psyche Zenobia. Citing as models a number of stories "of the sensation stamp" which he had published in his magazine, Mr. B. counseled his pupil:

> "Sensations are the great things after all. Should you ever be drowned, or hung, be sure to make a note of your sensations—they will be worth to you ten guineas a sheet. If you wish to write forcibly, Miss Zenobia, pay minute attention to the sensations."

Immediacy was above all the prime requirement:

> "The first thing requisite is to get yourself into such a scrape as no one got into before. The oven, for instance,—that was a good hit. But if you have no oven, or big bell, at hand, and if you cannot conveniently tumble out of a balloon, or be swallowed up in an earthquake, or get stuck fast in a chimney, you will have to be contented with simply imagining some similar misadventure. I should prefer, however, that you have the actual fact to bear you out. Nothing so well assists the fancy, as an experimental knowledge of the matter in hand."

The way in which Miss Psyche Zenobia carries through with Mr. B.'s advice affords some of the funniest bits in a very unfunny writer—Poe— who is here of course being ironic about the Gothic mode, which he himself had calculatingly adopted early in his prose writing, and in which he both lost himself and, later, found himself.

Melville had read Ames, and it is quite possible that he had read Poe's skit, since the line in *Moby-Dick* (Chapter 92), "How to cure such a dyspepsia [in the whale] it were hard to say, unless by administering three or four boat loads of Brandreth's pills, and then running out of harm's way, as laborers do blasting rocks," was probably suggested to Melville by one of Mr. B.'s suggestions: "Take a dose of Brandreth's pills, and then give us your sensations."

Reading Ames and Poe on sensations may have amused Melville and even may have added a greater zest to his writing as he saw himself following their suggestions. However this may be, two questions arise: Why did Melville introduce White Jacket's dramatic "fictional" fall from the mast-head in a book ostensibly documentary in nature? And why adapt an episode from the unknown Ames?

By Chapter 92 of *White-Jacket*, Melville was nearing the end of his story, with the imminent arrival of the *Neversink* at her home port. He had described in dense detail life in a man-of-war. Now, nearing the end, Melville needed a strong note, something more dramatic than the mere paying-off of the men in harbor. Even a documentary should end with some sort of climax rather than relying on mere accumulation to permit "Finis" to be written. The harmless but aimless trailing away of *Redburn* would not be repeated in this book, which might somehow be improved, strengthened—rather with a touch of bravura, perhaps than with a sober cessation. Melville, then, sought a strong note to focus attention again, emphatically and yet naturally, on the hero-narrator forgotten during the comical-heroical-tragical chapters on Ushant and the Mutiny of the Beards.

Poe's Miss Zenobia was even willing to hang herself in her garters for the sake of verisimilitude. Melville, on the other hand, had no need to fall, nor to have fallen, from an actual yard-arm in order to describe such a scene. Nathaniel Ames had already fallen and had described the fall, as he said, "for the benefit of future tumblers." Melville had come across this sensational (in Poe's sense) passage when seeking an effective way of concluding his own book—and more particularly, coping with the problem of getting rid of White-Jacket's white jacket. The jacket had supplied the title of the book; it had been the burden of the entire first chapter; and it had appeared frequently enough and dramatically enough in some of the book's high moments so that the elementary demands of "unity, coherence, and emphasis" called for its farewell appearance to the reader.

And how could this best be done? Reality, or direct experience, gave no help here ("I should prefer, however, that you have the actual fact to bear you out," said Mr. B. to Psyche Zenobia), for his own white jacket, the "veritable garment," had been ignominiously and unconsiderately dropped into the Charles River at the end of the voyage—at least so Melville told Dana. Such an end was too prosaic for the literary end of a garment which had been a leading property—almost, indeed, a character—in the book. An important thread of the story had, indeed, been White-Jacket *versus* his white jacket, and up to this point the jacket had won, clinging to its owner "like the hair-shirt of Nessus." Such a grotesque garment could not go out quietly; the villain must be defeated with a flourish and not allowed to sneak off unpunished, or worse, unnoticed. Previously the jacket had socially injured him and almost physically killed him, in events toward which the narrator had adopted a comic tone. Now in terminating the career of the jacket, Melville treats it as near-calamity. Reading Nathaniel Ames's *A Mariner's Sketches*, Melville's sensitive and searching attention found the striking episode, full of "sensations," wherein he could, and would, concentrate all his cunning in the writing craft, his deepened wisdom of the world, and his sense of symbolic significance.

•

. . . still—they fall from the mast-head.

Virginia Woolf, *Orlando*

Les ailes nous manquent, mais nous avons toujours assez de force pour tomber.

Paul Claudel, *Positions et Propositions*

Ripeness is all. Melville came upon Ames's vigorous episode in a state of creative readiness, alert to seize its narrative structure, imaginative to enhance its meaning. Zenobia's absurdity aside, even though Melville had never himself fallen from the mast-head of the *United States*—or any other ship—he had been a sailor, catlike and skillful in the main-top, and he had frequently confronted the danger known to Ames. Surely the description of Redburn's first venture into the rigging is a pure instance of the overflow of powerful emotion recollected in tranquillity:

> For a few moments I stood awe-stricken and mute. I could not see far out upon the ocean, owing to the darkness of the night; and from my lofty perch, the sea looked like a great, black gulf, hemmed in, all round, by beetling black cliffs. I seemed all alone; treading the midnight clouds; and every second, expected to find myself falling—falling—falling, as I have felt when the nightmare has been on me.
> I could but just perceive the ship below me, like a long narrow plank in the water; and it did not seem to belong at all to the yard, over which I was hanging. A gull, or some sort of sea-fowl, was flying round the truck over my head, within a few yards of my face; and it almost frightened me to hear it; it seemed so much like a spirit, at such a lofty and solitary height.
> Though there was a pretty smooth sea, and little wind; yet, at this extreme elevation, the ship's motion was very great; so that when the ship rolled one way, I felt something as a fly must feel, walking the ceiling; and when it rolled the other way, I felt as if I was hanging along a slanting pine-tree.

The basis of such a passage, one feels, is actual and not only imaginative experience. Did ever the novice sailor on his first climb into the rigging *not* experience the *frisson* of terror, not feel directly and forcefully the imminence of death? The first climb to the mast-head was for most sailors a major test of manhood; in *Redburn,* Melville made that first climb a critical test of courage, and Redburn's triumphant accomplishment is underlined by the subsequent failure of his friend Harry Bolton. In here describing such an experience as Redburn's, and his own, Melville employed some of his most significant, recurrent images: the sea-hawk, darkness, height, fall, and above all, the salt sea. In *White-Jacket,* encouraged by Ames's passage,[4] Melville took the peril only envisioned by young Redburn—"falling—falling—falling"—and dramatized it, transforming a boyhood experience of fear into a trope of the deepest and most far-ranging significance.

●

> But he sleeps on the top of his mast
> with his eyes closed tight.
> The gull inquired into his dream,
> which was, "I must not fall.
> The spangled sea below wants me to fall.
> It is hard as diamonds; it wants to destroy us all."
> Elizabeth Bishop, "The Unbeliever"

Melville's alterations of Ames were, in the actual fall part, verbally slight and artistically immense, the simple and slight touches whereby the ordinary becomes extraordinary. The difference, then, between what

---

4. As has been stated previously, Dana's *Two Years Before the Mast* was one of Melville's sources for parts of *White-Jacket,* and had possibly led him to Ames's book. It is interesting to read, too, Dana's opening paragraph in "Nearing Home," Chapter 34, which has echoes in Melville's Fall passage: "The same day I met with one of those narrow escapes which are so often happening in a sailor's life. I had been aloft nearly all the afternoon, at work, standing for as much as an hour on the foretopgallant yard, which was hoisted up, and hung only by the tie; when, having got through my work, I balled up my yarns, took my serving-board in my hand, laid hold deliberately of the topgallant rigging, took one foot from the yard, and was just lifting the other, when the tie parted, and down the yard fell. I was safe, by my hold upon the rigging, but it made my heart beat quick. Had the tie parted one instant sooner, or had I stood an instant longer on the yard, I should inevitably have been thrown violently from the height of ninety or a hundred feet, overboard; or, what is worse, upon the deck."

Ames wrote and Melville composed are decisive but delicate; they are something immediately felt, but the exact determination or tracing of those differences requires close attention.

One of these small but significant differences was the way in which Melville brought the scene closer to the reader as an event re-lived instead of merely re-told. Ames intruded his authorial consciousness, his awareness of writing "sensations." We seem to hear him muse, "I had an unusual experience; now how do I go about telling it?" This is to say that Ames was overly aware of his compositional tradition when he wrote, "I have often read different descriptions of one's sensations when drowning, hanging, starving, being buried alive . . ." so that he is writing to fill out the record of such rare experiences as Mr. B. advised Psyche Zenobia to record. This awareness ("If this don't fetch 'em, then I don't know—Providence!") plus a touch of jocularity, subtly dims the immediacy of the events. Ames thus mutes the emotional immediacy of his own dramatic experience. Melville recast Ames's words into a more intense physical and emotional event. The result is paradoxical. Ames could really say, "I was the man, I suffered, I was there," but *we* are less there in his version than we are in Melville's; Ames implies a distance which softens the searing experience for us. By erasing Ames's element of conscious composition, by deleting the author *as artisan,* Melville sharpened the physical and psychic impact of events, making them more truly a crisis on a physical and a spiritual level, confronting death and nothingness and rebirth with a felt force which makes Ames merely anecdotal.

A second significant alteration reinforces the argument that slightness is all. The pattern of a fall is basic, of a gravitational simplicity, but, in his rewriting of Ames, Melville needed one small bit to sharpen the visual quality, the *cleanness,* of the plunge. Ames wrote that when he fell from the futtock shrouds his descent had been momentarily arrested by his hitting a "spare maintop-sail yard." This Melville erased; White Jacket, falling from a greater height, plummets directly "straight as a die toward the infallible center of this terraqueous globe." So described, the Fall has a Luciferian largeness, the beauty of a knife-like dive rather than the ungainly puppet sprawl and splash described by Ames. Furthermore, Melville intensified the effect by the polysyllabic lilt of his language, phrases like "infallible center" and "terraqueous globe" imparting a new speed to the narration. Melville had already used *terraqueous* in *Mardi,* and he employed it twice in *White-Jacket* and yet again in the "Nantucket" chapter of *Moby-Dick.* It was a word he had appropriated from Carlyle's *Sartor Resartus,* from which he had taken so much else. *Terraqueous* was a happy variant of Homer's polyphloisbois, or of Shakespeare's "multitudinous seas," polysyllables favored for their suggestion in sound of the many-waved seas they connote—an onomato-poetic device used by many subsequent poets among them Whitman: "undulating waves, liquid, uneven, emulous waves"; Rossetti: "Like multiform circumfluence manifold / Of night's flood-tide"; or, in our time, Pound: "phantasmal sea-surge"; Stevens: "cadaverous undula-tions," "oracular rockings," "visible, voluble delugings"; Aiken: "the worldlong fruitfulness of assuaging sea"; or, perhaps most striking of all, James Joyce's "snot-green, scrotum-tightening sea."

A third detail argues the importance of the slight, but right, touch. Ames had written, in two places, that his chief fear during the crisis was of falling onto the quarter-deck guns. Melville reduced this to a single eloquent phrase—"conscious of a collected satisfaction in feeling that I should not be dashed upon the deck but would sink into the speechless profound of the sea"—achieving a new effect from the emphatic metrical motion of "collected satisfaction" and "speechless profound of the sea."

Among Melville's finest changes, however, was his handling of time. In Ames we are aware of seconds, but in Melville we are overwhelmed by eternities or even of time's very suspension. Ames's fall is protracted for the merest of moments through his striking the yard-arm, but that pause holds us in a closed, clock-time world; White-Jacket's plunge assumes temporal and spatial infinity: "Time seemed to stand still, and all the worlds seemed poised on their poles, as I fell, soul-becalmed, through the eddying whirl and swirl of the Maelstrom air." The repeti-tions and alliterations of the first two clauses, the assonance and onomatopaeia of "the eddying whirl and swirl of the Maelstrom air" and the contrast of the latter phrase with "soul-becalmed" are all of course part of the fine effect, but just as forceful—even if more ineffable —is Melville's sense of those infinite spaces which so terrified Pascal, or of those majestic constellations which awed Meredith's Lucifer when he beheld the stars, "rank on rank / The army of unalterable law."

These changes so far listed are considerable, but by far the most significant alteration by Melville of Ames was the structural one. As we glance at the two passages in parallel columns the difference, so long unnoticed, becomes obvious. Melville's passage is almost three times as long as Ames. We notice further that Melville really parallels Ames in the fall section alone, almost entirely abandoning Ames in the subse-quent scenes of submersion and emergence. What was simply a one-act anecdote in *A Mariner's Sketches*—its subject being what it is like to fall from a yard-arm into the ocean and to have "sensations"—becomes through Melville's elaboration a thumbnail three-act drama of Fall, Submersion, and Salvation. In Ames the Submersion is a mere detail passed over in the fewest words possible, an appendage, almost, required by narrative continuity. Ames's "sensations" had petered out. In Melville, on the other hand, the Submersion and the Salvation became the climax of the story to which the Fall had been the necessary prelude. On the un-Amesian sections of his story Melville now exercised his newly operative powers of poetic language and evocative symbolism.[5]

Melville abandoned Ames at this point—abandoned because there was little for him to use, and because he had meanwhile discovered new uses for such an adventure and had, characteristically, found other sources to supply him with help.

Ames said rapidly, directly:

> I kept going down, down, till it appeared to me that the seven fathoms and a half (the depth of the water at our anchorage,) had more than doubled since we let go our anchor.
> After a while I became stationary and soon began slowly to ascend. When I looked up, I saw high, very high above me, a dim greenish light, which became brighter and brighter till at last I bounced on the surface like a cork.

Melville's sinking is radically different from Ames, from whose words Melville takes off into profounder regions of fact and symbol.

> As I gushed into the sea, a thunder-boom sounded in my ear; my soul seemed flying from my mouth. The feeling of death flooded over me with the billows. The blow from the sea must have turned me, so that I sank almost feet foremost through a soft, seething, foamy lull. Some current seemed hurrying me away; in a trance I yielded, and sank deeper down with a glide. Purple and

5. Perry Miller, *The Raven and the Whale* (New York: Harcourt, Brace, 1956), pp. 55–56, has suggested that in Charles F. Brigg's popular novel, *The Adventures of Harry Franco* (New York: F. Saunders, 1839), "wonderfully occur anticipations of *White-Jacket*. There is a diatribe against the tyranny of the quarter-deck and against flogging. Franco escapes a whipping by climbing into the rigging; the fire of the marines cuts the cords, and he too falls from the yard-arm: 'The rush of the air as I fell, the many-voiced shriek of the crew, and the roar of the water as I sank beneath its surface, all sound in my ears even now while I write; and often since have I started from a deep sleep, with the same confusion of noises ringing in my brain.' "

pathless was the deep calm now around me, flecked by summer lightnings in an azure afar. The horrible nausea was gone; the bloody, blind film turned a pale green; I wondered whether I was yet dead, or still dying. But of a sudden some fashionless form brushed my side—some inert, coiled fish of the sea; the thrill of being alive again tingled in my nerves, and the strong shunning of death shocked me through.

For one instant an agonizing revulsion came over me as I found myself utterly sinking. Next moment the force of my fall was expended; and there I hung, vibrating in the mid-deep. What wild sounds then rang in my ear! One was a soft moaning, as of low waves on the beach; the other wild and heartlessly jubilant, as of the sea in the height of a tempest. Oh soul! thou then heardest life and death: as he who stands upon the Corinthian shore hears both the Ionian and Aegean waves. The life-and-death poise soon passed; and then I found myself slowly ascending, and caught a dim glimmering of light.

Quicker and quicker I mounted; till at last I bounded up like a buoy, and my whole head was bathed in the blessed air.

Melville's additions (not alterations) are of course everything, but perhaps they may be summed up, in the immersion scene, in words of Conrad Aiken:

The deep void swarming with wings and sound of wings,
The winnowing of chaos, the aliveness
Of depth and depth and depth dedicated to death.

The second detail refined by Melville from Ames was his hero's return from the depths—what, after *Moby-Dick,* he would have inevitably called the "breaching" of White-Jacket. Ames wrote that as he emerged from the depths of the sea he "bounced on the surface like a cork."[6] Melville appropriated Ames's kinesthetic image, altering it to read "bounded up like a buoy, and my whole head was bathed in the blessed air," so that the mechanical jerkiness of Ames's image is given a stronger, a tidal, rhythm by the buoy image. Melville also retuned the rhythm, throwing the accent on "up," and stressing the beat of the line by the emphatic "b" alliteration. Most important, perhaps, Melville weighted the passage, almost exalting it, with the adjective "blessed," by which he suggested not only the sheer physical relief which one feels

6. Recall a similar appropriateness of metaphor, when Rimbaud in *Le Bateau Ivre* wrote: "Plus léger qu'un bouchon j'ai dansé sur les flots."

on release from suffocation—indeed, it is every baby's first worldly experience—but also the haunting echo of the Ancient Mariner's "blessed release" from the burden of the albatross. Melville, far beyond Ames, jubilantly affirms the sheer goodness of being alive, coiled monsters though there be nearby.

•

You plunge poor soul,
From time's colossal brink into that chasm
Of change and limbo and immortal flux,
And bring up only, in your blood-stained hands,
One grain of sand that sparkles. Plunge again,
Poor diver, among weeds and death! and bring
The pearl of brightness up.
      Conrad Aiken, *Preludes for Memnon or Preludes to Attitude*

Sink deep or touch not the Cartesian spring!
      James Joyce, *Finnegans Wake* (301.24–25)

In general, however, the influence of Ames is scarcely evident in the immersion scene in *White-Jacket*. Ames's three bare sentences cannot explain Melville's three rich paragraphs. Did, then, Melville proceed solely on his own inspiration or did he find some author to help him continue? Using a crude, empirical logic derived from the many exposés by scholars of Melville's borrowing habits, we may assume that on abandoning Ames, who had now so little to give, Melville turned to another more fruitful source—or sources—from which to filch fine phrases or to gain suggestions. Or, to put it more politely, Melville's genius was now inspired by reading in some other book(s). Like Kepler predicting the appearance of Uranus, the sub-sub-librarian finds to his delight that his expectation and prediction are fulfilled as the new author, Johann Christoph Friedrich von Schiller, in *Poems and Ballads* as translated by Bulwer-Lytton (Leipzig, 1844), swims into his ken.

The influence of Schiller on Melville through this little volume of Bulwer-Lytton's translations has gone unnoticed save for the recognition that his poem "The Veiled Image at Sais"[7] furnished matter for the close of Chapter 76 of *Moby-Dick*. Just how far that influence went only close study will be able to determine, but Schiller touches from *Poems and*

7. *The Trying-Out of Moby-Dick*, p. 261.

Ballads may be easily noted in *Pierre* (1853), *Clarel* (1875), and *Timoleon* (1888).

However this may be, the part of *Poems and Ballads* which most deeply affected Melville was the poem "The Diver." This was natural, of course, to an author whose favorite verb was "to dive," who told Duyckinck that "I love all men who dive," and who even forgave the transcendentalisms of Ralph Waldo Emerson because he was at least a "thought-diver." The central meaning of Schiller's "The Diver," which a footnote describes as "the darkly hinted moral, not to stretch too far the mercy of heaven," is directly relevant to Ahab's mad hunt for the white whale.

"The Diver" is a ballad in three main scenes. It tells of a king who, hurling a golden cup into a whirlpool, offers a ring to the knight who will successfully recover it. A handsome youth accepts the perilous challenge. To the surprise of all he is successful. The King then hurls the goblet into the whirlpool a second time, now promising the hand of his daughter as a reward. The youth accepts this second challenge, plunges boldly into the maelstrom and disappears, forever.

The middle section of this three-scene ballad, in which the Knight tells of his first dive, of swimming in the depths and finding the golden cup, is the scene which significantly aided Melville.

> And he breathèd deep, and he breathèd long,
> And he greeted the heavenly delight of the day.
> They gaze on each other—they shout, as they throng—
> "He lives—lo the ocean has render'd its prey!
> And safe from the whirlpool and free from the grave,
> Comes back to the daylight the soul of the brave!"

> . . .

> And thus spake the Diver—"Long life to the king!

> "Happy they whom the rose-hues of daylight rejoice,
> The air and the sky that to mortals are given!
> May the horror below never more find a voice—
> Nor Man stretch too far the wide mercy of Heaven!
> Never more—never more may he lift from the sight
> The veil which is woven with Terror and Night!

> "Quick-brightening like lightning—it tore me along,
> Down, down, till the gush of a torrent, at play
> In the rocks of its wilderness, caught me—and strong

As the wings of an eagle, it whirl'd me away.
Vain, vain was my struggle—the circle had won me,
Round and round in its dance, the wild element spun me.

"And I call'd on my God, and my God heard my prayer
In the strength of my need, in the gasp of my breath—
And show'd me a crag that rose up the lair,
And I clung to it, nimbly—and baffled the death!
And, safe in the perils around me, behold
On the spikes of the coral the goblet of gold.

"Below, at the foot of that precipice drear,
Spread the gloomy, and purple, and pathless Obscure!
A silence of Horror that slept on the ear,
That the eye more appall'd might the Horror endure!
Salamander—snake—dragon—vast reptiles that dwell
In the deep—coil'd about the grim jaws of their hell.

"Dark-crawl'd—glided dark the unspeakable swarms,
Clump'd together in masses, misshapen and vast—
Here clung and here bristled the fashionless forms—
Here the dark-moving bulk of the Hammer-fish pass'd—
And with teeth grinning white, and a menacing motion,
Went the terrible Shark—the Hyeana of Ocean.

"There I hung, and the awe gather'd icily o'er me,
So far from the earth, where man's help there was none!
The One Human Thing, with the Goblins before me—
Alone—in a loneness so ghastly—ALONE!
Fathom-deep from man's eye in the speechless profound,
With the death of the Main and the Monsters around. . . ."[8]

It will be seen that Melville raided Schiller and Lytton—not for ideas, for structure, or for character—he raided for words. It is part of a poet's tactic to enrich himself from others' words. Schiller's language as rendered by Bulwer-Lytton is far above that of Ames; the resonant phrases which for many years now have been admired by Melville's readers as their author's own coining now prove to have been another's: "the wild elements," "the purple and pathless Obscure," "glided," "the fashionless forms," "the speechless profound," and "the thunder-

8. *The Poems and Ballads of Schiller,* translated by Sir Edward Bulwer-Lytton (Leipzig: Bernhard Tauchnitz, 1844), pp. 4–5.

boom" (from an earlier stanza)—these extensive, emphatic appropria-
tions supply much of the poetic power of the account in *White-Jacket,*
especially in the immersion scene.

So open, so barefaced is the character of Melville's theft that one must
wonder whether he did not feel a twinge of guilt. Perhaps he did, but it
can be argued that he erased that guilt by the strategic placement of his
borrowed passages, so giving each a new and different significance. The
difference between the two passages as a whole shows Melville's improvement of his source. Both are poetry, to be sure, although Melville's
is not regularly metered. Melville's lines are more evocative than the
cantering, overdecorated romanticisms of Schiller. Melville's narrative is
cleaner, tenser, more concentrated on a fundamental experience—sheer
survival—than that of Schiller's brave Knight, who is, after all, merely
playing a risky game for high stakes. As he did to Ames, so to Schiller/
Lytton Melville added majesty and infinitude, now transcending mere
fright and terror by his evocation of lovely and soothing death.

Melville borrowed from Schiller/Lytton for picturesque purposes,
but he made alterations to achieve a new intensity. Consider, for instance, such a slight, important change as his treatment of "the fashionless forms." Schiller, it will be noted, specifically names several of the
monsters—"Salamander—snake—dragon—vast reptiles," among others
—whereas in *White-Jacket* there is but one "fashionless form," one
"coil'd fish," used not as setting but as a significant actor, its species
properly unmentioned. Melville could not use the names of Schiller's
monsters; the salamander and the dragon were, after all, mythological
baggage inappropriate to a documentary travel book realistic in details
and atmosphere. Even had Melville wanted to use the romantic creatures
of "The Diver," he could not have done so without violating the very
tone of his book.

By the omission of the monsters' names and by their reduction to but
one fashionless form Melville did more than modify Schiller's Gothic
atmosphere. He heightened the psychological effect of menace and
terror, too much insisted on, overstated, by Schiller. The very obliquity
of Melville's monster, unseen as well as unnamed, frightens as it shocks
White-Jacket, as any swimmer may appreciate who has been unex-
pectedly brushed by a fish. Then, even the meanest minnow may seem a
menacing shark; it is a moment when one does not greet the unseen with
a cheer, nor did White-Jacket. Unnamed because unseen, the "coil'd
fish" of *White-Jacket* is far more frightening, shocking, than the
salamander, snake, and dragon which glided by Schiller's groping diver.

If Melville's use of the "coil'd fish" is brief here, it is powerful. That power comes from a long evolution of the "fashionless form" or "coil'd fish" image. It was an image developed over several years by an improving artist, an image now in *White-Jacket* receiving the polish of excellence, even greatness, which it is to display, in myriad ways, in *Moby-Dick*. The story of that image, the fashionless form which now brushes White-Jacket, may be seen in the history of its brushes with Melville's mind.

· 18 ·

The Last
of the Jacket

. . . schooled by the inhuman sea.

Clarel, IV, xiii, 7

WE have seen that Nathaniel Ames's influence on the entire Fall passage in *White-Jacket* had been primarily confined to the very fall, Ames's "tumble," itself. We have seen further that Schiller's influence was confined largely to verbal felicities, with perhaps the further suggestions of romantic tone. What literary source, then, we may logically ask, would have influenced Melville in the breaching of White-Jacket, wherein he rids himself of his jacket and saves himself?

A source may be suspected and a source has been found—found in as unlikely and obscure a place as was Ames's *A Mariner's Sketches*. Melville's theft for the third act of his miniature drama was from *Life on Board a Man-of-War, Including a Full Account of the Battle of Navarino,* by A British Seaman (Glasgow, 1829), the out-of-the-way little volume which had already served him so well in furnishing verisimilitude for Jack Chase's spirited account of his Navarino exploits. Parallel passages will show Melville's debt and his differences.

Melville (Chapter 92)

I had fallen in a line with the main-mast; I now found myself nearly abreast of the mizzen-mast, the frigate slowly gliding by like a black world in the water. Her vast hull loomed out of the night, showing hundreds of seamen in the hammock-nettings, some tossing over ropes, others madly flinging overboard the hammocks; but I was too far out from them immediately to reach what they threw. I essayed to swim toward the ship; but instantly I was conscious of a feeling like being pinioned in a feather-bed, and, moving my hands, felt my jacket puffed out above my tight girdle with water. I strove to tear it off; but it was looped together here and there, and the strings were not then to be sundered by hand. I whipped out my knife, that was tucked at my belt, and ripped my jacket straight up and down, as if I were ripping open myself. With a violent struggle I then burst out of it, and was free. Heavily soaked, it slowly sank before my eyes.

Sink! sink! oh shroud!

The British Seaman (pp. 120–121)

Towards the afternoon, I went aloft with others to set the fore-topmast-studsail, and being on the foreyard-arm, was busy cutting the stops with my knife, when the officer on deck hailed me with "Fore-yard arm there! Are you not ready with that sail yet?" "Not yet, sir," I replied; but my companion in the top mistaking my answer, sung [sic] out, "All ready, sir: hoist away!" I had my knife in my mouth at the time, and was busy trying to reach a stop that was rather high for me, so I did not notice what my companion said, but all at once heard the Lieutenant on deck give the order, "Run away with it, men! make a run!"—and before I could recollect myself, I was precipitated into the water from a height of above sixty feet. I cannot describe my sensations while descending into Davy's Locker, only I felt a horrid choking at the breast as if I had received a blow, and a roaring of waters in my ears like the fall of a cataract. I soon found myself ascending again, and

thought I; sink forever! ac-
cursed jacket that thou art!

"See that white shark!" cried
a horrified voice from the taff-
rail; "he'll have that man down
his hatchway! Quick! the *grains!*
the *grains!*"

The next instant that barbed
bunch of harpoons pierced
through and through the unfortunate jacket, and swiftly
sped down with it out of sight.

Being now astern of the
frigate, I struck out boldly toward the elevated pole of one
of the life-buoys which had been
cut away. Soon after, one of the
cutters picked me up. As they
dragged me out of the water
into the air, the sudden transition of elements made my every
limb feel like lead, and I
helplessly sunk into the bottom
of the boat.

when I reached the surface of
the water, being a good swimmer, I struck out for the ship,
which, by this time, was a
considerable way from me, although it was very calm. I found
myself much incommoded by
something hanging at my breast,
and putting my hand down,
discovered that a bag of water
had been formed by my shirt
between the waistband and the
neck, which prevented me from
swimming with ease. I succeeded in pulling up my shirt
with my left hand, which gave
me immediate relief, and soon
reached the Life Buoy which
had been flung out for me, but
I was so weak that I could
scarcely hold on. A dimness
came over my eyes, and I felt
very sick at heart. I heard the
voices of several people talk-
ing very loud, and was just
sinking, when I found myself
seized by the hair, and hauled
out of the water.

Even the hasty reader sees the closeness of Melville to his source. He
may see also Melville's subtle distance from it through alterations
whereby a routine rescue operation gains dramatic force suitable to the
death of the placental white jacket which throughout the entire novel
has been a mockingly destructive agent.

Two of the three sources of the whole Fall episode—first Nathaniel
Ames and now the "British Seaman"—had met Melville's narrative
need by describing an action to which the jacket might be easily added.[1]

1. Falls from yard-arms are of course frequent in sea-literature; we are concerned primarily with the ones which Melville had seen and which clearly assisted
him in shaping his passage. Some which he saw did not seem to give him much,
if anything, to use. An example of one of these falls is found in the fecund source
book, *Scenes* (p. 55): ". . . by some means or another the leech of the topgal-
lantsail got over the end of the yard arm, and in my laying out to clear it, she

In Ames, it will be recalled, the flapping sail which had caused his fall quite naturally translated in *White-Jacket* into the flapping jacket responsible for its owner's perilous plunge. In *Life on Board a Man-of-War,* the obstructing garment was a shirt, which Melville in turn transformed into a white jacket almost malevolent in its menace to the life of its wearer. All the way through the book Melville had utilized and dramatized the warning about the jacket which he had made in the first chapter, "And my shroud it afterward came very near proving, as he who reads further will find." Here is the "further," final episode of peril. To the anecdotal British Seaman, with his Peter Bell limitations, a shirt was but a shirt, nothing more! His factual account, so simple, so matter of fact, becomes intensely physical and symbolical by Melville's transformation.

It was inevitable that Melville should tighten the narrative line—the details of action—to sharpen sensations that the physical quality of the events might be felt with immediacy and intensity by the reader. Vague generalizations of feeling became strong images. For example, where the British Seaman wrote about being "very much incommoded by something at my breast," Melville tautened the slack phrase by use of a striking simile, "a consciousness of feeling like being pinioned in a feather-bed." Similar in creative borrowing was Melville's change of the British Seaman's "A dimness came over my eyes, and I felt very sick at heart," to White-Jacket's strong words: "the sudden transition of elements made my every limb feel like lead, and I helplessly sunk into the bottom of the boat." The fine pictorial detail of the "frigate slowly gliding by like a black world in the water. Her vast hull loomed out of the night" is absent from the sources.

The problem of encumbrance which the British Seaman solved with ease is a life-and-death struggle for White-Jacket, and the violent verbs give frightening force to what is in the source a faded matter-of-factness. The casual inconvenience and discomfort of removing a shirt have been heightened to an episode of rebirth, with obstetrical imagery which, effective and forceful in its place here, also foreshadows the familiar scene in *Moby-Dick* when Queequeg delivers Tashtego from the sinking head of the sperm whale in what Ishmael calls a "running delivery." Significantly different, too, is the fate of the shirt and of the

---

gave a heavy pitch, the sail disentangled itself, and with the jar I fell back a little, and as I grabbed one of the beckets on the yard to save myself, it carried away, and overboard I went; I struck something as I fell, for when I came to the surface of the water, I could scarcely strike out, I felt a kind of dizziness in my head. . . ."

jacket. The one is retained, the other rejected. The British Seaman does not bother to remove his shirt; White-Jacket violently rips his jacket open with a knife, struggles to take it off, and watches it disappear in the depths of the sea, like a snake's skin or a lobster's shell cast off in the growth process.

The jacket is sped downwards by the harpoons of the crew who mistake it for a shark, just as earlier they had mistaken it for another ill-omened creature, the albatross. For White-Jacket to resume his place on the main-deck this symbolic sinking is essential.

White-Jacket's protecting jacket, which did not really protect, has slid into the sea, his symbolized pretensions to purity, aristocracy, "his windy schemes and empty hopes" sinking as he emerges, half-naked, from the sea, ready to join his mates, received by them, saved by them, a White-Jacket no longer as, earlier in the book, both he and his jacket had been, rebuffed.

By now it is apparent that there is a close relation between the Fall passage in *White-Jacket* and the Epilogue of *Moby-Dick,* that strikingly different though they may be yet they are strikingly similar.[2] There, in each, is the strangling, suffocating salt sea; there, in each, is the swimming, struggling Everyman clinging to a buoy, wittingly made in *Moby-Dick* into a coffin-buoy; there, in each, is the menacing whiteness, jacket or shark or whale; and there, in each, the whiteness sinks or swims away; there, in each, death is defied and life affirmed.

•

My greetings to you, sir, whose memory,
the striped coat and colors—What is one man?
a man remembered still in the jacket
of his success? of the winning club?
in himself—successful? one man, alone?
This is that he who slights his fellows—
or else, as he is, plunges
to the wind-whipped swirl, hat, coat, shoes
and—as you did—drags in the body

2. Cf. Charles Feidelson, *Symbolism and American Literature* (Chicago: University of Chicago Press, 1953), p. 182: "The conclusion of the book anticipates the end of *Moby-Dick,* and recalls the end of *Redburn.* . . . He survives as the potentiality of experience, always about to lose himself in the flux and always emerging to face another world."

to the grapples defying death and the sea.
Not once but—again!
Is this the war—that spawned you? Or
did you make the war? Whichever, there you are.
                                   William Carlos Williams, "The Apparition"

A single passage of but one page has exuded sources like sap from an
unfrozen maple tree. Perhaps—but only perhaps—the essential sources
have now been traced, but this leaves unexplored those sources that are
too tenuous to prove, but which resound like echoes in Melville's episode. Edgar Allan Poe's *The Narrative of Arthur Gordon Pym,* which
later affected the composition of *Moby-Dick,* may possibly be detected as
we recall the close of that novel when Pym imagines falling:

> It was in vain I endeavored to banish these reflections, and to keep
> my eyes steadily bent upon the flat surface of the cliff before me.
> The more earnestly I struggled *not to think,* the more intensely
> vivid became my conceptions, and the more horribly distinct. At
> length arrived that crisis of fancy, so fearful in all similar cases,
> the crisis in which we begin to anticipate the feelings with which
> we *shall* fall—to picture to ourselves the sickness, and dizziness,
> and the last struggle, and the half swoon, and the final bitterness
> of the rushing and headlong descent. And now I found these
> fancies creating their own realities, and all imagined horrors
> crowding upon me in fact. I felt my knees strike violently together,
> while my fingers were gradually but certainly relaxing their grasp.
> There was a ringing in my ears, and I said, "This is my knell of
> death!" And now I was consumed with the irrepressible desire of
> looking below. I could not, I would not, confine my glances to the
> cliff; and, with a wild, indefinable emotion, half of horror, half of
> a relieved oppression, I threw my vision far down into the abyss.
> For one moment my fingers clutched convulsively upon their hold,
> while, with the movement, the faintest possible idea of ultimate
> escape wandered, like a shadow, through my mind—in the next
> my whole soul was pervaded with a *longing to fall;* a desire, a
> yearning, a passion utterly uncontrollable. I let go at once my grasp
> upon the peg, and, turning half round from the precipice, re-
> mained tottering for an instant against its naked face. But now
> there came a spinning of the brain; a shrill-sounding and phantom
> voice screamed within my ears; a dusky, fiendish, and filmy figure
> stood immediately beneath me; and, sighing, I sunk down with a
> bursting heart, and plunged within its arms.[3]

3. *The Complete Tales and Poems of Edgar Allan Poe,* with an introduction by
Hervey Allen (New York: Modern Library, 1938), p. 875.

It is possible, though by no means probable, that this passage served Melville as a source. Equally difficult to determine, and so dangerous categorically to assert, is the influence of the Biblical story of Jonah, especially in the following verses:

> The waters compassed me about, even to the soul: the depth closed
>   me round about, the weeds were wrapped about my head.
> I went down to the bottoms of the mountains; the earth with her
>   bars was about me for ever: yet hast thou brought up my life
>   from corruption, O Lord my God.

Many more echoes may be suggested;[4] perhaps other distinct sources, too, will be discovered. In any case, it is clear that, in bringing his book to its climax in the Fall of White-Jacket, Melville has cunningly united his finest patches with his most ingenious stitchery.

·

> Now from the darkness of myself
> I turn to let the lightness in.
> Is it the raging of the sun
> Or my own thoughts made free again?
> I between hills of light and light
> Stand and, composed of my own doubt,
> Wonder where they, where I begin.
>   Elizabeth Jennings, "Escape and Return"

We have looked at Melville's Fall passage genetically; we must now consider it psychologically. To quote Ahab: " 'Hark ye yet again,—the little lower layer.' "

Because of the special way in which this study has interpreted *White-Jacket,* arguing that the stitching of the jacket, the combinations of the patches and the pockets, and the like, were a conscious metaphor of the very process of composition, it is now possible, almost inevitable, to interpret in a smiliar manner the Fall passage, the very death of that jacket. Whether consciously or not, the sinking of the jacket is the determination of an artist moving to a new kind of writing, to a renewed attempt to capture a new kind of truth, higher than mere factuality.

4. Further ruminations on this Fall, written after this book went to press, are in my article, "And Still They Fall from the Masthead," in *Melville and Hawthorne in the Berkshires* (Kent, Ohio, 1966), pp. 144–155.

The Fall, then, must be construed also as a parable of Melville's own creative necessity, of his personal struggle with "the angel—Art." The parable, or rather the struggle, has shown itself before in his writing, especially in *Mardi,* and it shows with frankness at times engaging and at times almost embarrassing in his later writing. Even now, less than a year before breaking away from a "whaling voyage" to write a book "almost certainly to fail," Melville was anticipating that break-away, that sloughing off of the jacket which was threatening to drown his creative genius. The "immersion" of December 1850, seen in his remarkable letter to Duyckinck in which he describes his complete absorption in his compositional problems, is made more significant by remembering this interpretation of the Fall.

Before *Moby-Dick,* however, Melville had this great moment of achievement, of fulfillment, when the artless lines of Ames, the Bulwer-Lytton translation of Schiller, and the forthright narrative of the British Seaman came together in his mind, and were transformed by their conjunction in that mind into a passage of sheer genius. It reminds one of that remarkable night when John Keats and Charles Cowden Clarke read with delighted wonder the rolling lines of George Chapman's translation of the *Iliad,* developing latent images and unleashing hidden powers to transform the poetaster Keats into the poet of "On First Looking Into Chapman's Homer." Such a kindling occurred with Melville when his sources helped him to bring into coherence, order, and resonant power—and hence to a new spaciousness, a new depth—the significance of his dearest symbols, their dearness now realized and exploited. "The result produced in his little book was somehow a result beyond his conscious intention; it was as if he had planted his genius, had trusted his method, and they had grown and flowered with this sweetness." These words from Henry James's description in "The Middle Years" of Dencombe's experience as an author may seem a chic gloss arbitrarily placed against Melville's life, until Melville's own words in a letter to Hawthorne show his own awareness of the growth process in him through his authorship:

> Until I was twenty-five I had no development at all. From my twenty-fifth year I date my life. Three weeks have scarcely passed, at any time, between then and now, that I have not unfolded within myself. But I feel that I am now come to the inmost leaf of the bulb, and that shortly the flower must fall to the mold.

Melville reached his twenty-fifth birthday on 19 August 1844 while the *United States* was on the last leg of its homeward voyage. White-

Jacket's fall from the yard-arm would have taken place just about that time if the events of the book are equated with the reality of the log of the *United States*. We know that Melville never actually fell from that yard-arm, although biographers have had their day of fun and folly misunderstanding that pseudo-event—pseudo-event and metaphor of Melville's fall into life, into a constantly growing comprehension of the strikingly unusual experiences he had accumulated in three years of voyaging about the South Seas. Proust's self-reflection could be taken as the finest commentary on Melville's experience:

A new light arose in me, less brilliant indeed than the one that had made me perceive that a work of art is the only means of regaining lost time. And I understood that all the material of a literary work was in my past life, I understood that I had acquired it in the midst of frivolous amusements, in idleness, in tenderness and in pain, stored up by me without my divining its destination or even its survival, as the seed has in reserve all the ingredients which will nourish the plant. Like the seed I might die when the plant had developed and I might find I had lived for it without knowing it, without my life having ever seemed to require contact with the books I wanted to write and for which when I formerly sat down at my table, I could find no subject. Thus all my life up to that day might have been or might not have been summed up under the title: 'A vocation?' In one sense, literature had played no active part in my life. But, in another, my life, the memories of its sorrows, of its joys, had been forming a reserve like albumen in the ovule of a plant. It is from this that the plant draws its nourishment in order to transform itself into seed at a time when one does not yet know that the embryo of the plant is developing through chemical phenomena and secret but very active respirations are taking place in it. Thus my life had been lived in constant contact with the elements which would bring about its ripening. And those who would later derive nourishment from it would be as ignorant of the process that supplied it as those who eat the products of grain are unaware of the rich aliments it contains though they have manured the soil in which it was grown and have enabled it to reach maturity.

·19·

Conclusion

Melville fell
and the albatross
out of the rigging

Edam the moon
all angular else
mast and ropes

a feather fell
a claw
clutched the ladder

slipped
Melville fell
forty fathoms Melville fell

fathoms below the sea level
        Herbert Read, "Melville."

AND now," wrote Melville in Chapter 93, "that the white jacket has sunk to the bottom of the sea . . . what more remains?"

Little enough, it appears—Chapter 93 and the last, unnumbered chapter. Essentially the book is ended because the voyage itself is almost ended. The interior life of a man-of-war has been described in exact and generous detail, anecdotes have been related with irresistible zest, characters have performed entertainingly and instructively; and social evils, especially flogging, have been exposed and indicted with blistering scorn, with Swiftian indignation. Besides, Melville had almost four hundred pages ready for the printer. It was time to conclude.

The closing chapters of *White-Jacket,* then, move rapidly in the rounding-off process. Details are brushed together in a wide journalistic sweep: "Shall I tell . . ." this, that, and the other thing, Melville asks, listing points (the farewells and dispersals of messmates, the details of payment and dismissal, and so on), and he airily answers his own rhetorical question:

> No! let all this go by. . . . Let us leave the ship on the sea—still with the land out of sight—still with brooding darkness on the face of the deep. I love an indefinite, infinite background. . . .

But Melville is in a high mood and from this mockery he moves to lyricism: "It is night. The meagre moon is in her last quarter . . . the stars look forth in their everlasting brightness—and *that* is the everlasting, glorious Future, forever beyond us," concluding with a celebration of the love of comrades:

> We main-top-men are all aloft in the top; and round our mast we circle, a brother-band. . . . Hand in hand we top-mates stand, rocked in our Pisgah top. And over the starry waves, and broad out into the blandly blue and boundless night, spiced with strange sweets from the long-sought land. . . .

The entire outpouring, which had started with parody of the Weird Sisters in *Macbeth,* culminates in Jack Chase's recitation of apt lines from the ever-useful Camoëns. The effect is operatic, somehow, giving the impression of the close of a musical drama, the chorus of jolly tars striking up the final chorus; and one expects a line of sailors in a lively dance routine—a Dibdin operetta of naval life.

"What more remains?" Melville asked. One thing more there is to be skewered down, rounded off. Even though throughout the book it is a point—what Emerson would call "a spiritual fact"—which has been so timidly and delicately made—partly through the jacket symbol—it is well that it be brought out more forthrightly in the concluding chapter.

This last chapter of *White-Jacket* is a sermon, more or less, employing once again his iterated metaphor of the ship as the cosmos: "As a man-of-war that sails through the sea, so this earth that sails through the air." Even though this sermon lacks the verve and the dramatic relevance of Father Mapple's sermon in *Moby-Dick*, it nevertheless, too, undergirds the book. Melville here openly moralizes the metaphor so solidly developed earlier—the ship as a microcosm—but now he expands the comparison to the great globe itself, much in the manner of Whitman's little-known lines composed shortly before his death:

> One thought ever at the fore—
> That in the Divine Ship, the World, breasting Time
>   and Space,
> All peoples of the globe together sail, sail the
>   same voyage, are bound to the same destination.

What is most striking about Melville's chapter is that while employing a metaphor primarily social in character (ship equals world), his homily stresses the private individual, the unsocial, Ishmaelian element of the human self:

> Thus sailing with sealed orders, we ourselves are the repositories
> of the secret packet, whose mysterious contents we long to learn.
> There are no mysteries out of ourselves.

And shortly after, when he has allegorized the various parts of the ship—an allegory now made especially pointed and effective by our 400-page life on board that ship in its harsh physical and social realities—Melville returns again to the individual self with an almost existential directness: "Yet the worst of our evils we blindly inflict upon ourselves. . . . From the last ills no being can save another; therein each man must be his own saviour." Previously Melville had said, "I myself am Fate," and afterwards, in *Moby-Dick*, Ahab asserted "I am the Fates' lieutenant." In *Mardi*, Babbalanja had observed, "The world revolves upon an I."

White-Jacket is a series of recognitions of the nature of life; it exposes a finite world of which and in which we have infinite hopes ("a boundless future"); it is a dimly sensed consciousness of man's finitude and of his infinitude, of his alienation (from the mess) and of his acceptance (by the top, and by the deck after the loss of a harpoon-riddled jacket). White-Jacket has, insofar as he has let his mirror play on himself, known defeat and he has known joy, he has discovered comradeship and he has discovered his own existence. The "nothing" of the opening chapter, the wraith of Chapter 2, has now found his essential being, his form—found it now without his jacket, indeed because that jacket is no more—has found his naked self. Ishmael will more dramatically, more clearly, do the same.

●

> The prologues are over. It is a question, now,
> Of final belief. So, say that final belief
> Must be in fiction. It is time to choose.
> > Wallace Stevens, "Asides on the Oboe"

The prologue was indeed over, on 1 February 1850, for Herman Melville when his ship docked in New York, the English publication of *White-Jacket* assured. Melville had now written a prologue in five volumes, each moving closer to the final belief, and yet never attaining or capturing that final belief. A different weapon was called for, and now it had been forged.

It was time now for the fiction—not, as in *Typee* and *Omoo*, mere charming travelogues, a literature of escape; not, as in *Mardi,* a fiction of abstractions, a parade of metaphysical phantoms across an exotic stage set; not these, but a fiction fulfilled in precise, concrete forms—"No ideas but in things"—fiction found in the infinite space of the sky, in the shimmering surfaces of the sea and the darkness of its depths—in sky-hawk, ship, and shark and whale. Fiction unearthed from experiences lived and from experiences read in books, from the scars which seas and books had left on the body and on the heart and mind—"Blood, imagination, and intellect running together."

Now, Melville had achieved the mastery of a craft which could order the fleeting words, and he was ready for the composition of a whaling voyage. That he knew. What he did not yet consciously realize, but what we have seen in the promise of *White-Jacket,* was that he was ready for *Moby-Dick.*

> "Flame, sound, fury, composed. Hear what he says,
> The dauntless master, as he starts the human tale."

Appendix

A MAN named Cunningham paid a visit to the *United States,* and his firsthand description of the ship is worth quoting (From L. G. Carr Laughton, "John Cunningham's Journal," *The Mariner's Mirror,* IX [November 1923], pp. 334–336):

> I was received with much affability and civility by Commodore Hull, who did me the honour to introduce me to his Lady. . . . The Commodore's appearance pleased me much. He is a stout, thick set, rather shortish man, has a pleasing, rather handsome, honest-looking countenance, and very much beloved by his officers and men. Indeed, he brought to my recollection several of the captains of the *old school.* . . . His honest tar-like habits, the substantial fittings of the ship of the *Cambridge,* an 80-gun ship— the physical strength and excellent discipline of her crew . . . all

brought forcibly to my mind the Golden Days of our irresistible Navy before the Peace of Amiens. Indeed, that period of our service appears to be decidedly that which they copy from and may probably be accounted for from the following circumstance: that previous to that period we had a number of Americans in our navy for years together. Many were petty officers, some on the quarter-deck, even to the rank of acting-lieutenant. In several of the ships (chiefly boatswain's mates) were of that nation. They fought in all the general actions and many single ones. In short, they knew our service to a title; and it is very probable that many who did petty officers' duty in our service subsequently obtained still greater preferment in their own. . . .

The *States* is a tremendous frigate . . . and what may be called a bed of timber. Her scantling throughout is considerably above that of the *Cambridge,* according to actual measurement. Her sides are thicker by several inches. . . . Their fighting arrangements are admirable; and, having seen them at quarters, I could not help admiring several of their appointments. One especially—their boarding cap. It is of helmet form, the frame of pretty stout iron, covered outside with a stout, hard leather. Unless a cutlass were laid on by a very heavy arm, the head would scarcely be wounded. They are decidedly the best preservation I ever saw before in any service. . . .

I had not been five minutes on board before I ceased to wonder that my friend, Capt. Carden in the *Macedonian,* was forced to succombe to her. . . . Positively if she had closed the *Macedonian,* as she ought to have done, she ought to have blown her out of the water in 20 minutes. . . . They told me that during her late repairs a quantity of the *Macedonian*'s shot were taken out of her sides which had not penetrated.

There happened to be an American private gentleman on board on a visit, who appeared to be pretty conversant in naval matters. . . . The conversation led to an interesting piece of information respecting the *United States,* which seemed new even to the American officers. It was to the following import:

In 1790, when the American Congress had decided on commencing their military navy, President Washington sent for two shipbuilders then at New York. One was an Englishman, the other a Frenchman, and both eminent builders. He requested them to furnish him with a plan of a stout frigate, according to the models of their respective nations. When they were produced, he submitted them to the examination of a Mr. Humphries, a respectable American builder, who pronounced the following decision. That produced by the Englishman he considered best calculated for durability, but less for speed and a heavy force. That of the French builder he deemed best suited for speed, and capable of admitting a greater force, but less calculated for durability.

The President then requested his opinion whether an improvement might not be made on both plans, to which he replied in the affirmative, that strength, speed, and great force might be combined, and, at the same time, equal facility in management. He received the President's orders to put his conceptions into execution, and the *United States* was the result, combining all the qualities expected; and though now 24 years old, she has not yet had a thorough repair, and, is, by their account, the strongest ship in their navy. She certainly is the finest single-decked ship I ever had my foot on board of. She sails admirably well; is, they say, an excellent sea-boat; she speeds nearly, if not altogether, as much canvas as the Cambridge, and is in every respect a noble ship.

Index